MW00399658

THE INCIDENT AT ANTIOCH

L'INCIDENT D'ANTIOCHE

INSURRECTIONS: CRITICAL STUDIES IN RELIGION, POLITICS, AND CULTURE

INSURRECTIONS: CRITICAL STUDIES
IN RELIGION, POLITICS, AND CULTURE

Slavoj Žižek, Clayton Crockett, Creston Davis, Jeffrey W. Robbins, Editors

The intersection of religion, politics, and culture is one of the most discussed areas in theory today. It also has the deepest and most wide-ranging impact on the world. Insurrections: Critical Studies in Religion, Politics, and Culture will bring the tools of philosophy and critical theory to the political implications of the religious turn. The series will address a range of religious traditions and political viewpoints in the United States, Europe, and other parts of the world. Without advocating any specific religious or theological stance, the series aims nonetheless to be faithful to the radical emancipatory potential of religion.

After the Death of God, John D. Caputo and Gianni Vattimo, edited by
Jeffrey W. Robbins

The Politics of Postsecular Religion: Mourning Secular Futures,
Ananda Abeysekara

Nietzsche and Levinas: "After the Death of a Certain God," edited by
Jill Stauffer and Bettina Bergo

Strange Wonder: The Closure of Metaphysics and the Opening of Awe,
Mary-Jane Rubenstein

*Religion and the Specter of the West: Sikhism, India, Postcoloniality,
and the Politics of Translation*, Arvind Mandair

Plasticity at the Dusk of Writing: Dialectic, Destruction, Deconstruction,
Catherine Malabou

Anatheism: Returning to God After God, Richard Kearney

Rage and Time: A Psychopolitical Investigation, Peter Sloterdijk

Radical Political Theology: Religion and Politics After Liberalism,
Clayton Crockett

Radical Democracy and Political Theology, Jeffrey W. Robbins

Hegel and the Infinite: Religion, Politics, and Dialectic, edited by
Slavoj Žižek, Clayton Crockett, and Creston Davis

What Does a Jew Want? On Binationalism and Other Specters, Udi Aloni

A Radical Philosophy of Saint Paul, Stanislas Breton, edited by
Ward Blanton, translated by Joseph N. Ballan

Hermeneutic Communism: From Heidegger to Marx, Gianni Vattimo
and Santiago Zabala

Deleuze Beyond Badiou: Ontology, Multiplicity, and Event,
Clayton Crockett

*Self and Emotional Life: Merging Philosophy, Psychoanalysis,
and Neuroscience*, Adrian Johnston and Catherine Malabou

Alain Badiou

THE INCIDENT AT ANTIOCH
L'INCIDENT D'ANTIOCHE

A Tragedy in Three Acts / Tragédie en trois actes

Introduction by Kenneth Reinhard
Translated by Susan Spitzer

COLUMBIA UNIVERSITY PRESS

NEW YORK

COLUMBIA UNIVERSITY PRESS
Publishers Since 1893
New York   Chichester, West Sussex
cup.columbia.edu
Copyright © 2013 Columbia University Press
All rights reserved

Library of Congress Cataloging-in-Publication Data
Badiou, Alain.
    The incident at Antioch : a tragedy in three acts = L'incident d'antioche : tragédie
en trois actes / Alain Badiou; introduction by Kenneth Reinhard; translated by
Susan Spitzer. — First worldwide edition.
        pages cm. — (Insurrections: critical studies in religion, politics, and culture)
    In English and French.
    Includes bibliographical references.
    ISBN 978-0-231-15774-2 (cloth : alk. paper)—ISBN 978-0-231-15775-9 (pbk. : alk.
paper)—ISBN 978-0-231-52773-6 (ebook)
    I. Spitzer, Susan, translator. II. Badiou, Alain. Incident d'antioche. English.
III. Badiou, Alain. Incident d'antioche. IV. Title. V. Title: Incident at Antioch.

    PQ2662.A323I5313 2013
    842'.914–dc23

Columbia University books are printed on permanent and durable acid-free paper.

This book is printed on paper with recycled content.
Printed in the United States of America

c 10 9 8 7 6 5 4 3 2 1
p 10 9 8 7 6 5 4 3 2 1

Cover image: Caravaggio, *Conversion on the Way to Damascus,* 1601.
    Cerasei Chapel, Santa Maria del Popolo, Rome.
Cover design: Noah Arlow
Book design: Lisa Hamm

References to Internet Web sites (URLs) were accurate at the time of writing.
Neither the author nor Columbia University Press is responsible for URLs
that may have expired or changed since the manuscript was prepared.

CONTENTS

Preface vii

Translator's Preface xiii

Acknowledgments xix

Introduction by Kenneth Reinhard xxi

L'INCIDENT D'ANTIOCHE 2

THE INCIDENT AT ANTIOCH 3

Notes 121

A Discussion of and Around
The Incident at Antioch *137*

Bibliography 151

Index 155

PREFACE TO
THE FIRST WORLDWIDE EDITION
OF *THE INCIDENT AT ANTIOCH*

I began writing the first version of this play—a tragedy—during the summer of 1982, in the atmosphere of solitude that surrounded me and my activist friends at the time owing to our firm opposition, right from the start, to the government of François Mitterrand (elected in 1981), to which everyone around us had eagerly rallied. Between 1972 and 1977, I had already written a long play entitled *L'Écharpe rouge* (The Red Scarf). I had called it a "*romanopéra*" ("novelopera") because, in terms of both its length and its texture, it was more like a novel than a play, and because it was divided into "arias," "recitatives," "ariosos," "choruses," and so on. It was, moreover, as an opera that, after its publication by the illustrious Éditions Maspero in 1979, it was given its first performance at the Opéra de Lyon in 1984 and performed again, at the Festival d'Avignon, and ultimately in Paris, at the Théâtre National de Chaillot. Georges Aperghis wrote the music for it and Antoine Vitez directed.

I reworked *The Incident at Antioch* during the summer of 1984 at the same time as I was writing my first comedy, *Ahmed le subtil* (Ahmed the Subtle). I felt that the plot needed to be streamlined and especially that the chorus, which was very large in the first version, with many different voices, should be scaled down to more reasonable proportions.

Finally, between 1987 and 1989, I wrote a third version, the one that is being published here. This time around, the aim was to cut out all the too explicit references to the French political situation, to reduce the use of Marxist jargon, and to push the play toward a new form of universality, even if it were at the price of greater obscurity, or a more highly charged lyricism.

As can be seen, for about fifteen years—when I was between 35 and 50, say, and involved day and night in revolutionary politics—theater had nonetheless never been far from my thoughts.

After the staging of *L'Écharpe rouge* I thought that Vitez, the brilliant man of the theater, would someday or other be interested in the other two plays. And, sure enough, he gave two memorable readings of them, one (*Ahmed*) at Chaillot and the other (*The Incident*) at the Théâtre National Populaire in Villeurbanne. A few months after that second reading, he died suddenly, leaving all of us deeply bereaved. I put my plays away in a drawer and didn't even attempt to get them published. Theater disappeared from my writing and my concerns. It wasn't until 1993 that my interest in it revived, when Christian Schiaretti, the director of the Théâtre de Reims at that time, discovered the text of *Ahmed le subtil* and decided to stage it. It was thanks to him that I found my way back to the Festival d'Avignon and rediscovered my taste for writing for the theater again. Between 1994 and 1997—I was approaching 60 at the time— I wrote three new plays, all centering around the character of Ahmed: *Ahmed philosophe* (Ahmed the Philosopher), *Ahmed se fâche* (Ahmed Gets Angry), and *Les Citrouilles* (The Pumpkins). All these plays were published. They were also all performed, in several different productions, and are still being performed.

I take great pleasure in saying here that *Ahmed philosophe,* in a superb English translation by Joseph Litvak of Tufts University, is forthcoming from Columbia University Press and that we can look forward to seeing the whole collection of "philosophical comedies" published sometime soon and, who knows, maybe even performed for English-speaking audiences.

The fate of *The Incident at Antioch* is a different story altogether. Neither published nor performed, this tragedy completely disappeared, in a way, for almost twenty years. The only visible trace of its existence is a short film, based mainly on the beginning of Act III, which was directed by Élisabeth Boyer in 1989 under the title of *En partage.*

The play was in fact rediscovered by several British, American, and German scholars in 2005. A key role was played in all this by my friend Ken Reinhard of the University of California at Los Angeles and by Susan Spitzer, who promptly embarked upon the all-consuming adventure of translating it into English.

Among the signs of a keen interest in the play elsewhere than in France it is worth mentioning in particular two conferences, one that was organized in 2009 by Ward Blanton at the University of Glasgow, where several scenes from it were performed, and another, devoted more generally to my theater, that was held in Berlin in 2011 on the initiative of Ken Reinhard, Martin Treml, and Sigrid Weigel of the Zentrum für Literatur- und Kulturforschung. There too conference-goers could attend a performance of a few scenes from the play (combined with scenes from *Ahmed philosophe*).

To date, I have had the opportunity to hear fragments of *The Incident* in English and German, but never in French.

Why this belated, roundabout discovery? Why has there been such keen interest on the part of English-speaking philosophers and theologians in this long-forgotten play? And finally, and above all, why is there now this *en face* bilingual edition, the English side of which is a real, unexpected *tour de force*? To understand the reasons, we need to go into the details a little.

Of the six works for the theater that I have produced, four were written using famous classic plays as models. *Ahmed le subtil* reprised the plot of one of Molière's best-known comedies, *Les Fourberies de Scapin* (*The Tricks of Scapin*); *L'Écharpe rouge* follows the episodes of the first three "days" of Claudel's great play *Le Soulier de satin* (*The Satin Slipper*); *Les Citrouilles* follows the action of Aristophanes's *The Frogs;* and finally, *The Incident at Antioch* is modeled on another of Claudel's plays, *La Ville* (*The City*). I thus reprised one of the great traditions of classical theater: rewriting famous plays of antiquity. On one theme alone, *Amphitryon*, a Latin play by Plautus, there exists a play by Molière, one by Kleist, and one by Giraudoux.

What *The City*, a complex play of which there are several, ultimately very different versions, deals with is the fate of modern societies considered in the light of three different ideologies: one, an ideology inspiring socialist and communist revolutionaries (Claudel had the Paris Commune in mind); a second, a positivist ideology that ends up in the nihilism of pure technique; and a third that seeks to construct a new society based on religious law (Catholicism, for Claudel). As is always the case with this writer, it is a female character, Lâla, as she is called, who moves between these different orientations: she is their challenge, their irony, their stumbling block. She says she is "the promise that cannot be kept."

My intention was to take the same problem and present it in a somewhat different way. The same three orientations are all there again. First, there is the exhausted conservatism of our "democratic" societies, represented by two politicians, one on the Left and the other on the Right (the Maury brothers). Then there is contemporary nihilism, contemplating, with an eye at once amused and melancholic, the end of our world and the gradual advent of disaster. This is Villembray, formerly a dynamic, popular head of government but who, by the time the play begins, has very nearly become a derelict. And finally there is radical communist revolutionarism, represented by Cephas, a leader as lucid and efficient as he is ruthless.

The basic plot, the story line, akin to that of *The City*, recounts, to begin with, the refusal of Villembray, who has been approached by the Maury brothers to come be a savior, a sort of new De Gaulle, to stave off the collapse of the parliamentary regime; then, the revolutionaries' decision to take power by force, beginning with the execution of Villembray; and, finally, the destruction of the whole country by civil war, the revolutionaries' ambiguous victory, and the departure of Cephas, who believes that his task was to destroy rather than to build, and that it has therefore been accomplished.

What is significantly different from Claudel is the female role. Paula, the heroine of my play, in fact follows a path that is the opposite, as it were, of Claudel's Lâla's. Rather than being the irony of all the different doctrines, she is the rebellious voice of emancipatory truth. Although she is Villembray's sister, she has remained completely untouched by his nihilism. Quite on the contrary, inasmuch as she is linked to the people, to the workers, she will in a way be converted to the communist, revolutionary perspective. Having become an important leader, she opposes Cephas, because she thinks that the outbreak of civil war in the prevailing circumstances is doomed to end in terror. She attempts to save her brother, whom her comrades have decided to kill, but he accepts his death as a proof of the meaninglessness of all things. She has had a child, David, with a militant worker, Mokhtar. And then she vanishes. She reappears only much later. The revolutionaries are now in control, through terror, of a devastated country, and Cephas has abandoned power. David, Paula's son, has taken over the leadership of the Party. In a crucial scene, Paula attempts to convince him that power should be given up; that the revolutionaries should remain among the people and never be separated from them in the inevitably terrorist guise of the State of exception. Then she takes off again, leaving David and his supporters undecided as to which path to take.

Truth be told, my play superimposes on Claudel's story another source, which is quite simply my interpretation of the life and writings of the Apostle Paul. Paula's "conversion" to the revolutionary world-view is clearly akin to Paul's conversion on the road to Damascus. Afterward, Paula opposes the proponents of the violent law of revolutions; she opposes the idea that the only important issue for the revolutionaries is that of State power. Essentially, she opposes the communist law of the Party-State the way Paul opposed Jewish law as embodied in Peter (whose real name was Cephas). As is well known, the confrontation between Paul and Peter was a very violent one, especially in Antioch, when Peter refused to eat with non-Jews. Whence the title of my play. As is also well known, Paul said that political power should be left its prerogatives, because the true kingdom was not of this world. In the same way, Paula vehemently confronts Cephas, who wants the Party to have a monopoly on poli-tics, just as Peter wanted the true religion to be the Jewish community's monopoly. And she attempts to convince David that true politics consists in the general organization of working-class and popular thought and determination rather than the terroristic wielding of State power.

What the English-speaking philosophers and progressive theologians, Jewish and Christian alike, have discovered in my *Incident at Antioch* is that contemporary political thought can provide a new reading and interpretation of the Apostle Paul *by leaving aside the twin oppositions of Christianity versus Judaism and the religious spirit versus atheism.* Now that Paul has become Paula, he has functioned for them as a refer-ence they can all share, because what is involved is the revival of the theme of a politics of emancipation that avoids right-wing opportunism (cav-ing in to Western "democracy"), communist dogmatism (being oriented toward State terror), and leftist impotence (beautiful movements followed by endless reactionary restorations).

To bring all of this to the stage, what was needed, I thought, was a bold new language that would be neither academic (right-wing) nor Brechtian (classical Communist) nor avant-gardist (experimental leftism). Here too I followed Claudel, who invented a powerful, metaphorical language, accepting that there be obscurity in the service of his faith, in a complete break with the languages of the theater of his time, whether conventional (the bourgeois theater, also known as boulevard theater) or esoteric (the Symbolist avant-garde). In his wake, I created a sort of unknown language, because it is the language that must convey the message of a politics that is only just emerging.

I am, need I say, astonished, delighted, even overjoyed, that the first publication of this play—my favorite of my six plays—is occurring in the United States, in a bilingual version. I would like to take this opportunity to thank all my English-speaking friends who have devoted themselves to this feat. I have said enough about the French in which my play is conveyed for everyone to understand that transposing that language into today's English, not to mention its American variety, was well nigh impossible. For that impossibility, which constitutes the real of every true translation, may Susan Spitzer and everyone who assisted her be thanked, infinitely.

TRANSLATOR'S PREFACE

Differences, like instrumental tones, provide us with the recognizable univocity that makes up the melody of the True.

—Alain Badiou, *Saint Paul: The Foundation of Universalism*

I f the strategic decision made by Céphas and his followers lies at the tragic heart of *L'Incident d'Antioche*, the translation of the play into English, on an obviously less exalted plane, also demanded decisions at every turn regarding the style, register, and tone of the play's language as well as its overall cultural context. To enter the universe of *The Incident at Antioch* as a translator is to be confronted by a dizzying array of choices, for *language itself*, when all is said and done, might be considered the play's true subject. On the micro-level, the characters' search for a language, the necessity for naming, or formalization, underlies much of the action and provides an interpretative key, while on the macro-level the search for a new dramatic language in which to convey the play's political and philosophical concerns constitutes one of Badiou's self-confessed aims in rewriting Paul Claudel's play *La Ville*. The central issue of the latter work—the becoming-Subject of the individual, the struggle to accept a new, life-changing possibility opened to him or her—is also the crucial issue in *The Incident*, as it is in all of Badiou's philosophical work. Yet the challenge for the playwright, he remarked in an interview in Glasgow in 2009, included in this edition, was how to write something "that's really a *play*, that's really a piece of writing, not a proof, not an abstract text." In Claudel he found someone who had invented "truly a new language in French, a language with new images, and with an immanent relationship between abstraction and images, something like a new metaphorical way to examine the most important problem of human life."

Accordingly, *The Incident at Antioch* is characterized by a rich linguistic *mélange,* a virtual kaleidoscope of styles and genres: poetic or highly elevated literary language, language borrowed directly from the Bible or with religious overtones, pompous rhetoric, made-up proverbs, everyday French that often tends toward the colloquial, if not at times the vulgar, all overlain with the remnants of a certain Marxist vocabulary, or with terminology bearing the stamp of Badiou's own philosophical œuvre, and studded with allusions to, or quotations from, Marx and Engels, Goethe, Shakespeare, Racine, La Fontaine, Heraclitus, Parmenides, and Greek mythology, along with myriad references to the contemporary world.

What's more, the characters themselves switch effortlessly between one type of speech and another, defying all efforts to associate any of them with a consistent social register, a characteristic style of language-use from which their social stereotype could be inferred. The speech of the two workers in the play, Madame Pintre and Mokhtar, for example, is not only distinctly poetic at times but even what might be called prophetic in its sweep. Nor is Camille, the tough girl from the *banlieue,* limited to youthful colloquialisms or slang; she is often indistinguishable from her older comrades in her use of high-flown language. Normally, a translator will strive to maintain a consistent social register for, as Sandor Hervey has written, "if the *paysan* sounded like a cross between a gentleman farmer and a straw-chewing rustic, the effect could be ruined."[1] In Badiou's play, however, such inconsistency is precisely the sought-after effect. A constant fluctuation between everyday French and a more heightened, literary or poetic stage-language can be found in the speech of virtually every character in *The Incident.* Thus, the fundamental hybridization that characterizes the play as a whole inheres as well in its dramatic expression, a poetry that is entirely that of the theater.

The stylized use of a literary, frequently lyrical, brand of speech by characters from whom we would not necessarily expect it creates an "effect of strangeness,"[2] and an odd sense of unreality in the midst of the very concrete situation—an insurrection with its tragic consequences—depicted in the play. Perhaps only the two politicians, the Maury brothers, because they function as targets of ridicule, can be said to display a stable, if hollowly rhetorical, style of language. And it is this very stability that contributes to making them the characters we love to hate, if that is not too strong a term for such obviously satirical villains. Indeed, the intrusion of comedy, the way the play "plays" with its self-defined status as tragedy by incorporating farcical interludes or indulging in humor in the form of ironic barbs or otherwise comic exchanges between characters, bespeaks the essential strangeness at its heart and serves as the counterpart of the deliberate dislocation of time and place in which *The Incident* also revels.

The road to Damascus, Antioch, and Nicea—names or, above all, symbolic places in the play—are populated by a cast of characters who foreground the intentional connection to Saint Paul and the Acts of the Apostles announced in the play's title while remaining thoroughly contemporary figures. It goes without saying, then, that any notion of realism with respect to either time or place in the play had to be immediately abandoned. Remaining faithful to the flavor of this essential strangeness represented a major challenge of the translation. Faced with the decisions entailed by such a lyrical, ludic hodge-podge, I occasionally shared the sentiment expressed in Paula's plaintive question just prior to her "conversion": "Why is this confusing spectacle being left to me?"

The least fraught of the decisions that needed to be made at the outset concerned the possibility of domesticating the play by transposing it to an anglicized cultural context. Given its essential link to the events recounted in Acts, however, it clearly could not become *The Incident at Antioch, Ohio*. The retention of some of the play's "foreignness" in the translation is immediately apparent in the characters' names, for example, which I have left for the most part in French, with the notable exception of Paula and two others. Because the pronunciation of "Paule" in English sounds too much like "pole"—an unsuitable name for a heroine—her name had to be anglicized. (A different *French* name could not be substituted, without losing the crucial connection to Saint Paul.) The name Paula is joined by the anglicized versions of David and Cephas, so that there is actually a blend of French and English, as well as one Arab name, Mokhtar, in the translation, just as there is a mixture of place names: the conventional English equivalents Damascus, Antioch, and Nicea coexist with the dozen or so unchanged French *banlieues*—Nanterre, Vitry, Flins-les-Mureaux, and so on—that Paula evokes in Act I. Although this seemingly arbitrary mix of names may create a certain discordant effect in the translation, such incongruity is a hallmark of *The Incident*, where French-named characters of another time and place dot the landscape of an impressionistic early Christian Middle East. Adding another layer of incongruity, then, through the anglicizing of some of the names, seemed appropriate, reproducing as it does, on a purely linguistic level, the play's larger discontinuities and dislocations.

This cultural transplantation of names nevertheless represented only a minor aspect of the challenge involved in translating *The Incident*, for a distinguishing feature of the play is that it is already *itself* a translation: it "carries over" much of its language directly from the second version of *La Ville*, written in 1897. Rather than being "based on" Claudel's play, *The Incident* could be said to enact a sort of musical "sampling" of one playwright by another. Many of Claudel's lines are lifted intact, or only minimally changed, and set down in *The Incident* where they function as often as not to invert Claudel's conservative, religious message. In standing Claudel on his head, so to speak, Badiou freely appropriates the earlier playwright's lyricism for his own purposes. The essential decision regarding the translation of *The Incident*, then, concerned how to translate this unique "translation" of Claudel.

Because *The City*, the sole existing English translation of Claudel's play, dates from 1920, its language strikes the modern ear as somewhat stilted if not downright overwrought in places. Using similar language to translate *The Incident* would have added an unwanted exoticism to the play in English; clearly, an updating was in order. In fact, Badiou himself often modernized the language of the Claudelian text from which he borrowed. The standard modern French in which much of the play is written has been rendered by its equivalent in English so as to produce a translation that sounds contemporary, for the most part. Sometimes, however, a decision was made to leave intact in the characters' speech a certain "archaic" quality, occasionally religious in its overtones, in keeping with what I judged to be the playwright's intention. A balance needed to be maintained between the poetry in *The Incident*, which risked being flattened by too contemporary a translation, and the prose, which could sound too florid if it were not made contemporary *enough*.

Ultimately, the new relationship between abstraction and images in Badiou's richly innovative dramatic language generates striking similarities with music. It is perhaps no coincidence that his earlier drama, *L'Écharpe rouge*, was performed in the 1980s as an opera. While *The Incident*, unlike *L'Écharpe rouge*, is not subtitled a *romanopéra*, there can be no mistaking the ample use it makes of musical techniques. Badiou himself notes in the preface that an earlier version of the play included a chorus with a great number of voices, which he subsequently reduced.

In the later version published here, I think it fair to say that a certain choral effect persists, particularly in Act I, when the revolutionaries react to Paula's "conversion" and ultimately give what amounts to an antiphonal recitation of a passage from *The German Ideology*. Overall, what I have called the "sampling" of Claudel makes *The Incident* a unique aesthetic production, in which a variety of musical modes can be discerned. Long, aria-like passages contrast with short bursts of dialogue, lending the writing a distinctive rhythm throughout. Individual voices play off each other when characters speak at cross-purposes, as do Cephas or Villembray in confronting the banalities of the Maury brothers, who, in Act II, take their revenge in the form of a stichomythic duet. A more orchestral phenomenon can be noted at times in speeches begun by one character and completed by another. Mokhtar in Act I recites what Badiou described to me as a song. This list could easily be continued, but it is perhaps above all the subtle dialectic of sound and silence, in a work punctuated from beginning to end by numerous pauses and silences, that constitutes its essential musicality, some of which I hope to have conveyed in this first English translation of Badiou's remarkable play.

ACKNOWLEDGMENTS

A number of people generously assisted me with the translation of *The Incident at Antioch*. Among them were three colleagues at the University of California at Los Angeles: Eric Gans, who was the first to lay eyes on my earliest, very rudimentary draft, which he helped me improve immeasurably; my husband, Patrick Coleman, who contributed countless helpful suggestions and provided unfailing encouragement and support; and Ken Reinhard, who made many improvements to the translation and was with me every step of the way. I am deeply grateful as well to Isabelle Vodoz, whose invaluable explanations, in the course of our exchange of long, detailed emails, clarified much that was obscure for me in the play, and to Adrian Johnston of the University of New Mexico, Joe Litvak of Tufts University, and Steve Corcoran of the University of Cyprus, Nicosia, all of whom gave me useful comments and suggestions early on. Thanks are also due to Ward Blanton of the University of Glasgow, who invited me to attend the 2009 conference there at which a few scenes of my translation of the play were read, and to Wendy Lochner of Columbia University Press, who, as a dedicated supporter of this project from the start, awaited its completion with admirable patience. I also want to express my appreciation to Ron Harris for his scrupulous editing of this technically challenging *en face* bilingual edition. Last but not least, I owe a special debt of gratitude to Alain Badiou for his enduring confidence in my skills and for his forbearance in the face of my relentless interrogations.

INTRODUCTION

BADIOU'S THEATER:
A LABORATORY FOR THINKING

Kenneth Reinhard

Although he is primarily known as a philosopher, Alain Badiou's first major publications were the experimental novels *Almagestes* (1964) and *Portulans* (1967), and he continued to write and publish fiction through the 1990s, when *Calme bloc ici-bas* appeared (1997). In the years between, Badiou wrote a series of plays: the political tragedy, *L'Écharpe rouge* (The Red Scarf) (1979) and the four *Ahmed* comedies: *Ahmed le subtil* (Ahmed the Subtle) (1994 [written in 1984]), *Ahmed philosophe* (Ahmed the Philosopher) (1995), *Ahmed se fâche* (Ahmed Gets Angry) (1995), and *Les Citrouilles* (The Pumpkins) (1996). Badiou rewrote *L'Écharpe rouge* as an opera, and it was performed in this form almost two dozen times in the 1980s. The four *Ahmed* plays—especially *Ahmed philosophe*—have been staged numerous times, and continue to be performed frequently. But Badiou's other tragedy, *L'Incident d'Antioche*, which dates from 1982, has never previously been published and has not yet received a fully staged production. We are proud to present it here in the original French and in Susan Spitzer's translation, as the first of Badiou's literary writings to appear in English.

We could describe *The Incident at Antioch* as "political theater," except that all of Badiou's plays are political, and for Badiou theater has a distinctively close relationship with politics. *Incident*, however, directly addresses political questions in its setting, themes, and events: its characters are statesmen, revolutionaries, and workers, and their dialogue is almost exclusively about the nature and practice of politics. Badiou's earlier explicitly political drama, *L'Écharpe rouge*, was a play of its times, the "Red Years" following May '68 and continuing into the 1970s. It is a vast tableau of scenes of classical party politics, with multiple struggles, splits, and polemics surrounding a largely successful revolution; it brings out the intensities and exuberance of its historical moment through extensive borrowings from Paul Claudel's enormous baroque drama of 1929, *Le Soulier de satin*. But with the 1980s the "Red" political sequence seemed to be waning and a new one emerging, the "Black Years" of political disillusionment and compromise, redolent with the "elegant despair" of the anti-Marxist New Philosophers. Hence the question of revolution in *The Incident at Antioch* is more problematic than in *L'Écharpe rouge*, and the possibilities of transformation glimpsed in it are uncertain. *The Incident at Antioch* reflects on the situation of the '80s again as refracted through Claudel's drama, this time his earlier play *La Ville* (*The City*) and now also through events in the life of Saint Paul and the early history of the Church. In these two "Pauls," Badiou finds the primary resources for his literary and conceptual experimentation: Saint Paul and Church history provide a structural framework and conceptual material, as well as the titles of acts and names of characters and places; whereas literary texture—elements of setting, plot, style, and dialogue—are borrowed from Claudel, to create a language that is densely poetic, often surreal, and sometimes obscure, as well as concrete and surprisingly colloquial. Moreover, along with these two Christian "Pauls," the Apostle and the Playwright, I would like to suggest that we can find traces of a third, Jewish Paul in Badiou's play: the mathematician Paul Cohen, whose innovative concept of a "generic set" and remarkably generative technique of "forcing" were becoming increasingly important to Badiou's thinking in the late '70s and '80s. The presence of this third "Paul" is less overt than the other two but nevertheless plays a key role in Badiou's play. In a sense, Paul Cohen's ideas mediate between the other two Pauls, spacing and dialecticizing their relationship in Badiou's play, and proposing ways for each of them to produce more theatrical knowledge than they might appear to contain. *The Incident at Antioch* finally is an experiment in dramatic thinking whose materials are largely drawn from the work of these three Pauls.

BADIOU, THEATER, PHILOSOPHY

Before we examine some aspects of these "Pauls" and their functions in *The Incident at Antioch*, let us briefly consider some of Badiou's ideas on theater and its relationship to philosophy and politics. Readers familiar with Badiou's other writings will no doubt recognize echoes of them in *The Incident at Antioch*, including the central concepts of the event and the subject; the distinction between truth and knowledge (as well as opinion); the nature of political decision, act, and force; the status of groups, parties, collectives; the difference between unity (and the One) and universalism (and the multiple); and the "indifference" of conventional political oppositions such as Left and Right, and the possibility of cutting "diagonally" between them. *The Incident at Antioch* is of a piece with Badiou's other work in the late '70s and early '80s, especially *Theory of the Subject*, and it anticipates ideas he will explore in his later work, including his 1998 *Saint Paul: The Foundation of Universalism*. But we should not approach Badiou's dramas as merely the *mise en scène* of ideas articulated more rigorously elsewhere in his work. Indeed, one might argue that Badiou's theater doesn't reflect his philosophy as much as produce discoveries that his philosophy will develop or think otherwise, in nontheatrical modes; for Badiou theater constitutes a distinctive mode of thinking that produces its own characteristic ideas, neither simply derived from nor transferable to philosophy. In the preface to the recent edition of his *Ahmed* tetralogy, Badiou describes theater as "a particularly active form of thought, an *action* of thought" (*La Tétralogie* 21, emphasis added). According to Badiou, the activity of theatrical thinking takes place primarily in the movement from textual referent to theatrical performance and in relationships among its performative elements—actors, staging, audience, and so on. Any literary text is a kind of thinking, of course, but the thought proper to theater requires the additional movement from text to performance. Under the larger mode of thinking that is Art, theater is especially "active" insofar as each performance is a singular and transient occurrence that opens the possibility of a specific kind of truth. But what sort of ideas can theater generate, and what in this context does Badiou mean by truth? Why use such an apparently philosophical word in the context of art? In an essay from 1998, "Théâtre et philosophie," Badiou defines "the singularity of the theater-truth" succinctly as "an experimental quasi-political event which amplifies our situation in history" (13). Let us extract and expand four central ideas from this compressed formulation:

1. The "*experimental* dimension of theatrical truth" involves, first of all, the leap over the abyss that separates text and rehearsal from performance before an audience. In his long essay from 1990, "Rhapsody for the Theatre," Badiou writes that "the essence of theater lies in the existence of the opening night," which is not the culmination of a process of rehearsal but the interruption of repetition (189). Theater, properly speaking, does not occur prior to crossing the Rubicon of Opening Night, and its outcome is always uncertain, no matter how well laid the plans of directors, actors, and other contributors. Each subsequent performance, moreover, is another roll of the dice, the wager that tonight will not be merely another "dress rehearsal" in the presence of an audience, but the emergence of something new through the collective work of writers, actors, painters, musicians, audience, and so on. Theater is experimental in a sense characteristic of art rather than science: The results of its investigations can rarely be predicted and never replicated. Contingency and "noise" are not necessarily seen as contaminants to be avoided, but may be welcome, even cultivated; there can be no theatrical "control group" and no external or objective position from which results can be assessed, insofar as the theater-experiment is *subjective*—which is not to say individual, private, or impressionistic. For Badiou theater functions as a kind of laboratory for the experimental production and investigation of new subjectivities, new ideas, and new temporalities. As such, it may have implications for philosophy, which can learn from it (consider the originary case of Plato, for whom theater is philosophy's noble rival), but this is not a reciprocal relationship—theatrical experimentation produces results undreamt by philosophy, which has little to offer it in return. Nevertheless, through philosophy's mediation, theater may have productive implications for other fields, such as politics, love, and perhaps even science.

2. As an experimental activity, a theatrical performance is not intended to produce knowledge (or for that matter catharsis), but aims primarily at *truth*. For Badiou "truths" are not especially certain types of "knowledge," statements that correspond to something in the external world or are coherent within a given system of statements, but the emergence of

something *new* in a world or discourse through subtraction or decomple-
tion, and the *procedures* for evaluation and expansion developed around
the void suddenly laid bare. Badiou calls such a punctual and vanishing
hole or excess in knowledge an *event*, and the four types of truth procedures Badiou describes (art, politics, science, and love) are new ways of
linking and grouping the previously unrecognizable and unaccountable
elements that have become perceptible in the wake of an event. In the
world of tragic theater a key example of such an event goes under the
name of "Aeschylus"; but every theatrical performance is potentially a
small-scale event, as well as a truth procedure that explores its consequences. Theatrical truths are not everyday occurrences of going to see a
play; we probably experience much less Theater than what Badiou refers
to (using scare quotes) as "theater," mere entertainment that offers not
truth but only "opinions." Theater, however, is the condition of possibility for a kind of truth to which we would otherwise have no access.
Philosophy, for its part, does not produce truth at all; it is in no position
either to judge art (the project of aesthetics or art history) or to theorize
politics (the claim of political theory), but depends on the truths produced by each for its work.

3. Theater, as we suggested earlier, occurs as the exceptional intimacy
of the distinct truth procedures of *art and politics*. Badiou argues, "of all
the arts, theatre is the one that most insistently stands *next to* (or sup-
poses) politics" ("Rhapsody," 200). Theater can only break from the endless repetition of "theater" insofar as it appears in a world in which both
artistic and political truth procedures are vigorously pursued. Theater is
the space in which art and politics come into contact, without either polit-
icizing art or aestheticizing politics. Theater is art and politics in solidarity with each other—art offering its experimental resources for political
thinking, and politics lending art the possibility of collectivization—but
each retaining its own distinctive methods, materials, and kinds of truths.
Such a close relationship between fundamentally different truth procedures is possible because of what Badiou calls the "theater-politics isomorphism": the three conditions essential to theater (audience, actors,
textual or traditional referent) correspond to the three factors whose knot
is the political (masses, multiple subject-effects or positions, a thought
or conceptual referent). And just as true Theater is "rare," so too politics for Badiou is not the daily business of state administration, but its
occasional interruption. Moreover, theater is intrinsically "an affair of

the State," according to Badiou; unlike film, which can unspool just as well in an empty auditorium as in a full one, theater necessarily occurs in a public place before a group of spectators and in the shadow of an existing state: "theatre alone is tied to the State, cinema belongs only to Capital" ("Rhapsody," 188). And just as the state keeps a watchful eye on political activities that might disturb its administrative work, so it is also concerned with the ideological threat posed by theater, at times censoring or even closing it down entirely. In turn, theater observes the state with suspicion and tries to insert some moral distance into this uncomfortable proximity. And the fates of politics and theater are bound up with each other; when politics becomes entombed in the state, theater becomes "indecisive" and weak: "Theater," Badiou writes, "is sick of parliaments and cared for by unions of all kinds as one is cared for onstage by Molière's doctors" ("Rhapsody," 195). Theater is imperiled not only by state censure, but also by state support, which may turn it, we might say, into an "imaginary invalid," rendered impotent by the subsidies that prop it up. This isomorphism of theater and politics does not, however, imply reciprocity: If theater approaches the condition of politics in its relationship to the state, politics is not essentially theatrical (although it may of course involve demonstrations and other theatrical techniques). Theater is not political when it discusses political ideas, or even when it has social or political repercussions (as it occasionally does), but in its production of its audience as a new collective subjectivity—even if only in the person of a single spectator.

4. Theater's truth procedures are always addressed to *the present*, to "our situation in history," and as such they produce a new type of temporality. In "Théâtre et philosophie," Badiou elaborates on the particular historical present of theater: "Theater indicates where we are in historical time, but it does it with a kind of readable amplification that is proper to it. It clarifies our situation" (13). Whenever a play was written or in whatever period it may be set, theater reflects and *inflects* the historical moment of its performance. Its proximity to the State gives it special access to the language and structure of the current situation, which it makes readable in order to criticize (or in the case of "theater," merely reproduce), but insofar as theater is a truth procedure it also modifies its moment by supplementing the available experiences of time. Like politics, theater has a double temporal structure, involving both the long work of preparation that is broken by a singular performative act and

the retroactive assertion of a relationship between this act and a previous Event whose truth it expands. Theater, Badiou writes, proposes an "artificial temporality" that arises from the encounter between the "eternity" of a dramatic text, character, or idea and the "instants" of each embodied performance ("Théâtre et philosophie," 12–13). This is not the temporality of belatedness in which modern performances struggle against and thereby reassert the eternal authority of a past text, but the production of an experience of eternity *in* the present moment as an anticipation of its potentially infinite future expansion. Theater-truth involves a temporality "out of joint" with chronological history, like the messianic materialism described by Walter Benjamin, in which the string of present moments, "like the beads of a rosary," are shattered by the irruption of eternal "splinters of Messianic time," producing a revolutionary *Jetztzeit* or "now-time" redeemed from the constraints of historicism (397). This is a structure of both retroaction and anticipation, insofar as the theatrical performance not only contributes to and reconfigures a pre-existing idea, but also, in Paul Cohen's term, *forces* the future extensions of its truth to exist in the present moment. Finally, the question of such intervention is linked to Saint Paul's messianism in *The Incident at Antioch*: What can be done to bring about authentic change? If an "event" cannot be scripted or directed but must be awaited and responded to in its evanescence, what active strategies of transformation are available to the subject of politics or theater?

As we read *The Incident at Antioch*, it will be helpful to keep in mind these four aspects of Badiou's definition of theater, which we might reassemble as follows: Theater is *an experimental procedure for the production of an infinite and eternal truth in the present at the cusp of art and politics by finite, transient means.* We must not forget, however, that the text of the play by itself is only one of the several elements that contribute to a theatrical truth. Although Antoine Vitez's originary solo performance of the play actualized the possibility of *The Incident at Antioch* as a dramatic truth procedure, future performances will be the condition of its continuing expansion.[1] Nevertheless, Badiou's play as a text brings *resources* to the table of political and experimental theater, suggests *strategies* for performative realization, and deploys *techniques* in its orientation towards its sources, which we will now consider in more detail. My hope here is to provide background on these sources that may be helpful in reading Badiou's admittedly difficult play, and some ideas about ways to understand the relationships the play proposes among these three Pauls.

SAINT PAUL AND THE STRUCTURE
OF *THE INCIDENT AT ANTIOCH*

The three acts of *The Incident at Antioch* are named after three ancient cities—Damascus, Antioch, and Nicea—associated with events in early Christianity of major significance for the play, as well as frequent points of reference elsewhere in Badiou's work. Each act, moreover, is divided into a sequence of scenes that reflects the logic of the Christian episode it is named for as a movement through one or more of five allegorical places, or *lieux*: "The Official Place of Politics" (a big empty room), "The Place of the War Reserves" (a military port), "The Place of Truths" (the gates of a factory), "The Place of Choices" (a country road), and "The Place of Foundations" (a city in ruins). Act I, "The Road to Damascus," refers to the legendary conversion event reported in the Book of Acts where the Pharisee Saul, previously a zealous persecutor of the heretical cult of Jesus, encounters the risen Christ on the road from Jerusalem to Damascus sometime around 35 CE. Falling from his horse, he is temporarily blinded by the vision, but arises with eyes opened as "Paul": ex post facto Apostle of Christ to the gentile nations. For Badiou, the "road to Damascus" emblematizes the kind of evental break that is the condition for the emergence of a new subject; in his 1975 *Théorie de la contradiction,* he writes, "I admit, without any hesitation, that May '68 for me was . . . a veritable road to Damascus" (9). Paul's "conversion" on the road to Damascus is not for Badiou a "turning around" from some false idea or "turning toward" a new doctrine, but a "thunderbolt, a caesura" that shatters his very being and subjectivizes him as part of the collective known as the Body of Christ.[2] The experience will lead to new ideas, but in itself it involves no concepts, and requires nothing more than the faithful investigation and expansion of the event's consequences. Paul's model for this subjective reorientation is the faith of Abraham, and the Road to Damascus extends the unidirectional vector of Abraham's path out of Haran, when he heeds God's call to "go out from yourself" (*lekh lekha*) and unhesitatingly leaves his family, land, and his very self. This trajectory of departure or moving "out" seems reflected in the procession of scenes in Act I from one allegorical "place" to the next, without return: beginning in the Official Place of Politics, it moves to the Place of the War Reserves, from there to the Place of Truths, and ends in the Place of Choices—stopping short of the Place of Foundations, where the play will conclude. This sequence of scenes in Act I establishes a linear order in its continuous movement from one new Place to the next, a simple trajectory of Change that Acts II and III will complicate and modify.

Act II is "The Incident at Antioch" proper, named after the dispute between Paul and Peter in about 50 CE over the status of Jewish law in the Messianic era—an episode whose importance, Badiou writes in his book on Saint Paul, "it is impossible to overestimate" (26). The controversy arises at the famous Jerusalem Conference where Paul receives his mission to the gentiles and comes to a head when Peter later visits Paul's congregation in Antioch. The Christians centered in Jerusalem under the leadership of Peter ("Cephas," in Hellenized Aramaic) and Jesus's brother James insisted that Jewish Christians must continue to follow Jewish ritual law, including circumcision and the dietary rules of *kashrut*, and that gentiles too must become practicing Jews as part of their conversion to the messianic sect. For Paul such observation of the law fails to grasp the essential implication of faith in Jesus, because—at least according to one tradition of Jewish messianic speculation—all previous ritual law will be suspended when the Messiah comes. According to Paul's account of the "incident" in Galatians, when Peter first visited the Pauline church in Antioch, he ate freely with non-Jewish Christians, unconcerned about the laws of *kashrut*; but with the arrival of members of the Jerusalem church, Peter again observes the dietary regulations, and many members of the Antioch congregation follow his example, infuriating Paul, and opening a deep schism within emergent Christianity about the law. Paul argues not only that Peter's action is hypocritical, but more significantly that it denies the absolute sufficiency of Christ's sacrifice by implying that obedience to the law is still an effective means of "justification": Fidelity and lawfulness, Paul insists, are mutually exclusive relationships to the world historical transformations inaugurated by the Messiah's advent. In his book on Saint Paul, Badiou argues that Paul's position is not on behalf of Faith contra Law, but cuts a path diagonal to that opposition: "It is not that communitarian marking (circumcision, rites, the meticulous observance of the Law) is indefensible or erroneous. It is that the postevental imperative of truth renders the latter *indifferent* (which is worse). It has no signification, whether positive or negative" (23). For Paul, the "indifference" of the law means that one may indeed observe the law but only, as he writes in 1 Corinthians 7, *hōs mē*, "as if not," as if it were without force, not truly binding. The reciprocal implication would be that one may decline to practice the law, but only if nonobservance is not seen as an antinomian act of liberation, which would grant the law negative efficacy.

In *The Incident at Antioch*, this idea will be transferred to the controversy between proponents of revolutionary destruction and reformist reconstruction, and will allow Badiou's heroine Paula to articulate a new proposition incommensurate with conventional political discourses. The movement among scenic places in Act II describes a kind of static oscillation among opposed positions or irreconcilable interpretations of the events in Act I, like the conflict between Peter and Paul at Antioch. Skipping the Official Place of Politics, it begins in the militant Place of the War Reserves and moves in scene 2 one step forward (according to the sequence established in Act I) to the Place of Truths, only to return in scene 3 to the Place of the War Reserves; scene 4 sets out again, this time short-circuiting the Place of Truths and leaping directly to the Place of Choices, before again returning in scene 5 to the initial Place of the War Reserves. Each movement out and back proceeds either to "truths" or "choices," but neither passes through both, and each ends where it begins, in the Place of the War Reserves. These paths, however, do not describe the conflict of simple positions, one of which is more correct than the other, but the poles of a situation in relation to which a new path, diagonal to that opposition, is proposed.

Act III is titled "The Council of Nicea," after what we might call the "first international" of the Christian church convened by the Emperor Constantine in 325 CE, where fundamental doctrine was debated, including the vexed question of the substance of Christ's divinity, and the principles of a universal, or "catholic," Christian church were declared. The results of the Nicene Council and the Empire established by Constantine's merger of Rome and Christianity might seem to be the institutional closure of the radical subjective sequence opened by Saint Paul. For Badiou, however, the First Council of Nicea represents a radical new mode of dialectical thinking, one continued in the work of Hegel, Marx, and Mao, and still with resources to offer. In *Theory of the Subject* Badiou discusses the Nicene Council as exemplary of the dialectics of "one divides into two."

The debate at Nicea that produces Trinitarian theology involves the conflict between two positions that are both finally declared heretical: the "deviations to the right and left" of Arianism, which argues that Christ is God's finite creation, nondivine, fully human; and Docetism, which claims that the Son is absolutely divine, infinite, merely an extension or expression of God the Father. Badiou reformulates the results of the Nicene debate as the Hegelian dialectics of "force" and "place" (terms that anticipate his later concepts of "event" and "situation"): One God divides into two as the "force" of God is "placed" in historical time and space as Christ. The Nicene creed, Badiou argues, does not declare the mystical synthesis of Father and Son via the mediation of the Holy Spirit, but a rational dialectics of self-division, a spiraling "torsion" and periodizing "scission" from which novelty emerges, as "the pure passage from one sequence to the other" (19).

In Act III of *The Incident at Antioch*, set entirely in the Place of Foundations, the passage into a radically new sequence abandons spatial movement entirely. Instead its scenes are divided into a series of hours of the day, advancing from "dusk" in scene 1 to "the middle of the night" in scene 2, to "around 4 AM" in scene 3, to a gray "dawn" in scene 4, "10 AM" in scene 5, and concluding at the philosophical hour of "noon" in scene 6—the moment in Claudel's play *Partage de midi (Break of Noon)*, Badiou argues, of "the highest decision . . . the real event."[3] This cycle of hours, however, is not the abandonment of spatiality for a more fundamental or authentic experience of temporality—there is no mention of time or its passing in the act—but involves a kind of fold or twist of space and time, in which movement is no longer measurable in terms of either. We recall Parsifal's comment when he arrives at the Temple of the Grail: "I scarcely tread, yet seem already to have come far," to which Gurnemanz replies: "time here becomes space." Similarly, in Badiou's play traversing Nicea seems to require a new type of movement, unlike those in Antioch or along the road to Damascus. Here what appears to be a revolutionary putsch may be no more than treading water, and refusing state power may be a kind of act with unexpected force. Hence the Nicene Place of Foundations in Act III is not the resolution of the dialectics of Damascus and Antioch, but the "place outside of place," the "outplace" (*horlieu*), in Badiou's coinage in *Theory of the Subject*, from which a new political subject and sequence may commence. Nicea is the "foundation" for the possible emergence of an "impossible" political thinking, like a fragile flower, easily crushed and its longevity uncertain—nevertheless for the moment it is eternal, universal, and true.

We can diagram the movement of scenes in the three acts of *The Incident at Antioch* as follows:

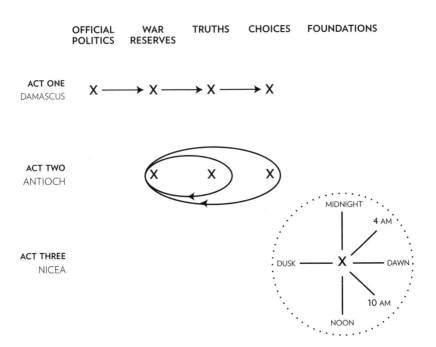

PAUL COHEN: FORCING AND THE GENERIC

Every reader of Badiou's philosophy knows that his thinking is profoundly based in set theory and other modes of contemporary mathematics. The suggestion that his drama also reflects mathematical ideas may be more surprising, but perhaps is not too outlandish. After all, when Paul Cohen sent his proof of the undecidability of the continuum hypothesis (which Badiou considers an "event") to Kurt Gödel in 1963, Gödel wrote back that "reading your proof had a similarly pleasant effect on me as seeing a really good play."[4] Although we might speculate whether seeing Badiou's play might have a pleasant effect similar to that produced by the demonstration of a really good mathematical proof, we can in any case find suggestions in *The Incident at Antioch* of Badiou's extension of Cohen's ideas into the realms of politics and art. Cohen's work goes back to Georg Cantor's 1877 "continuum hypothesis," which argues that the next largest infinity after the "smallest" infinity of whole numbers is the set of all real numbers, the continuum of points on the number line. Because this is the *next* biggest infinity, Cantor's hypothesis opened the door to perhaps infinitely more types of larger infinities than had previously been conceivable. In 1938 Kurt Gödel proved that the continuum hypothesis is indeed consistent with the standard Zermelo–Fraenkel axiomatization of Cantorian set theory (abbreviated ZF), a common foundation for modern mathematics; in 1963, however, Paul Cohen produced a model of ZF in which the continuum hypothesis is false. This led Gödel and Cohen to conclude that the continuum hypothesis is "independent" from ZF, part of a small group of statements in set theory that are "undecidable." The importance of this discovery is matched by the remarkable technique that Cohen developed to produce the new model of ZF, which he called *forcing*, and which continues to be enormously generative of mathematical innovation. Forcing involves adjoining to a fundamental model of ZF a "generic" set, one that, Cohen writes, "enjoys no 'specific' property" of the model it is added to, and that in a sense is hypothetical or "imaginary," insofar as it is an only partly known infinite set. Whereas the members of a "constructible" set are determined by particular conditions that they all satisfy, a "generic" set is a collection of elements that are not unified by any such condition, but determined merely by its members. By adding even one such unmarked subset to a given model, Cohen writes, "one would have a method to adjoin many and thus create many different models with various properties," new models that are "weakly forced" (as opposed to the "stronger" and more familiar function of implication), based on the promised future extension of the generic set.[5] The supplementation of a given set-theoretical model with such a barely discernible generic set forces the reevaluation of every statement in that model, with indeterminate and infinitely expanding consequences, leading, perhaps, to an entirely new mathematical world.

Badiou writes in the introduction to *Being and Event* that Cohen's concepts "resonate well beyond their technical validity, which has confined them up till now to the academic arena of the high specialists of set theory" (16). And this is precisely his project: to extend Cohen's concepts of forcing and the generic to other realms, including politics and art. Already in *Theory of the Subject* (based on seminars delivered between 1975 and 1979, and written more or less simultaneously with *The Incident at Antioch*), Badiou develops the distinction between constructible sets and logical implication, on the one hand, and generic sets and forcing, on the other, into the political question of how "immigrant workers" who "inexist" or are "internally excluded" in the larger political world can come into "existence" or (in his later terminology) *appear*. Is it a question of extending to undocumented workers the rights of "the documented"—that is, of "constructing" them as proper members of the nation according to well-defined criteria of citizenship? Perhaps this would be a welcome development, but the real political issue here, according to Badiou, goes beyond the project of increasing the number of recognized members of the state: "those who undergo the most important modification are not so much the immigrant workers themselves, even if they snatch up the right to vote, so much as the French: the French workers for whom the subversion of their national identity, provided they are swept up in the process, subjectivizes another vision and another practice of politics" (*TS*, 265—66). If we think of the immigrant workers as a *generic set*, not defined by any unifying characteristics, but as an infinite group of heterogeneous singularities, their addition as such a set *forces* the transformation of the entire nation, which can no longer be defined by the same "axioms" of identity. Such a transformation is not the function of historical necessity or logical implication; Badiou writes, "The 'no!' of the revolt is not implied by the local conditions. It is forced by the inexistence of an absolute constraint that would force submission to the immediate condition in a transcendent way" (*TS*, 273).[6] Forcing in this sense involves a subjective attitude, being "swept up in the process" and wagering that the generic set "will have been" completed. This is not exactly "blind faith," but what Badiou calls "confidence": a new form of verifiable *knowledge* with immediate consequences in the world.[7] If forcing seems "weak" compared with the "strength" of logical implication, this is precisely its strength: Forcing does not argue, for example, that social contradiction *implies* the necessity of revolution, but rather that there is *nothing that requires the continuing dominance of the local conditions,* nothing preventing that generic set from extending into the conditions of a radically new political world.

In his 1997 book on Saint Paul, Badiou suggests a link between Cohen's concepts and Saint Paul's messianism. Explaining his affinity for Paul's thinking, despite his frank disbelief in the content of Paul's revelation, Badiou writes that Paul's "*fabulous forcing of the real* provides us with mediation when it is a question of restoring the universal to its pure secularity, here and now" (*Saint Paul*, 5, emphasis added). Paul's discourse is "fabulous" for Badiou, merely a fable, but nevertheless it *forces* the production of new knowledge about the universal, outside of any religious conviction. Badiou's characterization of Saint Paul's project as "forcing the real" links him with the controversial Jewish concept of "hastening" or "forcing" the advent of the messianic era, in effect compelling God to act through human agency. Such "forcing" was a plausible accusation against all Messianists, including the early Christians: Wasn't the declaration that Jesus was the Messiah precipitous and demonstrably erroneous, since, for one thing, he had lived and died without effecting the radical social and political transformations traditionally associated with the Messiah?[8] In Badiou's reading, Paul's response is that Jesus *will have been* the Messiah, through the confidence of those like himself who pursue the "generic" universalism implied by his resurrection. That is, just as Paul Cohen "forces" the future perfect production of myriad new set theoretical worlds by the minor addition of a generic set, so Saint Paul "forces" Jesus to have been the Messiah by the addition of the generic set of "Christians," a set, we recall, that is not determined by outward markings such as circumcision or uncircumcision. And just as Cohen enables the creation of strong new models for mathematics through the "weak" technique of forcing, so Paul's "militant discourse of *weakness*" has had the strength to invent several new worlds (53).[9] We recall

Walter Benjamin's discussion of Kafka, for whom, he writes, the Messiah "will not wish to change the world by force but will merely make a slight adjustment in it" (*Selected Writings,* Vol. 2, 811). This is the messianism not of force but of *forcing,* in which the "slight adjustment" produced by the addition of the almost nothing of a generic set is enough to change almost everything. And this is the possibility of transformation that Paula will obscurely invoke in *The Incident at Antioch.*

PAUL CLAUDEL AND THE MATERIALS OF *THE INCIDENT AT ANTIOCH*

If Paul Cohen seems an unlikely resource for drama, Paul Claudel—political and religious conservative, career diplomat, perhaps even apologist for Pétain—might seem to be an unlikely literary ally for Badiou. Although Claudel is less read and performed today than he once was, Badiou is not alone in considering him to be the most important modern French dramatist before the war.[10] Claudel's theater was unlike anything before it in France, and it is still singularly demanding: linguistically dense, nonpsychological, often drenched in Catholicism, and sometimes enormously long, it is a symbolist theater of passionate ideas. In a letter from 1894 to the dramatist Maurice Pottecher, Claudel speculates on the possibility of "a theater of thought," and this above all is what Badiou finds essential in him: a drama in which ideas are not only represented but also *constituted* by what happens on stage.[11] In *The Century,* Badiou makes the unexpected comparison of Claudel with Brecht, arguing that for both dramatists "what touches the real is never either knowledgeable wisdom or ordinary morality. What is required instead is a definitive and deracinating encounter, together with an absolute stubbornness in pursuing the consequences of this encounter to the very end" (fn. 15, p. 207). This could just as well describe Badiou's own dramatic practice, which aims to produce an evental encounter with a "real" exceptional to the horizon of reality, and vigorously pursues its unpredictable consequences, wherever they may lead. What this suggests, moreover, is that for Badiou Claudel is not so much a literary *auctoritas,* an imitable source of poetic ideas or moral intelligence, as a text to be "encountered." Hence we find that a remarkable quantity of Claudel's language passes directly into Badiou's play, often untouched or only lightly modified. Moreover *The*

Incident at Antioch closely follows much of the plot of *La Ville*: Both plays begin with an obscure political crisis and a vacuum in leadership, a dire situation without evident solution. Both plays are written in the aftermath of a great French political event that seems to have run its course: for Claudel, the Paris Commune, for Badiou, May '68. Both plays confront the question of how to recover some part of these events beyond their apparent termination; how, that is, to *force* the current situation through our confidence that the barely discernible traces of those events do indeed constitute elements of a new and expanding generic set.

Because Claudel's play is so constitutive of Badiou's, some familiarity at least with the plot and texture of *La Ville* will be helpful for reading *The Incident*. Claudel wrote a first version of *La Ville* in 1890 (published in 1893), and in 1897, while a diplomat in China, significantly revised it. It is this second version, published in 1901, that is the primary model for *The Incident at Antioch*. The first act of Claudel's revised text is set in a garden above the unnamed city, where the world-weary former politician, Lambert de Besme, expects to be called to return to government to lead the city's recovery from economic collapse and to quell the growing social and political chaos. He is cynical about politics and fatalistic about the city, however, and plans to marry his young ward, the beautiful Lâla (her very name a song of the feminine) and to retire with her in domestic tranquility. With him is the misanthropic Avare, who scoffs at Lambert's romantic aspirations and the desperate attempts to restore order to the city, and calls instead for its fiery destruction. Lambert's wealthy brother, Isidore de Besme, the engineer, plutarch, and "Father of the City," enters along with the alienated and disillusioned poet Cœuvre (usually taken as something of a proxy for Claudel himself). Lâla taunts and flirts with Cœuvre, her onetime teacher, and it becomes clear that she has not yet decided to marry the much older Lambert. When deputies enter and plead with Lambert to accept the offer of leadership, he leaves the decision with Lâla: If she agrees to marry him he will return to politics, even though he has little faith that anything can be done. Lâla, however, throws herself at Cœuvre's feet and begs him to marry her. Cœuvre seems contemptuous of her self-abasement but claims her as his own, derisively summoning her to follow him as the curtain falls.

Act II takes place in a cemetery overlooking the city, where Lambert digs graves for the victims of Avare's purge. Lâla has had a son with Cœuvre, but she has left them to reside with Avare, and she now returns to tell Lambert that "inequality among men exists no more" and to urge him to join her and the rebels. Lâla doesn't seem to be describing a political reality as much as expressing her own inexplicable prophetic ecstasy and a feminine knowledge that remains mysterious to the men. For Avare, however, "equality" means that all men are equally worthless, and to realize this nihilistic vision he relentlessly burns the city and murders its citizens. Most of Act II involves complicated political discussion among Avare and Lâla, more or less on the "left," and Besme and Cœuvre, apparently defending the state, while Lambert witnesses from a grave. But the rioters are approaching, and the act concludes with the murder of Besme, his head carried by the mob on a pike.

Act III is set fourteen years later, when Avare has fulfilled his political vision of destruction: The city is in ruins, "millions" were killed, and through military force he has established "peace." He has no further desires but to let "this devastation have authority," and so he suddenly departs. He passes his command to Ivors, the son of Lâla and Cœuvre, who joined the clergy and has now returned to the city as a Bishop. Cœuvre calls for an end to the "strife and litigation" and tells the people to prepare for peace. At first Ivors is suspicious of his father's religious turn, seeing little value in his inexplicable vision of "absolute happiness," and seems more concerned with reconstructing the government. The poet-turned-priest Cœuvre urges him not to stop there, but to look for a deeper satisfaction and a more profound transformation of both the city and its subjects: "Happiness is not some luxurious ornament," he argues, "it is in us like ourselves, it is blent with the subject of our consciousness" (103). Ivors declares his faith in God, and asks his father for advice in founding a new society. Cœuvre replies in a familiar Platonic metaphor that, although there is no "sovereign recipe" for politics, the "incomprehensible Truth," like the "sun" from which all things "derive their form and life," will guide him. The king is "the sacred being, the one among all men" and the "heart" of the body politic; society in turn "absorbs the leader" and then "restores again his image" to him. Suddenly, in the last moments of the play, Lâla returns, her hair gray but her beauty strangely undimmed with time; at first Ivors denounces her as "the Queen of Madness, the mother of the aberrant multitude," a "witch," but Lâla pleads that she has been misunderstood: No one knows, she says, "the secret of my joy." She salutes Ivors as king, the fruit of his father's poetic religiosity and his mother's joyful liberation. Like a holy spirit who will dwell among them, Lâla enigmatically proclaims herself "the promise that cannot be kept," "the sweetness of that which is with the regret of that which is not," and "truth with the face of error," even as she leaves to die (114). It is noon, and Ivors announces that he will constitute the city's new laws.

In the original version of his well-known poem "In Memory of W. B. Yeats," Auden wrote that "Time . . . will pardon Paul Claudel"—"pardon" him, presumably, for his politics and possibly for his Catholicism. But even though he is an atheist and considerably to the left of Auden politically, Badiou seems to feel no need to forgive or apologize for Claudel in *The Incident at Antioch*. For Badiou, Claudel's personal religious or political "opinions" are irrelevant compared with his conceptual and aesthetic struggles in *La Ville*: his attempt to invent a new dramaturgical language, a language for the production of new ideas concerning how we shall live. The particular content of those ideas is finally not as important as the confidence in the possibility of the new that they signal. For Badiou, Lâla is the central figure in Claudel's play, and the role of Paula in *The Incident* greatly expands her function, especially in the third act, while shifting the inflection of her revelation from religion to politics. For Claudel, Lâla's return at the end of the play symbolizes the promise of renewed political-theological life, under the auspices of her spiritual joy. There is, however, no indication that Ivors or Cœuvre has been affected by her final ecstatic utterance, or that their plans for the City will be influenced by it. As Ivors tells her, "Woman, your place is not with us"—and this is precisely her point as well: Lâla has no place in the renascent City. She does not represent a particular position among the various voices on stage; she is, in Badiou's sense, "outside of place," and her strange appearing and disappearing signals the eventa nature of the truth she announces. Lâla is the cause of the desire for change, without specification or limitation. As she says, "he who hears me is cured of repose forever and of the thought that he has found it": She offers no solutions, only restless confidence in the possibility of transformation. As "the promise that cannot be kept," she is not a promise that will be broken, but an impossible promise—indeed, the promise *of* the impossible, the index of a path not limited to the pragmatic questions of "what is possible" that the city's new leaders will no doubt need to confront. Badiou understands this line, "the promise that cannot be kept," as Claudel's definition of woman (*The Century*, 24). This does not mean, however, that Lâla is a "typical" woman or the type of Woman; rather, we might say that Lâla is "unconstructible," in Paul Cohen's sense:

Lâla is woman precisely insofar as she is both singular and generic. As she says in her final speech, "I am truth with the face of error and he who loves me is not concerned with dividing the one from the other." Lâla is indifferent to the oppositions and categories that organize the world of *The City* as it is; she has no place there, but instead points to *another world*, as yet obscure, but undetermined by existing political categories. Lâla's final ecstatic annunciation, before she turns to greet death, concludes with a compelling image: "He who sets himself to follow me will not know how to stop." Whether the new City will indeed follow her remains uncertain, an open question. There is nothing that implies that it must, but perhaps we will be able to say, through the intervention of *The Incident at Antioch*, that the knowledge of its possibility will have been forced.

THE INCIDENT AT ANTIOCH

Despite its references to the *banlieues*, media, the fall of communism, Arab workers, and other markers of modern France, the setting of Badiou's final version of *The Incident at Antioch* is abstract and underdetermined, much like the second version of Claudel's *La Ville*. Both revisions are simplified and generalized, as if to avoid the particularity of historical and geographical context for the sake of the immediacy of a drama of ideas. The world in which Badiou's play takes place, composed of shards and fragments of Claudel's poetic language, is a world in which the Paris of May 1968 and the Paris of the 1871 Commune converge—not as similar historical events, but as singular Events that fall out of any historical continuum. *The Incident* offers us access to Paul Claudel's City through the technique of forcing practiced by Paul of Tarsus and formalized by Paul Cohen.

Act I, "The Road to Damascus," begins in the Official Place of Politics, where the current situation is laid out: The unnamed City has been ravaged by economic crises, and the government is collapsing. Politicians on the right and left, the clownish brothers Jean and Pierre Maury, put aside their differences to call for the return of the retired elder statesman Claude Villembray to form a "national unity government," as the only remaining hope of averting disaster. The radical Cephas, on the other hand, broods on the "worthlessness" of all existing political discourse and rejects what he sees as desperate attempts to salvage the state; he dreams of a new political order and gazes up at the "star of power" that now seems within reach. The scenario here closely follows the opening of *The City*, with Villembray in the role of Lambert de Besme, and the part of the melancholy revolutionary with a passion for destruction played by Cephas. Badiou "samples" here liberally from Claudel, borrowing individual words, snatches of dialogue, and sometimes entire phrases from *The City*, at times leaving them intact, at other modifying or recombining them. But a consistent one-to-one relationship between *dramatis personae* in the two plays cannot be established: Sometimes Badiou's characters speak lines drawn from several different figures in Claudel's play, and sometimes lines from one of Claudel's characters are divided among more than one figure in Badiou. So Villembray's speeches combine lines from both Lambert and Isidore de Besme, and Paula's include elements of both Lâla's and Cœuvre's discourses in *La Ville*. It often feels as if Claudel's play constitutes an unconscious storehouse of phrases and images that move into Badiou's play of their own accord, like elements of a dream work; but elsewhere, Badiou's appropriations and modifications of Claudel seem precise and strategic. For example, in Act I, scene I both Avare and Cephas recollect primal scenes of their political rage: In Claudel's play, it is Avare's memory of public indifference in the face of a personal loss that makes him now yearn "with a force like the rigor of love" to restore the "glory" of death to the world. He looks down at the City, where he sees the people locked in the prisons of their own conventionality, and wants to "liberate" them from the corruption that is their lives. In Badiou's version, it is a scene of police brutality, the obscenity of the Law, that galvanized Cephas, and drives him now to purge the city through fire and terror. And whereas it is *death* that Avare wants to restore to a world that has forgotten it, Cephas seeks a new *language*, new rules—indeed, consistent with his Petrine name, a new Law "where ordinary law leaves off." The desire of each is to re-establish a limiting, regulatory principle (death, law) that has been corrupted: Thus both Avare and Cephas are *reactionary* revolutionaries, each caught in the vicious circle of his own *ressentiment* and each working to transform the old rather than to discover the new. And by putting Law in the place of Death in Claudel's text, Badiou tacitly makes the Pauline argument that it is the law itself that has brought death into the world. Both Avare and Cephas are motivated by memories of injustice that they wish to rectify, and neither is simply condemned by their authors.[12] But each is limited by and to the terms of the primal scenes that structure their revolutionary desires and tie them to the past. Those scenes are in a sense the inversion of Badiouian events, and to be "faithful" to them is to linger in the particularity of private wounds. Once their initial destructive vision is achieved there is nothing left for either Avare or Cephas to do but disappear without trace or consequence.

Scene 2 of Act I is set in the Place of the War Reserves, the allegorical locus of ammunition for the consideration of politics by other means. Here we see the cynical Villembray, who no longer believes in the possibility of change: "Action merely obeys a pointless necessity," he comments, "everything comes about with completely predictable results." Paula, Villembray's beautiful and strangely charismatic sister, agrees with Cephas that nothing will be gained through reformist policies, but she is neither resigned to political decay like her brother nor committed to Cephas's revolutionary vision. Paula feels inexplicably liberated from the constraints of history and women's conventional roles. She believes that all existing accounts of political power are inadequate, but as yet she is unsure how to pursue the transformation—one finally more radical than the total destruction envisioned by Cephas—that she obscurely senses: "What do you measure power by?" she asks her brother. "The powerful fragrance of misty gardens, where the boxwoods have just been pruned? The power of truths in the *banlieues*, at the factory gates, on public transport? The powerful melancholy of the Arabian sands? Doesn't Venice draw its force from having no force at all anymore?" Paula's idea of a certain kind of *power of powerlessness* is central to the play, and over the course of Act I her uncertain musings will develop into subjective certainty. Paula believes that the materials for change are already at hand, but her confidence is intuitive and inchoate—more existential than conceptual. When a dilapidated battleship appears in the harbor, representing the obsolescence of conventional military might, Paula salutes the "overly symbolic ship" by throwing her overdetermined "red scarf" (*l'écharpe rouge*) into the water, but she acknowledges that the gesture is "ambiguous": Does she anoint the battleship with the emblem of revolution, or is she taking leave of both symbols? As if following the orthodox Marxist location of political reality in the means of production, scene 3 continues Paula's investigation at the gates of a factory, The Place of Truths. There Paula, her Arab husband Mokhtar, and a factory worker, Madame Pintre, salute the workers for their concrete experience of the real. But for Paula there is no longer any certainty here. The workers are silent and the revolutionary discourse of the truth of Labor belies the conventionality of the party politics at the factory, which for her reeks with "the stench of a dead State." The city is already in flames and the old models no longer apply, and she alone senses the immanence of a new world in this void. For Paula "the world is starting today," every moment is a new beginning, on the verge of redemption, and the path to the new world she obscurely senses leads from the ecstasy of "this very nothing that I am" to "the dispersion of being" as such, a destitution beyond the material destruction called for by Cephas.

In Act I, scene 4 we have reached the Place of Choices, the road where Paula will have her "Damascus" event. The Maurys continue to press Villembray to take control of the foundering government and enact the drastic cuts required to salvage the economy. And as in *La Ville*, where Lambert announces that his decision will depend on Lâla's response to his marriage proposal, so Villembray here leaves the decision to Paula. But rather than answering, Paula falls to the ground, her arms outstretched in ecstatic revelation, as in Caravaggio's painting of Saint Paul falling off his horse: "Chance, illusion of meaning, whereby I know what it knows! The pebbles in my mouth are changing into clear words." Paula's revelation overflows in a rush of surreal images, her subjective conversion experienced as an impersonal "it knows" of unconscious truth, beyond the personal "illusion of meaning." Like Socrates's *daemon*, Paula's revelation calls her back from precipitous action, the "feverish exaltation" of revolutionary enthusiasm. She arises, shattered, "a woman broken in two," and transfigured, a radiant new subject with "the precision of an axiom," no longer bound by the world she lives in. In language that recalls Lacan's description of the terrible splendor of Antigone, she sees herself as "the sudden flash of light, the magnificent imminence" of a new subjective possibility. She is possessed too by new ideas, indeed the *idea* of new Ideas, "the inexistent's ability to be thought"—*political* ideas that she embodies as much as understands: "I exist in the splitting of the law." The "splitting" of the law is neither hairsplitting obedience to state authority nor political disobedience, but indifferent or diagonal to such oppositions. The revolutionaries are swept up in Paula's revelation and commit to follow her; they experiment with different militant interpretations of the event, but they don't really understand her. And how can they? Her experience is literally beyond their frame of reference; as she says, "I'm taking place out of place [*J'ai lieu hors lieu*]." "The road to

Damascus" in Act I has led from Place to Place until finally taking Paula entirely beyond the coordinates of the political discourses surrounding her. This "place out of place" (the *horlieu* or "outplace" of *Theory of the Subject*) in which Paula now finds herself, at the center of the new revolutionary movement but also strangely excluded by it, recalls Lacan's notion of "extimacy" (*extimité*), the topological folding of outside and inside, subject and other, characteristic of the *objet a*. Paula is the catalyst of the crowd's excitement—and like the *objet a*, the cause of their desire—but according to Badiou's stage directions she is "almost completely hidden" behind them, again like the *objet a*, shrouded by their projections and recontained by their imaginary embrace.

As the revolutionaries wrap themselves together in the red scarf, Paula recites a long list of great women (including Sappho, Hypatia, Joan of Arc, Emily Dickinson, Rosa Luxembourg, and Camille Claudel), concluding that "this marks the end of all the exhausting efforts to bring you to light. The declaration of the end of exceptional circumstances." Paula is not associating herself with these women as representatives of Woman or an underlying feminine essence, but *breaking* with such an account: As Madame Pintre (the canniest of the revolutionary chorus) will say, "after the woman of the ages comes the woman of the hour" (*A la femme éternelle succède celle de l'instant*). In fact, Paula's list is remarkably heterogeneous, insofar as there is little that associates these women with each other besides the fact that they are all heroic exceptions, each was "the woman of the hour." And by marking the *end* of historical "efforts to bring [them] to light," their determination in terms of particular "exceptional circumstances," what is truly exceptional in them is formalized as *generic*, as lightly marked as possible; indeed, the very fact that it is a list of women would seem to emphasize this point for Badiou, insofar as his own symbol of a generic set is ♀.[13] But the revolutionaries close around Paula, and it is not clear that they fully comprehend her revelation and the new political topology it demands. Villembray, however, understands her experience as implying that he should not engage in conventional politics. He is repulsed by the "primitive ritual" enacted by the revolutionaries wrapped in the "Red Scarf," taking refuge in it as a symbol of "the insularity of the revolution." Similarly, the comfortable familiarity of a passage from *The German Ideology* circulates among them, concluding with the declaration that "it's incumbent upon us to put an end to the state," and this becomes their single clear goal, unlike the strange restraint called for by Paula, whom they now designate "the indiscernible one." Villembray condemns them all, politicos and revolutionaries alike, as "the eclipse of every subject" (*Éclipse de tout sujet*), which for him implies the abandonment of subjectivity as such. In the same words that concluded the first act of *La Ville*, Act I ends with Mokhtar contemptuously calling Paula to follow him, "Come on, you!" (*Toi, viens!*), the strangeness of her revelation forgotten as she is elevated to the status of glorious symbol of the revolution, both "invisible and essential." Paula's "road to Damascus" has led her off the map of all conventional politics, beyond the opposition between conservative attempts to salvage the state and revolutionary attempts to grab state power, but it is unclear if anyone will follow her on the path she obscurely indicates.

In Act II, the Incident at Antioch proper, the conflict between Paula's critique of power and the scorched earth politics of Cephas comes to a head. Cephas's vision of "the total disruption of everything" is gaining adherents, and without Villembray's influence, the government will surely collapse. The people love the spectacle of destruction, and Cephas knows that faced with the prospect of endless anarchy they will call for the restoration of law and order, allowing him to assume full dictatorial power. Although some of the revolutionaries are skeptical about Cephas's motivations and plans, they don't really understand Paula's position, which, it must be admitted, she does little to explain and may not fully understand herself. Whereas for the revolutionaries Paula's refusal to take power is an inexplicable failure to act, for Paula not taking action is a new kind of act. Paula senses that a politics that abandons the endless oscillation between State and Revolution, power and powerlessness, is possible, but she doesn't have a positive language for it. And whereas the charismatic event of her "conversion" experience had produced powerful, if confused, positive responses in her fellow revolutionaries, now her act involves a *negation*, a resolute "no!" to the political as it stands. Susan Spitzer has characterized Paula's negation as an act of *subtraction* in which her refusal to participate in the dialectics of state and revolutionary counterstate reveals the void concealed by that opposition. Paula rejects Cephas's revolution as pure repetition without development or transformation, just as Villembray realizes that moderate reform will merely continue political business as usual.

Act II begins in the Place of the War Reserves, where Paula finds Villembray fishing in the harbor, as he says, "practicing nothingness." Like

Lâla to Lambert in Claudel's play, Paula tells her brother that she has left Mokhtar and their son David, both of whom have been swept up in the revolutionary momentum, and now she intends to confront Cephas directly. Paula tells Villembray that "the people are taking shape," are becoming political once again, and she urges her brother to join them in "the rapture of a new day" and the project of "inventing a politics" hitherto unknown. But Villembray can only see himself as part of a superannuated past, and refuses. Scene 2 advances to the Place of Truths, where the terms of the disagreement between Paula and Cephas are elaborated. The people are torn between Cephas's stark vision of "the total disruption of everything," despite their suspicions of his motivations, and Paula's apparent quietism, although her insistence that "power, even if it's there for the taking, isn't always the right thing for us to take," is a provocation: "Paula's turning our patience into an endless waiting game." As we saw, the biblical "incident at Antioch" was not the conflict between Peter's legalism and Paul's antinomian liberation from the law, but the difference between the dialectic of prohibition and transgression, on the one hand, and Paul's "indifference" to that dialectic, on the other. In Badiou's play this proposition is expressed in Paula's refusal to support either the political reformers (the Maurys) or their revolutionary antagonists (Cephas and the others), who represent state and revolution as two sides of a coin. The difficulty of moving from this distinction to a new political practice remains to the very end of the play.

Scene 3 of Act II returns to the Place of the War Reserves, where the two conventional politicians of the Left and Right, Pierre and Jean Maury, again try to persuade Villembray to save the crumbling government. But he has only contempt for their pleas, and the surreal scene pokes fun at their empty sloganeering. The powder of conventional political munitions is evidently damp here, and their great white hope is fading into the bitter irony of his solipsism. In scene 4, however, a new sequence begins again by jumping over the question of truth to the Place of Choices, where, at a large conference table, surrounded by all the other revolutionaries, Paula and Cephas have their "incident at Antioch." Paula is called on to defend her inexplicable resistance to taking power, which is beginning to tire even those sympathetic to her. Even her former ally, Madame Pintre, calls her to join with Cephas, "so that we can muster the forces for continuing and bend our action to support what's becoming" (*afin que nous rassemblions la durée, et pliions l'acte à la consolidation de ce qui devient*). Another revolutionary, René, calls on Paula to help them "put an end to the way things are" so "those who exist can come into their rightful place of superiority" (*afin que nous interrompions ce qui est, et que celui qui existe advienne à sa suprématie*). The terms in which the revolutionaries plead with Paula reveal how far apart they are: "To support what is becoming" may sound like revolutionary progressiveness, but for Paula "becoming" is simply a transitive mode of "being," and what she is calling for is, we might say, *unbecoming*, the emergence of the inexistent as such, the abandonment of the entire state of things, not the circular "revolution" imagined by the partisans of Cephas, in which the existent takes the "rightful place of superiority," like the meek, inheriting the earth. Paula argues that the easy victory that Cephas offers them would fail to achieve real change, it would only be a local modification, "revolution" merely as rotation, and at enormous human cost:

> The action I'm calling for is valid at all times anywhere on the face of this earth. An endless working on oneself, reproducible everywhere. St. Paul's rejection of the old law had the time-honored power to afford the child and the slave, the Persian and the Viking, the opportunity for grace and salvation. So now we've come to the second foundational moment, when the unprecedented act consists in *not* seizing a power that's there for the taking. Because that's how the world will learn that the law has been split in two and that we're no longer burdened by having to take power. Revolution: the nominal pride of people everywhere. But, thereafter, the prelude to Empires. Let's rule that word out, valiantly. It brands us with the obsolete law, the law in which the subsumption of our thinking of equality by the social bond is not yet mature. Just as circumcision was for St. Paul, revolution is nothing and unrevolution is nothing.

While the revolutionaries wait impatiently for Paula to act, she insists that her nonaction announces a *new kind of action*. This is not nonviolent resistance or any other mode of passive aggression or turning the other cheek, but the decision to reject the oppositions that structure the conventional political vocabulary as local, particularist, and in this case, merely in the service of Cephas's personal rage. Paula realizes that the revolution Cephas proposes would simply lead to another empire, more of the same; her revelation was of a "splitting of the law" that requires an entirely new politics. Paula wants to "light a bright fire whose mystery will be interpreted by everyone all the way to the horizon." There is no doubt that Paula's idea is still inchoate, she is working more from the strength of her conviction than from clarity about what the change she intuits will involve. However, this obscurity is not her youth or lack of vision, but the very nature of the truth she has discovered: Indeed, from within the old situation, the new truth is precisely *indiscernible*. The revolutionary women seem to hear some of what Paula is saying, but the men still reach for the brass ring of power Cephas dangles before them: While Mokhtar argues that "the decision seizes the chance," Madame Pintre knows that "the decision remains outside of place [*hors lieu*]." The truth that was subjective, but evanescent, and without consequences in Act I is extended and expanded here, into the beginnings of a *theory of the political*. Nevertheless, most of the people rally around Cephas, Villembray is murdered, and Paula disappears.

Act III, "The Council of Nicea," is set fifteen years later in "the Place of Foundations," when Cephas's revolution has ended in ruin: Everything—state, industry, nature—has collapsed and the survivors keep watch over the still smoldering fires, struggling to imagine a new beginning. Cephas understands that his role has come to an end, that "beyond victory there's only defeat"—the defeat that "restores the State's power." His destructive function exhausted, he departs, like Villembray in Act I, leaving his gun with Paula and Mokhtar's son David, whom the revolutionaries embrace as their new leader. But David is unsure, wondering if rebuilding the state would make the entire revolution meaningless, and all its "sacrifices" in vain. He is groping for something, but he only knows that it can be neither a renewal of the old order nor the radical disorder left by Cephas, and he wonders if such "going around in circles" is simply the nature of politics. Suddenly Paula returns, elegantly dressed, still young and more fascinating than ever, and this last act focuses on Paula's struggle with her son over the political future. Paula advises the revolutionaries once more to "give up power! Let things run their course without you. . . . Start your group over on the basis of this renunciation. Scatter among the people, whose hatred is already pursuing what you yourselves were going to attack. Take one more step toward State coercion and History will remember you as no more than a bloody national struggle reduced, where justice is concerned, to mediocrity or even worse. [. . .] Our generation knows the hidden blackness in the red. It's up to us, by making an unprecedented decision, not to let that knowledge go to waste." The logic of revolution practiced by Cephas was "classical," of another time; he tried to put an end to repetition, but his ideas and techniques are no longer effective: "Today . . . when every classical revolution leads only to Empire, there's no neo-classical purity save death." Paula tries to stop David from leading the transition from revolution to reconstruction, and to convince him that restoring the state is not the solution: David must work for a more profound political subjectivation that is the *exception* to the law of domination and the dominated. Forget the state, she insists; grasp the thread of multiplicity, against the logic of the One that the state inevitably requires. Rather than constructing a revolutionary counter-force to state force, "scatter among the people," as elements of a generic set—not merely another party, but the forcing of a new *part* whose addition opens the possibility of a much more profound political transformation. It won't be easy, but we must go beyond the localization of politics in the state apparatus; politics is what is *subtracted* from the state. The event from out of which a political truth may arise *is* fleeting, Paula tells David, but it is all we have to work with: "Politics is like an event, as unrepresentable as all the hard work, in the theater, that ends up making the play we see before us a mysterious, one-time thing."

The truth that Paula experienced "on the road to Damascus" was singular; the question is how to work to extend it, how to remain *faithful* to it, how to *force* it to produce knowledge. And there is something *theatrical* about this work, in two senses. First, it is as invisible as all the work that prepares for a theatrical production but that must vanish for the theatrical event. Truth is subjective; its universality unfolds in the infinite sequence of its investigative extensions. Second, the truth-event, like the theatrical event, vanishes in its very emergence; it is essentially transient as a performance, and each iteration is unique, with only the possibility of being extended by a faithful subject.

But, David asks, reasonably enough, where to begin? Paula replies, "Find the people who matter. Stay connected to what they say. Organize their consistency, with equality as the goal. Let there be core groups of political conviction in the factories. And committees of popular will in the cities and the countryside. Let them change the way things are and rise to the generality of situations." David objects that what Paula suggests is no strategy at all; and indeed we might better characterize it as an *investigation*, an aleatory process of finding the people who have already sensed the void in the existing structure of politics, organizing them into

L ◆ INTRODUCTION

groups based on nothing more than the conviction of equality (their indifference to existing differences), and letting them "rise to the generality
of situations"— that is, gather themselves into immanent generic multi-
tudes, rather than factions located on the continuum of the political Left
and Right. At first they will indeed be indiscernible, invisible to the rest of
the world, but finally this is precisely what will allow for the emergence of
previously unthought possibilities as new knowledge. David finally seems
to understand Paula's point when he concludes, "Politics is about making
politics exist, so that the State should no longer exist." That is, a political truth, such as radical equality (at this point only partially knowable),
may be *forced* and in the future perfect (that is, by assuming its eventual
completion) it may produce knowledge that we can work with *now*; but
it is a risk, always subject to appropriation by the demagogues of the Left
and Right, the Fools and Knaves. Nevertheless, confidence that there *is* a
politics that is "free from the State's grasp, unrepresentable, and endlessly
decoded," a politics of "infinite liberation," is what David finally learns
from his mother; and although there are no guarantees, this confidence
may have been enough to change the world.

At the end of the play, Paula disappears, but David is ready to pursue
the truth that she encountered and to force it to imply new knowledge. In
nearly the final lines of the play, everyone seems to experience a radical new
truth, based on the dual accounts of Paula and her brother, Villembray:

> Eclipse of every subject.
> But that's the very subject.
> [*Eclipse de tout sujet.*
>   *Mais c'est le sujet, même*]

For Villembray in Act I, the "eclipse" of the subject meant the disastrous
end of subjectivity, but now a new subject may indeed emerge at and *as* the
site of the disappearance of the reactionary and obscure subjects gathered
at the end of the play in the Place of Foundations. A new kind of revolutionary subject can arise only through a process that includes the "eclipse"
of the old. David may instantiate this new faithful subject— a new "Jew,"
born of the "Christian" Paula and the Arab Mohktar—but there is no
promise that a new foundation will indeed be forced to appear; left alone
on stage, David wonders what the new century will have to tell us.

The Incident at Antioch is a nodal point in Badiou's *oeuvre*, bringing together art and politics, theology and mathematics, the Paris of 1871 and the Paris of 1968, while building on *Theory of the Subject* and anticipating *Being and Event*. As an experimental procedure, it investigates the text of Claudel's *La Ville*, seeking to discover in it the materials for new theatrical possibilities and political ideas. Because Claudel's play is already "Christian," we might say that Badiou's experimental procedure involves adding to it something that is already there—Saint Paul—through a remarkable adaptation of the technique developed by Paul Cohen. But the "addition" of this supplement, the overlay of Paul Claudel's story with Saint Paul's structures, brings out something immanent to Claudel but not yet clear in his text: the generic nature of Lâla's ecstatic prophecy, its apparent contentlessness. In this sense, *The Incident at Antioch* forces *La Ville* to reveal a revolutionary knowledge it will have had, by expanding the Pauline truth of the event and its generic extension, with potentially unlimited new possibilities for thinking. The results of Badiou's experimental forcing can be seen in his extraordinary extension of the concept of the generic in *Being and Event*, and in his book on Saint Paul, where the theory of the event is instantiated in perhaps its most crystalline form. The bilingual publication of *The Incident at Antioch* now, thirty years after its writing, has enormous implications for the great and still expanding corpus of Badiou's writings and ideas. Moreover, I am hopeful, nay, *confident* that we will not have to wait another thirty years for a full production of the play.

THE INCIDENT AT ANTIOCH

L'INCIDENT D'ANTIOCHE

L'INCIDENT D'ANTIOCHE

TRAGÉDIE EN TROIS ACTES

LISTE DES PERSONNAGES

JEAN MAURY: homme politique de droite
PIERRE MAURY: homme politique de gauche
CÉPHAS
CLAUDE VILLEMBRAY
PAULE: sœur de Villembray
MOKHTAR: ouvrier arabe de cinquante ans
CAMILLE: louloute de banlieue
RENÉ: paysan
MME PINTRE: ouvrière
DAVID: fils de Paule et de Mokhtar

LISTE DES LIEUX

Le lieu officiel de la politique: une grande salle nue
Le lieu des réserves de la guerre: un vieux port militaire
Le lieu des vérités: une porte de grande usine
Le lieu des choix: une route départementale dans un champ de
   betteraves
Le lieu des fondations: une ville détruite

THE INCIDENT AT ANTIOCH[1]

A TRAGEDY IN THREE ACTS

CHARACTERS

JEAN MAURY, a right-wing politician
PIERRE MAURY, a left-wing politician
CEPHAS[2]
CLAUDE VILLEMBRAY
PAULA, Villembray's sister
MOKHTAR, an Arab factory worker, age 50
CAMILLE, a tough girl from the *banlieue*[3]
RENÉ, a farmer
MADAME PINTRE, a factory worker
DAVID, son of Paula and Mokhtar

PLACES

The official place of politics: a big bare room
The place of the war reserves:[4] an old military port
The place of truths: the gates of a big factory
The place of choices: a country road running through a beet field
The place of foundations: a city in ruins

ACTE PREMIER

Le chemin de Damas

SCÈNE 1: Dans le lieu officiel de la politique.

LES DEUX MAURY *sont assis sur des chaises d'école, l'un côté cour, l'autre côté jardin, vers le fond.* CÉPHAS *est en avant, le dos tourné au public.*

JEAN MAURY: Il faudra bien qu'ils se décident à faire revenir Villembray. (*Silence.*) Claude Villembray. Il n'y a plus que cela de possible.

CÉPHAS: Alors, désirons l'impossible.

PIERRE MAURY: Collègues dont l'Occident désert compose tout l'ennui! Prospérons à l'abri fracassé des empires d'Orient.

CÉPHAS: Que je témoigne n'être à jamais aucun d'eux.

JEAN MAURY: Nul n'est aucun, qui ne soit nous.

CÉPHAS: Ô nullité de tout emblème existant!

PIERRE MAURY: Qui a parlé que je n'entends point?

CÉPHAS: Et moi j'entends bruire un vol de palombes, monotonement. Détestable cliquetis d'ailes, au cœur du terrestre témoin!
Les gens sont ici rassemblés par vols migratoires comme qui va se prendre aux filets des sapins. L'endroit n'est pas plus fait pour l'existence que ces taches grises à l'intérieur d'où dégoutte le sang des chasseurs en ligne. Au nom du ciel! Cela sent la plume, la fiente et la tuerie! (*Silence.*) Vous n'avez rien à dire?

JEAN MAURY: Nous jouissons de la tombée de la nuit.

CÉPHAS: La nuit, la nuit même ne vous sert plus à rien.

PIERRE MAURY: Ne sert, ce qui s'appelle servir, que ce dont les journaux vont parler.

JEAN MAURY: Comptes de la nation! Balance des paiements! Tenue de la monnaie! Onzième choc pétrolier! Restructuration du tissu industriel! Europe supra-nationale! Excédents de lait de chèvre!

ACT I

The Road to Damascus[5]

SCENE 1: In the official place of politics.

THE MAURYS *are seated on school chairs toward the rear of the stage, one stage left and the other stage right.* CEPHAS *is downstage with his back to the audience.*

JEAN MAURY: They'll have to bring Villembray back. (*Silence.*) Claude Villembray. There's nothing else possible now.

CEPHAS: Then let's wish for the impossible.[6]

PIERRE MAURY: O colleagues whose trouble all comes from the desert of the West![7] Let's thrive in the shattered shelter of the empires of the East.

CEPHAS: Let me swear never to be one of them.

JEAN MAURY: No one is, who's not one of us.

CEPHAS: O worthlessness of every current emblem![8]

PIERRE MAURY: Did someone just say something I couldn't hear?

CEPHAS: While *I* hear a flock of wood pigeons mournfully rustling. An abominable whirring of wings, in the heart of the earthly witness![9]

People are gathered here in migratory flocks like ones about to be snared in the fir tree nets. This place is no more fit for living than those gray stains inside from which the line hunters'[10] blood is dripping. In the name of heaven! It reeks of feathers, droppings, and butchery! (*Silence.*) Don't you have anything to say?

JEAN MAURY: We're enjoying nightfall.

CEPHAS: Night, night itself, is of no use to you anymore.

PIERRE MAURY: The only thing that's of use, really of use, is what will be in the news.

JEAN MAURY: National accounts! Balance of payments! Currency performance! Eleventh oil crisis! Industrial base restructuring! Supranational Europe! Goat milk surpluses!

PIERRE MAURY: Plan social! Du chômage, mais social! Une insertion
entièrement sociale! Des immigrés, s'ils sont sociaux, et non cas
sociaux! Aucune exclusion, à moins qu'elle ne soit sociale! L'Europe,
mais carrément sociale! Le social comme âme, comme finalité,
comme entéléchie, de tout le corps démocratique! Mon cheval pour
du social.

CÉPHAS: Harcèlement du rien aux lucarnes de l'été. Le monde est comme un papier d'emballage que tamponne la mention d'un destinataire
inconnu.

Moi aussi je suis né de ce pays phraseur. Mon père était dans les
honneurs au parlement, oui, oui. Homme droit et disert, il tenait
son épouse dans l'anarchie muette. Et moi, son fils, je fais parler à ce
silence la vieille langue du conflit. Je vois partout la guerre. Réjouis-
sance!

Toutefois, suis-je indemne? N'ai-je pas été blessé? Considérant les
grands pins des landes au ras de la mer, je suis tenté de tout absoudre,
comme si la nature de ce pays me faisait le prêtre d'un monde usé
jusqu'à la corde. Ou bien je n'ai d'œil que pour cette femme qui vient
de délinéer la clôture de sa gloire. Et je rêve d'un intemporel été sur
quatre lacs, aux espaliers des monts du sud.

PIERRE MAURY: Technologies modernes. Soin porté à l'écologie des
rivières. Citoyenneté des femmes, des enfants, des animaux, des
handicapés, des mal voyants, du cresson des vieux puits.

CÉPHAS: La vraie terre fume et remue sa foule et ses tracteurs sanglants
sur la motte salée! Les hommes abrutis mangent à leur faim, et pé-
nètrent en foule dans les bureaux aux vitres d'or!

Métropole dévastée! Je t'aime et te proscris! (*Il lève son poing au-
dessus de sa tête.*)

JEAN MAURY: Cet homme, à la fin, est-il connu des services de police?

CÉPHAS: Je suis inconnaissable. Un jour, j'étais ailleurs, et je me suis
connu. Une maigre foule courait sous la pluie, talonnée par les flics.
On assommait sur le pavé les moins véloces, ou les plus courageux.
Tout à coup je sentis que je n'endurerais jamais plus de voir ainsi la
traque et le gibier. L'envie me prit d'en finir avec la solitude de l'œil.

PIERRE MAURY: Socially responsible downsizing! Unemployment, but only if it's socially responsible! Absolutely socially responsible integration! Immigrants, provided they're socially responsible, not social work cases! No discrimination, unless it's socially responsible! Europe, but only if it's positively socially responsible! Social responsibility as the life-blood, the ultimate purpose, the entelechy of democratic society as a whole! My horse for social responsibility!

CEPHAS: Torment by nothingness at the windows in summer.[11] The world is like a piece of brown wrapping paper stamped "Addressee unknown."

I'm a product of this country of phrasemongers, too. My father was a big man in Parliament; yes, he was. An honorable, eloquent man, he kept his wife in a state of mute anarchy. And I, his son, am making that silence speak the old language of strife. I see war everywhere. Jubilation!

Yet have I escaped unscathed? Haven't I been wounded? When I gaze at the big pines at the shore, I'm tempted to give absolution to everything, as if nature in this country were making me the priest of a worn-out old world. Or else I only have eyes for that woman who has just erased the contours of her fame.[12] And I dream of a timeless summer on four lakes, in the terraced vineyards of the mountains in the south.

PIERRE MAURY: Modern technologies. Commitment to river ecology. Citizenship for women, children, animals, the disabled, the visually impaired, the watercress growing in old wells.

CEPHAS: The real earth fertilizes and turns over its bloody masses and tractors on the salty turf! The stultified[13] people eat their fill, and swarm into the golden-windowed offices!

O ravaged city! I love you and repudiate you! (*He raises his fist above his head.*)

JEAN MAURY: Honestly, is this man known to the police?

CEPHAS: I'm unknowable. One day, I was somewhere else, and I suddenly knew who I was. A sparse crowd of people were running in the rain, with the cops at their heels. They were clubbing the slowest, or the bravest, ones on the pavement. All of a sudden I realized I could never again bear to see hunters stalking their prey that way. I felt an urge to put an end to the eye's solitude.[14]

Et je l'ai fait, car une langue existe! Elle vous indique où s'interrompt la loi commune. Si vous suivez son ordre, vous voici dans l'appareillage de tout ce que la cité contient d'absence. La vie est anonyme, on ne connaît plus vos actes, qui ne sont plus les vôtres, mais ceux du manquement lui-même à tout le convenable du lieu. Vous viennent des compagnons malaisément identifiables, gens sans décoration ni entours. Avec eux vous existez dans les pliures de la langue, vous nommez ce que vous êtes et devenez dans la filiation d'un siècle et demi d'innocence.

Je ne serai connu que trop tard, quand l'arène ancienne de la connaissance aura flambé, quand l'ignoré ancien sera source unique du savoir.

Nous chasserons du lieu tout ce qui ne consent pas d'y faire exception!

Nous voyons briller dans la nuit l'étoile du pouvoir. Comme elle paraît lointaine! Mais proche aussi, si proche qu'il nous est enjoint, à nous, les inconnaissables, de la saisir comme on fait de la lune à la demande d'un enfant.

Et cette fois, soyez-en sûrs: il ne s'agira plus de la captivité d'un reflet dans quelque lessiveuse peinte en rouge!

(CÉPHAS *sort brusquement.*)

SCÈNE 2: Dans le lieu des réserves de la guerre.

VILLEMBRAY: Chère Paule, vous me remplissez d'étonnements, et le moindre n'est pas de te nommer: sœur! Sœur fallacieuse!

J'ai examiné les choses de la politique dans leurs balances. De toute décision dont je suis saisi je suis prêt à calculer les conséquences et à rectifier les emphases.

Je sais que l'action ne fait que suivre une vaine nécessité, et que tout s'accomplit sans que rien vienne à manquer de prévisible au résultat.

Aussi tout ce qui est fait s'annule.

Voilà qui est une certitude et une satisfaction.

Mais vous, Paule, à quoi donc servez-vous? Et comment vous compter dans le total?

And I did, because there's a language! It lets you know where ordinary law leaves off. Follow its rules and there you are in the bustling heart of all the absence contained in the city.[15] Life is anonymous, no one's aware anymore of your actions, which are no longer your own but the actions arising from the very failure to respect the local proprieties. Companions who are hard to place seek you out, people of no particular distinction, with no close friends or relations. With them you live in the folds of the new language, you name what you are and are becoming as heirs to a century and a half of innocence.[16]

I'll only be known when it's too late, when the old arena of knowledge has gone up in flames, when what was unknown in the past has become the sole source of knowledge.

We'll drive anyone out of this place that won't be an exception to it!

We see the star of power shining in the night sky. How far away it seems! But close, too, so close that we, the unknowable, are required to reach out and grab it the way you do the moon when a child asks you to.

And this time, you can be sure, it won't be about capturing a reflection in some old washbasin painted red![17]

(CEPHAS *rushes out.*)

SCENE 2: In the place of the war reserves.

VILLEMBRAY: Dear Paula, you fill me with amazement, not least because I can call you: sister! Fake sister!

I've studied political affairs and weighed them in the balance. I'm prepared to reckon the consequences of any decision I'm called upon to make and correct any imbalances.

I know that action merely obeys a pointless necessity and that everything comes about with completely predictable results.

Thus, every action cancels itself out.

That's a sure thing and a source of satisfaction.

But what about you, Paula, what purpose do you serve? And how should you be counted in the total?

PAULE: Voyez-vous, Claude, pour nous comprendre, il est besoin désormais de nous voir dans l'exacte étendue de notre visibilité.

Ce n'est pas qu'il faille soustraire les femmes à la raison du monde. Ce n'est pas que leurs humeurs et leurs enfantements les règlent sur les astres.

Mais je me tiens droite, pour fournir au monde l'éclat d'instant, la royale imminence.

Nulle cause ne me rattache à l'avant-hier du monde. Si tu me demandes à quoi je sers, tu m'as déjà capturée et détruite.

VILLEMBRAY: Certes, quand vous parlez à partir de cette inclination de la tête et des mains retenues l'une à l'autre dans le dos comme pour y tenir caché votre signe distinctif, je sens, irrépressible, venir une paix, j'assiste à la descente en pleine mer des grands buffles d'herbe.

PAULE: Je ne dis pas ce que je veux, je dis l'excès qu'il y a à ne plus rien vouloir. Je ne peux vous expliquer, c'est l'explication qui m'est retirée. Vouée du fond du temps à la transmission de la vie, j'ai le caprice de transmettre la mort.

VILLEMBRAY: Ainsi je parviens à cerner votre angoisse. Car qui vous interroge, et à qui répondez-vous?

PAULE: Exact, Villembray, je dois vous dire: «Touchée!» Je ne puis faire le partage entre l'indécidable et le doute.

Rien ne vaut, sinon ce rien même que je suis, jeune femme rebelle au rapt et méfiante à l'amour. Et rien ne dispense de transmettre la nouvelle, pour faire existence de cette transmission.

J'appréhende d'avoir à rencontrer l'obstacle des femmes elles-mêmes, que cette révélation irrite, trop soucieuses de se soustraire à l'errance qu'elle contient.

VILLEMBRAY: Ainsi vous vous tenez isolée entre toutes les femmes, n'étant à nulle rattachée par le lien de la parole. Mais, Paule ! Parlez à tous!

Ne soyez pas l'inutile et l'excommuniée!

PAULE: Nulle foi dont je puisse être exilée.

(*Silence.*)

VILLEMBRAY: L'idée générale qui promet à qui n'est rien de devenir tout, et du passé faisons table rase, n'est-ce-pas, tout cela ricane avec les morts.

PAULA: Well, you see, Claude, if we're to understand each other, from now on we need to see each other to the true extent of our visibility.

Women needn't be excluded from the realm of reason. Just because they have moods and give birth doesn't mean they're regulated by the stars.[18]

No, I stand firm, to show the world the sudden flash of light, the magnificent imminence.

No destiny binds me to ancient history. When you ask me what purpose I serve, you've already captured and destroyed me.

VILLEMBRAY: Of course, when you speak with your head cocked that way and your hands clasped behind your back as though trying to keep some distinguishing feature of yours out of sight, I feel an overwhelming sense of peace come over me, I'm watching the big prairie buffalo come down on the sea.[19]

PAULA: I'm not expressing what I want; I'm expressing the extreme joy there is in no longer wanting anything. I can't explain it to you; explanation's been taken away from me. Destined from the dawn of time to spread life, I have a sudden impulse to spread death.

VILLEMBRAY: So now I'm able to understand your anxiety. For who is questioning you, and who are you answering?

PAULA: Right, Villembray, or should I say "Touché!" I can't distinguish between the undecidable[20] and doubt.

Nothing matters, except this very nothing that I am, a young woman resistant to abduction and leery of love. And there's no excuse for not spreading the news, to make it widely known.

I dread having to face the obstacle of the women themselves, who are annoyed by this revelation, so anxious are they to avoid what's unsettling about it.[21]

VILLEMBRAY: So you keep aloof from all the women, being unconnected to any of them by the bonds of speech. But, Paula! Speak to everyone!

Don't be someone useless and excommunicated!

PAULA: I have no faith to be exiled from.

(*Silence.*)

VILLEMBRAY: The common idea promising those who are nothing the chance to become everything, and "let's make a clean slate of the past,"[22] of course–that's all laughing from the great beyond.

Derrière la révolution s'ouvraient de grandes fosses communes. La tour de guet pour le matin radieux n'était qu'un mirador. Comme disent les journaux, le communisme s'est effondré. Chacun, assis devant son feu, fait sa gamelle. D'autres calculent en haut lieu la probabilité du désastre.

Et moi, Paule, que direz-vous que je suis?

PAULE: Claude, mon frère, je vous apprécie de partager avec moi, très loin de moi, la conviction du grand creux des choses. Tu en fais un élément de distinction, et le ressort de la supériorité politique.

Certes, je ne te reprocherai pas d'être au milieu de tant d'hommes inutiles celui qui sait que l'inutilité est le matériau de toute présupposition relative à l'État. À force de scruter le mécanisme des amendements, de prévoir le résultat des sondages et de placer qui il faut au sous-secrétariat à la pêche aux crabes, tu parviens à l'ajustement des silences populaires et de la rhétorique d'en-haut.

VILLEMBRAY: Il est très vrai, Paule, n'en doutez aucunement. Vous pouvez m'appeler le garant de ce régime. Nul doute que demain au plus tard, désorientés par la crise économique, inquiets des proclamations de Céphas, ils vont venir me demander de former l'union nationale.

Dans le rôle du capitaine debout sur la dunette qui exhorte son équipage en déroute à couler la tête haute, je suis, chère Paule, inégalable.

PAULE: Oui, je le crois.

VILLEMBRAY: C'est ainsi que j'ai été fait le recours et qu'ils me haïssent tous.

Chacun sait qu'à mon entrée au Palais, l'énergie et le devoir national vont figurer à l'ordre du jour.

J'annoncerai d'un air sévère des réformes et des sacrifices. Si quelques clients africains font mine de chercher de l'air du côté des rivaux allemands ou japonais, je leur dépêcherai un bataillon parachutiste, ne serait-ce que pour défendre les droits de l'homme, qu'ils auront très certainement bafoués.

PAULE: Voilà! Par ces temps sans couleur aucune, votre cynisme est ce que les hommes de votre espèce ont de mieux. Vous méritez votre gloire, votre sœur en reçoit noblement la lumière portée.

(*Silence.*)

Behind the revolution huge mass graves gaped wide. The watchtower for the glorious new dawn was nothing but a prison observation tower. As they say in the papers, Communism collapsed. Everyone's sitting alone around their campfire now, preparing their own little meal. Others, at the top, are calculating the likelihood of disaster.

And as for me, Paula, what would you say I am?

PAULA: Claude, dear brother, I appreciate your sharing with me, however far apart we may be, your belief in the utter meaninglessness of things. You make it a badge of honor and the source of political greatness.

Naturally, I could never blame you for being the only one among so many useless[23] men to know that uselessness is the basis of every assumption about the State. By closely studying the workings of amendments, forecasting the outcome of opinion polls, and appointing the right person as Under Secretary of State for Crab Fishing, you manage to reconcile the people's silence and the rhetoric from above.

VILLEMBRAY: That's very true, Paula, no doubt about it. You can call me the mainstay of this government. There's no doubt that by tomorrow at the latest, confused by the economic crisis and alarmed by Cephas's pronouncements, they'll come and ask me to form a national unity government.

In the role of captain standing on deck urging his crew in disarray to go down with their heads held high, I, dear Paula, am second to none.

PAULA: I don't doubt it.

VILLEMBRAY: That's how I became the one they turn to and why they all hate me. Everyone knows that, once I take office, willpower and patriotic duty will be on the agenda.

I'll sternly announce reforms and sacrifices. Should any of our African clients act as if they might try their luck with our German or Japanese competitors, I'll send them in a division of paratroopers, if only to defend human rights, which they'll most certainly have abused.

PAULA: There you go! In these totally dreary times, your cynicism is the best thing about men of your kind. Your reputation is well deserved; your sister proudly basks in its reflected glow.

(*Silence.*)

VILLEMBRAY: Ah! Qu'on me change de siècle! Ou n'avoir pas reçu ce don figuratif, par quoi je tiens, dans l'obsolescence de tout, un absurde flambeau de papier!

PAULE: Voyons! Ne soyez pas si sérieux! Qu'importe votre âme?

VILLEMBRAY: Écoutez, certainement vous savez. Il y a de ces moments où la trame des occupations laisse deviner que l'ensemble est vain et que les significations de toutes choses, mises bout à bout, ne composent aucun texte lisible. Pour moi je connais pire.

PAULE (*indifférente*): Allons donc.

VILLEMBRAY: Il y a la certitude où l'on est d'être tombé sur une basse époque, où nul n'a de vos talents le goût ni l'emploi. Vous vous sentez plein de ressources et d'habileté à saisir ce qui est dans son conflit central. Vous êtes très fourni en sûretés et en règles d'emprise sur autrui. Rien ne vous manque. Eh bien, si la circonstance fait défaut, le lieu est désert, l'époque a échoué votre pays sur le sable. D'autres ont pris le relais de la puissance, et dont la langue même vous est inconnue. Civilisé plus que quiconque, mais pour des tâches qui n'existent plus; et au regard de ce qui importe, plus démuni et barbare qu'un enfant. Sur la scène politique, où votre agitation fait un tabac provincial, vous ne valez pas mieux qu'une troupe de patronage en train d'écorcher *Britannicus*.

Moi aussi, finalement, dans une longue enfance on m'aura fait vieillir. Mon pays est trop vieux pour mes ambitions. Et les vraies puissances n'en ont cure, si elles peuvent à tout instant m'écraser comme une mouche.

PAULE: Quelle mesure avez-vous de la puissance? La puissante odeur des jardins embrumés, dont on vient d'équarrir les buis? La puissance des vérités aux banlieues, aux portes, aux transports en commun? La puissante mélancolie des Syrtes? Venise ne tire-t-elle pas sa force de n'avoir plus de force aucune?

VILLEMBRAY: Mais sans la main serrée sur la gorge des Turcs, et la richesse inouïe de ses doges, Venise n'aurait même pas existé!

Voyant notre campagne remplie, la modération de nos allées forestières, nos villes mesurables, je déchiffre aussitôt le cimetière et l'orphéon.

VILLEMBRAY: Oh, if only I could live in different times! Or if only I hadn't been cursed with this gift for metaphor, on account of which I'm standing here, with everything crumbling all around, holding a ridiculous paper torch!

PAULA: Oh, come now! Don't be so serious! What does your soul matter?

VILLEMBRAY: Look, I'm sure you know. There are moments in the midst of your ordinary activities when you get a sudden glimpse of how pointless the whole thing is, and how the meanings of all things, when lined up end to end, don't add up to a text that makes any sense. In my case it's even worse.

PAULA (*uninterested*): Oh, come on.

VILLEMBRAY: You're sure you've fallen on dark times, when no one appreciates your talents or knows how to put them to good use. You feel resourceful and clever enough to grasp the contradiction at the heart of the way things are. You've got plenty of self-assurance and ways of influencing people. You lack for nothing. Well, if the right circumstances aren't there, it's all a wasteland, your country's been run aground by the times. Other people have taken over power, and even the language they speak is one you don't know. You're better trained than anyone, but for tasks that no longer exist; and as for what really matters, you're more helpless and naive than a child. On the political stage, where your campaign's only a minor hit, you're no better than some amateur theater company mangling *Macbeth*.[24]

By keeping me a child for so long they'll have aged me, too, in the end. My country's too old for my ambitions. And the real powers-that-be couldn't care less, so long as they can squash me like a fly whenever they please.

PAULA: What do you measure power by? The powerful fragrance of misty gardens, where the boxwoods have just been pruned? The power of truths in the *banlieues*, at the factory gates, on public transport? The powerful melancholy of the Arabian sands?[25] Doesn't Venice draw its force from having no force at all anymore?

VILLEMBRAY: But without its chokehold on the Turks and the phenomenal wealth of its Doges, Venice would never even have existed!

When I see our contented countryside, the quiet restraint of our forest lanes, the human scale of our cities, I instantly sniff out the graveyard and the funeral procession.

Dans la voie brutale des profits et des ruines, nous ne sommes pas allés assez loin. Nous avons trop aimé nos monuments, nos vieilles gares, nos tuiles.

Rasez tout cela! De la vitre, de l'acier, du bitume! Une centrale nucléaire dans chaque site classé!

Qu'on donne pleins pouvoirs aux capitalistes pourris les plus grandioses, aux militaires, aux entrepreneurs fantasques et violents! Qu'on triple la flotte en cinq ans! Qu'on annexe le voisin le plus faible!

Mais non. On ne part pas.

Ô lieu tardif et dérisoire! Ô lieu d'humanité où s'aménage un tombeau! L'homme d'État que je suis ne sert qu'à dessiner les ornements tributaires.

(Silence. Un grand navire de guerre entre dans le port, assez vétuste, mais encore impressionnant.)

PAULE: Cependant le mugissement de la mer engendre au-dessus d'elle un monstre mélancolique. Et comme à votre appel, ce lieu préfectoral essaie de nous donner ce qu'il y a de mieux pour combler votre désespoir de puissance.

Voici l'appareillage en beauté de notre vieillissement, voici que se peint sur la mer l'ombre dorée de vos nuages!

VILLEMBRAY: Salut, sympathique ferraille!

PAULE: Ovation à l'orgue rouillé, blason de notre demi-gloire!

Tu manifestes, sans le détruire, le mystère de la machine aux prises avec l'emblème. Car, comme la suscitation d'une force inemployée, tu parcours l'océan pour signifier notre grandeur éteinte. Tu es la forme d'acier de nos livres d'histoire.

Vieux poème à l'aplomb de la souille marine! Aime-moi, mon présent est plus équivoque que ta célébration.

Navire outre-signe! Une femme te salue, ne t'offrant rien d'autre, avec cette couleur.

(Elle enlève à son cou l'écharpe rouge qu'elle portait et la jette à l'eau.) Un jour nouveau s'exerce à notre rencontre insensée.

Along the brutal road to profit and ruination we haven't gone far enough. We've been too enamored of our historic monuments, our old train stations, our tiled roofs.

Tear that all down, I say! Let's have glass, steel, and asphalt! A nuclear power plant in every registered historical landmark!

Let's give full powers to the biggest, baddest capitalists, to the military men, to the reckless, ruthless entrepreneurs! Let's triple the size of the fleet in five years! Let's annex our weakest neighbor!

No. It's not going to happen.

O pathetic, backward place! O place of humanity where a tomb is being built! The statesman that I am is good for nothing but designing funeral wreaths.

(*Silence. A big battleship, quite outdated but still impressive, steams into the harbor.*)

PAULA: Yet the roar of the sea is producing a melancholy monster above it. And as if in response to your appeal, this little prefectural site is trying to give us the best thing there is to relieve your despair about being powerless.

Behold the glorious ship of our obsolescence; behold how the golden shadow of your clouds is reflected on the sea!

VILLEMBRAY: Hello, you wonderful old tub!

PAULA: A round of applause for the rusty old gunship, the emblem of our quasi-fame!

You manifest, without destroying it, the mystery of the machine in its struggle with the symbol. For, like the awakening of a dormant force, you ply the seas as witness to our faded glory. You are the steel version of our history books.

You old poem floating above the muddy ocean floor! Love me; my present is more ambiguous than your song of praise.[26]

You overly symbolic ship! A woman, giving you only this, salutes you with these colors.

(*She removes the red scarf*[27] *she was wearing from around her neck and throws it in the water.*) A new day is dawning on our incredible encounter.

SCÈNE 3: Dans le lieu des vérités.

MOKHTAR: Bonjour, Paule du matin.

Si chez les prêtres on ânonne que « Mohamed va à l'école, Mohamed achète le pain, Mohamed, qui est chômeur, va à l'Agence pour l'Emploi », vous nous mettez en bride des mots lourds et proches des récits de notre mère d'exil avec la cadence qu'il faut. Quand la voiture amène à mon pistolet sur le train du vacarme sa vingt-cinquième aile, je dis:

De l'ombre si tu viens sois l'or
Pour ce que fait d'un tel été ton fer.
Nul ouvrier n'a part à ce qu'il tient d'enfer
Et d'ombrelles aux files d'un or-
Age.

Pénultième je viens face à la porte.
Ô sentier des villes! Aigle inhérité
De ceux d'en bas! Ici le lac à plat de vérité.
Celui qui n'a dit mot vêtu de boue j'attends qu'il sorte.

PAULE: Vous savez rire. N'auriez-vous pas l'idée que je suis folle?

En dehors de ce nom, Paule, je ne conviens qu'à qui ne convient à personne. Quand je vous parle, c'est vous qui avez ma conviction.

MOKHTAR: Et tu nous as trouvés muets. Aucune voix dans aucune presse.

PAULE: Là où réside ce dont nul ne parle, là s'entend la communication du vrai.

Puisque partout ailleurs sévit le bruit qui recouvre.

Et qu'il en est des paroles comme de tout ce qui importe, si elles ont sens c'est d'être rares, et de qui on ne les attend pas. Et si au contraire elles sont mécaniquement répandues dans tout l'espace où l'écran du diseur les comprime, elles sont égarées dans l'écoulement des significations.

SCENE 3: In the place of truths.

MOKHTAR: Good morning, Paula Sunshine.

In Catholic school they recite in a drone: "Mohammed goes to school, Mohammed buys the bread, Mohammed, who's out of work, goes to the unemployment office," but *you* have us warm up[28] with weighty words akin to the tales our mothers of exile tell, with the right rhythm. When the car on the deafening track brings its twenty-fifth fender around to my paint gun,[29] I say:

> Be the gold, though you come from the night,[30]
> For what your iron makes of such light.
> In his own hell no worker need share
> Or in the parasols of the awful din there-
> In.

> Penultimate,[31] I come before the door.
> O cities' bitter path! Eagle, stripped bare,
> Of all the have-nots there! The dried-up lake of truth is here.
> He who said nothing cloaked in mud, it's him I'm waiting for.

PAULA: You sure can mock. You probably think I'm crazy, don't you?

Apart from this name, Paula, I only suit those who don't suit anyone. When I speak to you, it's from you that I get my conviction.[32]

MOKHTAR: And you found us silent. No say at all in any of the press.

PAULA: There where resides that about which no one speaks, there the message of truth is heard.

Since everywhere else it's drowned out by noise.

And since it's the same for words as for everything that matters: if they mean anything it's because they're rare, and come from the least likely person. But if, instead, they're mechanically spread all over the space into which the speaker's screen constricts them, they get washed away in the flow of meanings.

C'est ainsi que jadis, avec la vision dans le cœur d'un vieil arabe absolument droit je poussai mon vélomoteur jusqu'aux noms pour moi garants du lieu du vrai: Nanterre, Thiais, Villemomble! Vitry, Choisy, Malakoff! Genevilliers! Puteaux et Bagnolet! Les Ardoines, Senons! Et plus loin encore: Garges-les-Gonesse, Livry-Gargan, Flins-les-Mureaux! Poissy que je conjoins à Aulnay 3000! Ô banlieues! Trame vraie de l'étoffe! Sens gris des couleurs du non-sens! À qui donc le poème, sinon à ce désert sans étoile, où vivent les derniers nomades, rivés?

Or ce lieu m'est acquis et c'est moi qu'on interroge. « Qu'aviez-vous à nous dire? » demandez-vous. Jeune femme, je manque aux mots qui font lever les mots des autres. Au bord de l'inutile, je me tiens dans le lieu sans en avoir trouvé la langue. Je défaille à la transmission de la mort.

MME PINTRE: Et tu nous as trouvés muets.

MOKHTAR: Nous sommes venus forcés de loin car le fleuve est à sec, où nous élevions des truies. Nous sommes seuls, sans femmes, et logés dans le semblant d'un chenil. Nos droits sont nuls, nos papiers résiliables. Cependant la grande usine nous refait à neuf pour plus d'un monde confirmé. (*La porte de l'usine s'ouvre.*) Je te salue lourde porte du service! Je te salue préambule du lieu!

MME PINTRE: Porte de la pensée vague pour l'incapable instant! Usine! En fonction d'origine et de disparition!

MOKHTAR: Salut, matinale et claire! Porte noire de l'usine! Entrouverture de la conscience entremise! Salut, franchissement ouvrier! Là où tu vas, qui ne me nommes, gît ma nomination.

PAULE: Inutile survie d'une langue étrangère.

MOKHTAR: Très peu à nous savoir, nous maintenons l'échelonnement. Frères de Juin, de Mars et d'Octobre, ou du Janvier des antipodes ou de l'août méridien, quand les eaux se retirent et qu'il est dur de comprendre tant d'algues desséchées, trois ou six avertis du neuf font de l'usine histoire, et ancienneté persistante, et le tout de la mer!

PAULE: Prose d'ailleurs en place du poème d'ici.

MOKHTAR: Salut, au nom de ceux qui cherchent le nom de votre patience.

(*Les ouvriers commencent à sortir de l'usine pressés et nombreux.*)

So it was that once, with the image of a perfectly honorable old Arab in my heart, I rode my motorbike all the way to the names that are the guardians of the place of the true for me: Nanterre, Thiais, Villemomble! Vitry, Choisy, Malakoff! Genevilliers! Puteaux and Bagnolet! Les Ardoines, Senons! And even farther away: Garges-les-Gonesse, Livry-Gargan, Flins-les-Mureaux! Poissy, which I combine with Aulnay 3000![33] O *banlieues*! True weave of the cloth! Gray meaning of the colors of meaninglessness! Who is the poem for, if not this starless desert, where the last nomads live, rooted to the spot?

Yet this place is mine and I'm the one being questioned. "What was it you wanted to tell us?" you ask. I'm just a young woman and I'm missing the words that elicit other people's words. On the verge of uselessness, I stay on in this place, though I haven't figured out its language. I'm a failure at spreading death.

MADAME PINTRE: And you found us silent.

MOKHTAR: We were forced to come here from afar because the river's dried up where we used to raise sows. We're here alone, without our wives, and housed in something resembling a kennel. Our rights are nonexistent; our documents can be revoked at any time. Meanwhile, the big factory is retooling us for another cruel world. (*The factory gates open.*) Hail, heavy gates of servitude! Hail, prelude to the place!

MADAME PINTRE: Gates of irresolute thinking leading to the ineffectual moment! Factory! In terms of appearance or disappearance![34]

MOKHTAR: Hail, bright and early! Dark factory gates! Half-opening of consciousness lodged in between! Hail, place the worker passes through! Where you, who don't name me, go is where my naming abides.

PAULA: The needless survival of a foreign language.

MOKHTAR: We few who are known to each other assign the order of the tasks. Brothers of June, March, and October,[35] or of January in the Antipodes or of meridional August, when the waters recede and it's hard to fathom so much dried-out seaweed, three or four people in the know about the new restore the factory to history, and its enduring memory, and the whole of the sea!

PAULA: Prose from somewhere else in lieu of the poem from right here.

MOKHTAR: Hail in the name of those who seek the name for your endurance.[36]

(*A crowd of workers starts streaming hurriedly out of the factory.*)

PAULE: Salut de celle qui transmet son étroitesse d'existence.

MME. PINTRE: Salut, excès sur rien!

PAULE: Pur creux du trop-plein du monde! Vous qui en commençant votre jour savez que le jour est fini. Le temps revient de dormir, et entre deux sommeils, vous seuls allumez la torche.

Ailleurs, l'œil est clos, toute bouche s'est tue. Ou bien sévit le mécontentement. Plus de maîtres ni d'intelligence. On se met sur le ventre. L'homme agité dort. Il vaque à l'absorption du surplus. Ou, menacé de le perdre, il sécrète autour de ce qu'il a la coquille en calcaire des temps de crise.

Mais trois choses de vous sont enviables : l'astreinte mécanique, qui garde d'oublier où le réel se fait; la révolte d'atelier, qui délibère sur qui conserve au plus haut prix le respect de soi-même; le langage matériel, qui coupe court à l'apitoiement sur soi.

MOKHTAR: Effervescence de midi, stupeur studieuse de minuit. Ô foule d'usine dégagée, énigme de ce qui sera et de ce qui ne sera pas. Volonté de refaire . . .

MME PINTRE: . . . un sujet, parti de si peu qu'il doute, mais de son doute même il délibère, et de son doute il alimente . . .

MOKHTAR: . . . ce qui se dit antérieurement dans la ressource apprise et inventée de sa langue natale.

PAULE: Oserez-vous encore prononcer le mot qui fit au-dessus de vous le drapeau de l'histoire? Tous les pays racontent avec amertume ce qui devient après que dans la gloire et la victoire des servants du rouge ouvrier on ait cru arrivé le temps de votre règne.

Quel rapport, dites-moi, entre la traque ici de votre pensée vraie, que dicte le seul lieu qui ne soit pas encore surnuméraire, et ces polices de flagorneurs trafiquant sans excès des biens de l'État?

Quand moi, femme du grand rivage, je cherche parmi vous la langue où chaque mot désormais a la puanteur d'un État mort.

Si quelqu'un d'ici est mon ami, qu'il tolère que je ne sois qu'une amie ambiguë. Car celui qui s'organise ne fait plus de poème, et s'il a du temps, il le consacre à préparer la réunion du soir. Quand elle a lieu, il parle à son tour, et trouve sa satisfaction s'il n'a pas dit un mot que l'autre n'aurait pu dire.

PAULA: Hail from one who declares the narrowness of her own existence.

MADAME PINTRE: Hail, excess over nothing!

PAULA: Pure void of the overflow of the world! You who when beginning your day know that it's already over. The time for sleeping returns, and between two slumbers, you alone light the torch.

Elsewhere, eyes are closed, every mouth has fallen silent. Or else discontent is rampant. No more thinkers[37] or thinking. One lies on one's stomach. The restless man sleeps. He attends to the absorption of the surplus. Or, threatened with losing it, he secretes around what he has the chalky shell of times of crisis.

But three things about you are enviable: the physical workload, which keeps you from forgetting where the real occurs; the shop-floor rebellion, which deliberates about who maintains his self-respect above all else; and concrete language, which puts a quick stop to self-pity.

MOKHTAR: The hustle and bustle of noon, the studious stupor of midnight. O factory masses released, you riddle of what will and won't be. The desire to change . . .

MADAME PINTRE: . . . a subject, who has come from so little that he doubts, but on his doubt itself he reflects, and with his doubt he contributes to . . .

MOKHTAR: . . . what was previously expressed in the learned and invented resource of his native language.

PAULA: Will you still dare to utter the word that became the flag of history waving over you? Every country tells the bitter tale of what happens after people thought the time of your reign had arrived through the triumph and glory of the soldiers of the workers' revolution.

Tell me, what connection is there between the pursuit of your true thought here, dictated by the only place that's not yet superfluous, and these hordes of bloodsuckers casually selling off state assets?

While I, a woman from a distant shore, am here among you seeking the language in which each word now has the stench of a dead State.

If anyone from here is my friend, he'll have to accept that I'm only an ambivalent friend. Because anyone who gets involved in politics no longer writes poetry, and if he has any time, he devotes it to getting ready for the evening meeting. Then when it's held, he takes his turn speaking and is gratified if he hasn't said a single thing that someone else couldn't have said.

MOKHTAR: Ne méprise pas ce soin de n'intervenir que d'après ce que l'autre est en train de penser, jeune femme têtue.

PAULE: Je ne méprise personne. Je me suis portée malgré moi de l'autre côté d'un fleuve. La ville se démembre sous les pas. Les seuls monuments crachent la fumée jaune du sulfure, et l'éclairage, la nuit, vient des torchères.

Je m'adresserai seule à vous. Je vous dirai que le monde commence aujourd'hui, partant de rien, et qu'il n'est que de suivre le dispersé de l'être, comme fait dans l'herbe sous la brume le grand chien blanc des poésies.

C'est ainsi que je m'avancerai, jusqu'à ce que parmi vous l'unique héritier se lève à la faveur de mon entêtement.

MME PINTRE: Va, Paule ! Tu ne nous es pas ennemie. Le poème du lieu se fait à mille voix.

SCÈNE 4: Dans le lieu des choix.

MOKHTAR, CAMILLE *et* MME PINTRE *sont alignés au bord de la route comme s'ils regardaient passer les autres.* VILLEMBRAY, *sur le goudron, est entouré des* DEUX MAURY. PAULE *est de l'autre côté de la route, dans un champ de betteraves.*

JEAN MAURY: Villembray, nous avons des torts envers vous.

VILLEMBRAY: Crachez le morceau, je vous prie.

PIERRE MAURY: La situation n'est pas excellente.

JEAN MAURY: Elle est pire. J'accompagne mon collègue de la gauche, mais je suis absolument pessimiste. Il y a une logique de la crise.

VILLEMBRAY: La guerre vous renflouera un jour.

PIERRE MAURY: Vous conviendrez avec nous qu'il faut briser le cycle infernal. Il faut, il faut absolument, rétablir les grands équilibres, respecter la démocratie, soutenir les droits de l'homme, augmenter les investissements, sauver la monnaie, contrôler sévèrement l'immigration, qu'elle soit sauvage ou civilisée, clandestine ou officielle, et bien entendu, assurer par tous les moyens le rayonnement culturel de notre pays.

VILLEMBRAY: Magnifique! Votre programme est magnifique. Vous n'avez nul besoin de moi.

MOKHTAR: Don't look down on that concern with only saying something based on what someone else is thinking, you headstrong young woman.

PAULA: I'm not looking down on anyone. I came over here reluctantly from the other side of a river. The city is breaking apart underfoot. There are only big buildings belching yellow sulfurous smoke now, and at night the lighting comes from the torches.

I'll speak only to you. I'll tell you that the world is starting today, from scratch, and that all you have to do is go after the dispersion of being,[38] the way the big white dog of verse does in the fog-shrouded grass.

That's how I'll proceed now, until the sole heir appears among you owing to my doggedness.

MADAME PINTRE: Get going, Paula! You're not our enemy. The poem of the place is for a thousand voices.

SCENE 4: In the place of choices.

MOKHTAR, CAMILLE, MADAME PINTRE, *and* RENÉ *are lined up on the side of the road as if they were watching people go by.* VILLEMBRAY, *standing right on the road, is flanked by* THE MAURYS. PAULA *is on the other side of the road, in a beet field.*

JEAN MAURY: Villembray, we've been unfair to you.

VILLEMBRAY: Be my guest; out with it.

PIERRE MAURY: Things are looking pretty bad.

JEAN MAURY: Terrible, actually. I've come along with my colleague on the left, but I'm absolutely pessimistic. There's a certain logic to the crisis.

VILLEMBRAY: You'll be bailed out by war one of these days.

PIERRE MAURY: We're sure you'll agree that the vicious cycle has got to be broken. Economic stability has *absolutely* got to be restored, democracy respected, human rights upheld, investment increased, the currency rescued, immigration—whether controlled or uncontrolled, legal or illegal—strictly limited, and, of course, the cultural prestige of our country spread by every means possible.

VILLEMBRAY: Brilliant! Your platform is brilliant! You have no need of me whatsoever.

JEAN MAURY: Il faut tailler dans le vif. La situation demande un chirurgien, et non un rebouteux. Choisissons nous-mêmes l'homme au couteau. C'est vous.

VILLEMBRAY: Messieurs, votre démarche n'appelle aucun remerciement, étant, de votre propre aveu, nécessaire. Vous ne venez me chercher que pour vous faire rempart.

S'il est possible, par quelques mesures ajustées que votre peur me permettra de prendre, de donner un bref éclat à votre submersion, je le ferai. Je saisirai où il est requis le couteau.

Je n'ai nullement l'intention de voir plus loin que l'heure présente, et du reste vous ne me confierez rien au-delà.

Bien entendu, je vous réprimerai à l'égal des autres. Mais vous savez attendre et vous courber.

Toutefois regardez cette jeune femme (*il montre* PAULE). Tournez-vous vers elle car elle dispose de ma décision.

Paule, dites-moi, considères-tu, oui ou non, que je dois accepter en ces termes leur proposition gouvernementale?

Qu'elle dise oui, et je prépare avec vous l'investiture. Qu'elle dise non, et je renonce au labeur d'extirper de ce feu mort quelques étincelles de parade.

JEAN MAURY: Ainsi l'État vient-il à trouver son hasard essentiel.

PIERRE MAURY: Parlez, chère camarade. L'heure est partout aux femmes.

(*Silence.*)

PAULE (*vers* MOKHTAR, CAMILLE, MME PINTRE *et* RENÉ): Vous, vous!

MOKHTAR: Regarde, écoute, songe.

PAULE: Étrangeté du visible! (*Silence.*) Pourquoi me laisser cette vision sans choix? Donnez-moi le nom. Me laisserez-vous saisie par l'édifice des lumières?

CAMILLE: Laisse ce mec venir à ce pour quoi il est fait.

PAULE: Qui parle de mon frère? O syllabaire de l'encheminement!

MOKHTAR: Lieu d'un hasard absolument quelconque.

(*Silence.*)

PAULE (*tombe à terre les bras en croix*): Hasard, fiction du sens, d'où je sais ce qu'il sait!

Les cailloux de ma bouche se changent en mots clairs.

Ô j'avançais, périlleuse, et sous l'acte

JEAN MAURY: We've got to make drastic cuts. The situation requires a surgeon, not just some quack or other. We should choose the man with the scalpel ourselves. You're the one.

VILLEMBRAY: Gentlemen, your initiative doesn't call for any thanks from me, since, as you yourselves admit, it's unavoidable. You're only seeking me out so I can act as a shield for you.

If it's possible, with a few appropriate measures that your panic will allow me to take, to lend some momentary luster to your total collapse, I'm game. I'll wield the knife where necessary.

I have no intention of looking any further than the present moment, and you won't entrust anything beyond it to me anyway.

Naturally, I'll crack down on you just like on everyone else. But you're good at being patient and doing what you're told.

Yet look at that young woman (*he points to* PAULA). Turn and face her because my decision is in her hands.

Paula, tell me, yes or no: Do you think I should accept their proposition that I head the government on these terms?

If she says yes, I'll go with you and prepare for my investiture. If she says no, I'll turn down the chore of trying to pull a few sparks out of this dying fire just for show.

JEAN MAURY: Thus does the State discover its essentially random nature.

PIERRE MAURY: Speak, dear comrade. Women's time has come.

(*Silence.*)

PAULA (*to* MOKHTAR, CAMILLE, RENÉ, *and* MADAME PINTRE): *You* decide! *You* decide!

MOKHTAR: Look, listen, and think it over.

PAULA: How strange the visible is! (*Silence.*) Why is this confusing spectacle being left to me? Give me the name for it.[39] Don't let me be overwhelmed by this huge mass of lights!

CAMILLE: Let the guy come and do what he's cut out for.

PAULA: Did someone say my brother? O syllabary[40] for the road ahead!

MOKHTAR: Place of an absolutely indeterminate chance event.

(*Silence.*)

PAULA (*falling to the ground, arms outstretched*):[41] Chance, illusion of meaning, whereby I know what it knows![42]

The pebbles in my mouth are turning into clear words.

Oh, there I was, going dangerously along, in the grip

D'un embrasement où s'effondrent l'obstacle et la rétraction du désir, me voici dans la minceur du matin.

Voyez, toute l'extension d'un corps, tel un lac en la surprise
Des sapins du ciel, la transparence infime où je me résous!
Où donc l'abri, vertu du soir, accueil de la pénombre?
La lumière écarquille sa gloire! Les poissons d'or giclent sur le cil des eaux!

Ô route obsolète, droiture soudain sciée! J'ai mis ma propre chute au plateau des justices.

J'avais, illuminée, le sensible et l'épars.

Qui donc me plie? Qui m'instruit du stratège?

Forme du casque et de la chouette, renaissante à rien qu'à la déesse impalpable! Je me courbe, et la lumière fait bouclier de mes genoux.

Mot d'un acte par trop durable.

Je définis, inémotive, la pensée qui vous fonde.

C'est moi! (PAULE *se lève, diction légèrement changée.*) Seigneuries de la politique, relevez-moi! Le coup qu'il faut porter! La consistance qu'il faut avoir!

De peur que je vacille, de peur que je cède à l'oubli de ce qu'il faut oublier, tenez-moi debout, femme cassée en deux, fendue par l'éclat!

Dictature! Capacité pensable de l'inexistant!

Pourquoi n'ai-je plus ni frère, ni sœurs, ni amants, sinon pour que je sois votre emblème? Afin que je vous appartienne.

Ô jeunesse en ferrailles, en fumées! Je rencontrais, j'avais rencontre, oui, pour tenir droite, et m'accable

Qu'il faille la langue et la nomination perfectible.

Au nom des fleurs! Au nom du brasier!

Parlez-moi, je vous répondrai.

J'existe! J'existe dans la scission de la loi. (*Silence. Le groupe* MOKHTAR, CAMILLE, MME PINTRE, RENÉ, *considère* PAULE, *de l'autre côté de la route.*) Parlez, délégation du Deux.

RENÉ: Nous réfléchissons, l'œil circulaire orienté sur toi.

PAULE: J'ai lieu hors lieu.

CAMILLE: Nous te regardons sans aucune joie.

Of a feverish exaltation in which the obstacle and the shrinking of desire both give way;[43] now here I am in the tenderness of morning.

See, the full extension of a body, like a lake bedazzled

By the fir trees of heaven, and the imperceptible transparency into which I'm being dissolved!

Where is the haven, goodness of evening, welcoming twilight?

The light opens wide its splendor! The goldfish spurt out onto the filament of the waters!

O obsolete road, rectitude suddenly shattered! I placed my own fall on the scales of justice.

I had, aflame with zeal, the sensible and the scattered.[44]

Who is forcing me into submission then? Who is telling me about a strategist?[45]

The image of the helmet and the owl,[46] coming back to life as none other than the ethereal goddess! I bow down, and the light turns my body into a shield.

The name for an overly long process.[47]

I define, without emotion, the thought that founds you.

It is I![48] (*She stands up, her manner of speaking slightly different now.*) Your Highnesses of politics, help me to my feet! The blow that must be dealt! The fortitude that must be had!

For fear that I might falter, for fear that I might give in to the forgetting of what must be forgotten, hold me up, a woman broken in two, shattered by the light!

Dictatorship! The inexistent's capacity to be thought![49]

Why have I no brother or sisters or lovers any longer, except so that I might be a symbol for you? So that I might belong to you.

O youth in rubble, in ruin! I used to encounter, yes, I had chance encounters to hold my own in life, and it devastates me

That language and ever-perfectible naming are necessary now.[50]

In the name of the flowers! In the name of the blazing furnace!

Speak to me, and I'll answer you.

I exist! I exist in the splitting of the law.[51] (*Silence. From the other side of the road,* MOKHTAR, CAMILLE, MADAME PINTRE, *and* RENÉ *all stare at* PAULA.) Speak, delegation of the Two.

RENÉ: We're reflecting, as we look you all over.

PAULA: I'm taking place out of place.

CAMILLE: We're looking at you without any enthusiasm.

PAULE: Vous déteniez sous la lampe un fragment de langage, refrappé. Je vaux mieux que ce fer. À l'instant vous m'avez à la retrempe.

MOKHTAR: Pourquoi ne pas accepter la preuve étrange?

MME PINTRE: Te voici! Jeune femme dans la satisfaction du nouveau.

CAMILLE: Dénombrement des feuilles, liste du sorbier rouge!

MOKHTAR: Telle tombée en croix sous la lumière, et ce n'est pas le dieu qui lui parle. Car c'est d'en perdre l'ornement qui la renverse et la fait rejaillir pour la précision d'un axiome.

RENÉ: Ne convoitons rien d'autre qu'elle. Quand la saison est celle de l'attente, qu'il y a dehors le froid gris, le champ labouré, on frappe, vous ouvrez, tout le temps se propose à l'étonnante discussion.

MOKHTAR: Divisiblement prête à changer la loi de l'Un.

PAULE: Donnez-moi l'écharpe rouge que porte la très jeune fille parmi vous. J'ai jeté ma couleur dans le port.

(CAMILLE *traverse, et met l'écharpe rouge au cou de* PAULE. *Pendant ce qui suit,* MOKHTAR, RENÉ *et* MME PINTRE *vont traverser la route pour se tenir, le dos au public, du côté de* PAULE.)

CAMILLE: Je te salue dans l'insularité du rouge.

MOKHTAR: « L'écart entre le 'je suis' de la personne et la prégnance en lui d'une contrainte n'apparaît qu'avec notre engendrement collectif.

RENÉ: La haine des individus mis en rivalité productive nomme enfin la contingence de ce qui les fait exister. Nous sommes plus libres sous la domination du capital, parce que nos conditions d'existence nous sont à nous-mêmes contingentes.

MME. PINTRE: Mais nous sommes naturellement moins libres, puisque régis entièrement par une puissance objective.

CAMILLE: La contradiction entre notre être subjectif intime et ce qui nous est imposé dans le travail, sur le fond d'un sacrifice fait dès l'origine, entre au jour de la conscience.

MOKHTAR: Pour advenir comme sujets, nous devons par conséquent abolir jusqu'aux ultimes conditions de notre propre existence.

MME PINTRE: Et donc ce sur quoi repose toute société jusqu'à nos jours.

PAULA: You were holding a fake chip of language under the lamp. I'm worth more than that old metal. I've just been freshly minted.

MOKHTAR: Why shouldn't we accept the strange evidence?

MADAME PINTRE: Here you are! A young woman experiencing the joy of the new.

CAMILLE: Counting the leaves, cataloguing the red ash trees!

MOKHTAR: Like one fallen spread-eagled under the light, but it's not God speaking to her. For it's giving up those trappings that's knocking her down and making her spring back up to achieve the precision of an axiom.[52]

RENÉ: Let's not want anything but her. When it's cold and gray out and the field's been plowed, a knock comes at the door, you open it, and all of time presents itself for the startling discussion.

MOKHTAR: She's divided enough to be ready to change the law of the One.

PAULA: Give me the red scarf that that young girl is wearing. I threw my own colors into the harbor.

(CAMILLE *crosses over and wraps the red scarf around* PAULA'S *neck. During what follows,* MOKHTAR, RENÉ, *and* MADAME PINTRE *will cross the road and stand next to* PAULA, *with their backs to the audience.*)

CAMILLE: Hail in the insularity of the revolution.

MOKHTAR: "The gap between the 'I am' of the individual and the hold on him of an inner constraint appears only with the emergence of our collective self-creation.[53]

RENÉ: The antagonism between individuals forced into competition with each other ultimately names the accidental character of what engenders them. We are freer under the dominance of capital, because our conditions of life are accidental to us.[54]

MADAME PINTRE: But we are naturally less free, since we are wholly controlled by an impersonal force.[55]

CAMILLE: The contradiction between our inner subjective selves and what is forced upon us by labor, against the backdrop of a sacrifice made right from the start, becomes evident to us once we become conscious.[56]

MOKHTAR: In order to come into being as subjects, we must therefore abolish the very conditions of our own existence.[57]

MADAME PINTRE: Which is to say, what all society has been based on up to the present.[58]

CAMILLE: De là que nous sommes en opposition directe avec la forme que les sujets virtuels du social ont jusqu'à présent choisie pour expression d'ensemble.

RENÉ: C'est-à-dire l'État. Il nous est dévolu pour réaliser le sujet que nous sommes de faire cesser l'État. Exister, dès aujourd'hui, revient à l'exercice encore minime de cette cessation.»

(PAULE *est presque dissimulée par* LES QUATRE.)

CAMILLE: Nous te désignons l'indistincte.

PAULE: Voici que je vous suis absente et majeure.

MME PINTRE: Donne l'écharpe. (LES QUATRE *et* PAULE *se passent l'écharpe rouge comme un fil d'Ariane.*) Incorporation de l'une aux préambules du texte.

PAULE: Mokhtar et Mme Pintre, bonjour. Également Camille et René, bonjour.

MOKHTAR: Toile de tente au désert, quand le renard suit vers le creux le dix-septième nom de l'eau. Au-dessus de chacun son dix-septième nom entre au lexique de sa langue fanée.

MME PINTRE: À la femme éternelle succède celle de l'instant, qui prodigue, outre l'idée, la persuasion et le commandement.

PAULE: Louise Michel, Hypatie, Elizabeth Dmitrieff, Jeanne d'Arc, Virginia et Catherine.

Sapho, Marie Curie, Camille Claudel et Sophie Germain.

Émilie Nœther, Vera Zassoulitch, Louise Labé; Emily Dickinson et les sœurs Brontë, Bettina von Arnim, Djuna Barnes.

De La Fayette et du Châtelet, Victoria, Elizabeth et Catherine la deuxième aussi bien.

Sainte Thérèse d'Avila, Zénobie, Alexandra Kollontaï, et Théodora de Byzance.

Jane Austen, Anna Seghers, Gertrude Stein et Cyvia Lubetkin. Dame Murasaki.

Chiang Ching avec Rosa Luxembourg.

Ici la fin de tout harassement à vous mettre en lumière. Procédure de la fin d'exception. Que l'écrit soit livré avec ma signature dans l'orthodoxie successive.

Car je suis dans la main du temps.

CAMILLE: Hence we are directly opposed to the form in which the virtual subjects of society have until now given themselves collective expression.[59]

RENÉ: That is, the State. In order to become the subjects that we are, it is incumbent upon us to put an end to the State. From now on, to exist comes down to the still negligible effort to bring about that end."[60]

(PAULA *is almost completely hidden behind the* OTHER FOUR.)

CAMILLE: We designate you the indiscernible one.

PAULA: Now I'm both invisible and essential to you.

MADAME PINTRE: Hand me the scarf. (PAULA *and the* OTHER FOUR *wrap the red scarf around themselves like a thread connecting them.*) The incorporation of some-one into the preamble to the text.[61]

PAULA: Mokhtar and Madame Pintre, hello. Camille and René, hello to you, too.

MOKHTAR: The tent in the desert, when the fox follows the trail of the seventeenth name of water into the hollow. Rising above everyone, its seventeenth name enters the vocabulary of their worn-out language.

MADAME PINTRE: After the woman of the ages comes the woman of the hour, who, in addition to the idea, propagates conviction and authority.

PAULA: Louise Michel,[62] Hypatia, Elisabeth Dmitrieff, Joan of Arc, Virginia, and Catherine.[63]

Sappho, Marie Curie, Camille Claudel, and Sophie Germain.

Emmy Nœther, Vera Zassulitch, Louise Labé; Emily Dickinson and the Brontë sisters, Bettina von Arnim, Djuna Barnes.

Madame de La Fayette and Madame du Châtelet, Victoria, Elizabeth, and Catherine the Second as well.

Saint Theresa of Ávila, Zenobia, Alexandra Kollontaï, and Theodora of Byzantium.

Jane Austen, Anna Seghers, Gertrude Stein, and Zivia Lubetkin. Lady Murasaki.

Jiang Qing with Rosa Luxembourg.

This marks the end of all the exhausting efforts to bring you to light. The declaration of the end of exceptional circumstances.[64] Let the document be delivered with my signature in successive orthodoxies.

For I am in the hands of time.

MME PINTRE: Rien n'est dit quand la parole, telle au matin l'enlèvement de l'air dans le coulis des brumes, n'a pas encore l'émission ni le timbre.

Femme! À refaire, le trajet d'Athéna, la loi qu'insupporte ton abdication. Ô glaciation des ailes d'un aigle bref! L'amère idole ici est consommée. Ici l'inconnaissable vient à la ferme forme de sa dissolution d'État.

(LES QUATRE *se regroupent en silence, fermés autour de* PAULE.)

VILLEMBRAY (*quelques pas vers* PAULE): Paule, laisse-moi te saluer au terme de la cérémonie barbare. Car je m'en vais. Adieu.

JEAN MAURY: Villembray, n'aurons-nous point votre réponse?

VILLEMBRAY: Vous l'avez.

PIERRE MAURY: Vous présenterez-vous devant la chambre?

VILLEMBRAY: Non.

JEAN MAURY: La gauche est d'accord avec nous, je vous l'assure, pour vous remettre tous les pouvoirs requis.

VILLEMBRAY: Éclipse de tout sujet.

PIERRE MAURY: Soyez.

VILLEMBRAY: Éclipse de tout sujet.

PIERRE MAURY: À cause de cette jeune femme, absorbée sous vos yeux dans un groupuscule fanatique?

VILLEMBRAY: Éclipse de tout sujet.

JEAN MAURY: Allez-vous mettre en balance le hasard de l'État et cette vaticination?

VILLEMBRAY: C'en est fait.

Reçois-moi dans le quelconque, haute nation si ramenée à son jardin que la jeunesse n'a d'issue qu'aux mains des prophètes secrets.

C'est en vain que je me suis mêlé à la clameur publique. La parole que je voulais assourdir parle plus haut dans les bouches que mon cliquetis compétent.

Capitaux et frontières, sentences télévisées, sommets aux tapis, quelle infortune!

Barque pourrie qu'aucun flot ne supporte, je te considérerai.

Désolation innocente, du plus bas de tout ce qui est anonyme, je t'alimenterai froidement.

(VILLEMBRAY *sort*.)

MADAME PINTRE: Nothing's been said when speech, like the air borne aloft in the currents of the morning mists, still lacks its emission and timbre.

Woman! Athena's life journey, the law outraged by your renunciation, must be done all over again.[65] O glaciation of a brief eagle's wings! The cruel idol here has been destroyed.[66] Here the unknowable achieves the definitive form of its State dissolution.

(THE FOUR OF THEM *silently gather together, closing around* PAULA.)

VILLEMBRAY (*taking a few steps toward* PAULA): Paula, let me say goodbye to you at the conclusion of this primitive ritual, because I'm leaving now. Goodbye.

JEAN MAURY: Villembray, won't we have an answer from you?

VILLEMBRAY: You have it.

PIERRE MAURY: Will you appear before the Chamber?

VILLEMBRAY: No.

JEAN MAURY: The left, I can assure you, agrees with us about handing all necessary powers over to you.

VILLEMBRAY: The eclipse of every subject.[67]

PIERRE MAURY: So be it.

VILLEMBRAY: The eclipse of every subject.

PIERRE MAURY: On account of this young woman, swept up into a fanatical sect right before your eyes?

VILLEMBRAY: The eclipse of every subject.

JEAN MAURY: Are you going to weigh the fate of the Nation against this ranting and raving?

VILLEMBRAY: It is done.

Welcome me into the ordinary, once proud nation now so reduced to a little patch of earth that the young have no alternative but to fall into the clutches of shady prophets.

It was all in vain that I joined in the clamor of public opinion. The words I wanted to muffle speak louder now than all my expert claptrap.

Capital and borders, televised verdicts, luxurious summit meetings, what a disaster!

O rotting boat that no waves can keep afloat, I'll observe you.

O stupid devastation, from the depths of anonymity I'll coolly assist you.

(*EXIT* VILLEMBRAY.)

PIERRE MAURY: Voici, je crois, le bout de la route. Je vais rentrer à la maison. Le boulot de bonne heure, demain.

JEAN MAURY: Un jour dans la menace de sa similitude à tout autre. Partons.

(LES DEUX MAURY *sortent.*)

MOKHTAR (*à* PAULE): Toi, viens!

PIERRE MAURY: This, I believe, is the end of the road. I'm going home.
Back to work early, tomorrow.

JEAN MAURY: A day under the threat of being just like every other.
Let's go.

(*EXEUNT* THE MAURYS.)

MOKHTAR (*to* PAULA): Come on, you!

ACTE SECOND

L'incident d'Antioche

SCÈNE 1: Dans le lieu des réserves de la guerre.

VILLEMBRAY, *délabré, un chapeau de paille sur la tête, pêche à la ligne dans le port.*

VILLEMBRAY: Je trempe ce fil dans la pourriture de l'eau.

    Petite poissonnaille engraissée de marins morts! Accroche tes barbes à mon épingle à nourrice! Je te ferai frire dans l'huile de machine.

    Sonne-t-on encore la messe à l'Église du quartier général? J'aimerais l'ornement d'une cloche, car je m'entraîne ici à la perfection du rien.

    Avant que la catastrophe n'éreinte la ville, je rassemble les affaires d'un mutisme. Je plaide pour l'inutilité. Non.

    L'inutile n'a pas à valoir au lieu de l'utile. Plein de douceur, je regarde l'eau et le bouchon.

(*Il se tait un moment. Entre* PAULE.)

PAULE: Villembray! Claude Villembray! (*Elle lui lance des petits cailloux.*)

VILLEMBRAY: Qui êtes-vous?

PAULE: Paule. Je suis Paule. C'est moi. Ne reconnaissez-vous pas votre sœur, très cadette?

VILLEMBRAY: Que venez-vous faire ici, ô âme retardataire?

PAULE: Et que faites-vous vous-même au bout de ce bâton, batelier à baleine?

VILLEMBRAY: Je suis comme la danaïde, sauf que c'est l'eau qui perce mon hameçon, d'un trou où passent d'exécrables nageoires.

PAULE: Claude Villembray, j'ai bien des choses à te dire. Ce peuple à nouveau prend figure. Claude! Ce qu'il veut et ne veut pas est désormais dicible.

    Le commandement s'exerce à parfaire le lien de la confiance. Les enfants ont pour jeu de savoir ce qui en est.

    C'est pourquoi jette ton attirail et viens.

ACT II

The Incident at Antioch

SCENE 1: In the place of the war reserves.

A scruffy-looking VILLEMBRAY, *a straw hat on his head, is fishing in the harbor.*

VILLEMBRAY: I'm dunking this line in the foulness of the water.

Hey, little fishy fattened on dead sailors! Hook your gills on my safety pin! I'll fry you up in machine oil.

Are the bells still ringing for mass at the headquarters church? I'd like to have a bell as an accompaniment because I'm practicing nothingness here.

Before the city's wiped out by the disaster, I'm putting together a case for silence. I'll defend uselessness. No.

The useless needn't be valued over the useful. Mellow as can be, I'll look at the water and my float.

(*He's silent for a moment. ENTER* PAULA.)

PAULA: Villembray! Claude Villembray! (*She tosses some little pebbles at him.*)

VILLEMBRAY: Who are you?

PAULA: Paula. I'm Paula. It's me. Don't you recognize your baby sister?

VILLEMBRAY: What are you doing here, O obsolete creature?

PAULA: And what are *you* doing at the end of that fishing pole, you fisher of whales?

VILLEMBRAY: I'm like one of the Danaides,[1] except it's the water that's piercing my hook, with a hole that hideous finned creatures are swimming through.

PAULA: Claude Villembray, I have lots to tell you. The people are taking shape once again. Claude! What they want and don't want can now be expressed in words.

The high command is working at strengthening the bonds of trust. The children have made a game out of knowing what's what.

So drop your fishing gear and come along.

Tu fis ma décision, et je peux te la rendre.

J'ai quitté celui avec qui j'étais.

VILLEMBRAY: Tu l'as quitté?

PAULE: J'ai eu un fils de lui, nommé David, sache ce nom.

VILLEMBRAY: Vas donc en prendre soin!

PAULE: Qui est David, mon fils? Qui est cet homme nommé Mokhtar? Je
lui dis: « Laisse là le complot des armes et des ordres du jour. Quelle
obscurité bien connue prépare ton obsession de l'assaut? Va avec moi
dans l'égalité des gens comme ils pensent, et suscite, valant pour elle-
même, leur persévérance. »

Mais lui, gagné par Céphas, comme un homme qui regarde au lieu
d'écouter, s'exalte, et se hâte vers l'entrée militaire dans le plus grand
nombre de palais.

Comme nos routes s'écartent, je le quitte, je viens ici à la source,
parler à Céphas.

Toi, sors de ta poubelle, viens! Tu es assez nihiliste pour reconnaître avec gaîté la consistance. Tu la cherches dans le vide. Mais
s'effectue son plein. Nul ne t'écartera.

VILLEMBRAY: Et qui rôtira mes petits poissons? Je suis l'artisan du minuscule, je ne suis pas le prêtre du grand Tout.

PAULE: Laisse là l'injonction de la petitesse! Nous avons changé tout
cela. Ce pays devient sous notre emprise l'invention d'une politique.
Chacun y fera loi du devenir de l'illégal.

VILLEMBRAY: Je n'y crois pas. Laisse-moi être le bœuf attaché à un
bouchon jaune. Pourquoi venez-vous me chercher? As-tu besoin de
ma ruine pour y faire trébucher Céphas? Je suis l'oubli d'une ville
plus ancienne.

Dans les rues de cette autre ville qui nous entoure, noire comme
d'un incendie qui fait défaut, tout le jour montent des cortèges. Est-
ce vous? Est-ce les autres? Est-ce Céphas? Moi, je me tiens à l'écart
de tous ceux qui arrivent. Ils entrent, stupidement joyeux, dans leur
future maîtrise. La cité n'a qu'une loi morte, où chacun serre contre
lui, cachée à ses propres yeux, l'angoisse qui le guide.

PAULE: Viens dans le courage d'un été! Viens et je t'aimerai encore!
Viens, et sois ce qui de toi résulte!

You made up my mind for me and I can return the favor.

I left the man I was with.

VILLEMBRAY: You did?

PAULA: I had a son by him, named David—remember that name.

VILLEMBRAY: So go take care of him!

PAULA: Who's David, my son? Who's that man named Mokhtar? I told him: "Forget about the armed plot and its orders of the day. It's that old obscurantist mindset²that's feeding your obsession with attacking. Come with me into the equality of people as they think and inspire them to carry on, which is something worthy in itself."

But he, under Cephas's influence, like a man who looks instead of listening, got all fired up and rushed off to the military gate in as many fortresses as he could.

As our paths diverged, I left him, and have come here to the source, to speak to Cephas.

Hey you, come out from under your rock! Come on! You're enough of a nihilist to cheerfully acknowledge political consistency. You've been searching for it in a vacuum. But its fullness is at hand. No one will turn you away.

VILLEMBRAY: Then who will fry my little fish? I'm the artisan of the miniature, I'm not the priest of the great cosmic Whole.

PAULA: Forget about everything having to be small! We've changed all that. Under our influence this country is becoming all about inventing a politics. Everyone will make the spread of illegality the law here.

VILLEMBRAY: I don't believe it. Let me just be an old ox tied to a yellow cork float.³ Why have you come looking for me? Do you need my downfall to trip up Cephas? I'm the forgetting of an older city.

Up the streets of this other city surrounding us, as black as from a failing fire, processions of people file by all day long. Is it you? Is it the others? Is it Cephas? *I* keep my distance from everyone coming here. Mindlessly elated, they're taking up their future position of command. Law is dead in the city, where everyone tightly clutches the anxiety, hidden from their own view, that drives them.

PAULA: Come with me in the rapture of a new day! Come and I'll love you still! Come, and be what results from yourself!

SCÈNE 2: Dans le lieu des vérités.

CÉPHAS: Ouvriers de l'usine, voici l'hiver de l'Autre.

La ville entre les mains des vieux gèle ses tubulures. Partout le craquement du solide des fleuves. L'essence en pénurie ne laisse plus patiner sur les flaques que des autobus extrêmement verts.

Si vous regardez dans la fente de mes yeux, vous y verrez en surimpression sur les glaciers du monde une foule qui court et crie.

MOKHTAR: Certes, la foule se tourne vers notre imminence. Quelles instructions?

CÉPHAS: La désorganisation de tout va son train. A défaut de Villembray, l'action gouvernementale jette ses coups d'épée dans l'eau.

Le soir, les rues s'absentent d'elles-mêmes et ne sont que des tranchées. La police rase les murs à la recherche de son ombre.

La monnaie ne vaut plus qu'on se chauffe au feu de bois qu'elle allume.

L'attente étend sur tous un empire de nécessité.

Cependant l'hiver tient la cité dans son carcan, et nous délibérons du point où faire céder ce qui déjà de soi seul est interrompu.

CAMILLE: Il est mauvais d'attendre, dans la fascination de l'instant. Car c'est la durée qui prévaut.

CÉPHAS: Horreur de la perpétuation! Ce qui dure ne fait que pourrir. Non pas le corps, l'articulation seule, là où casse un élan sec.

Notre office, savant de toute une ombre avide, est de changer en destruction le lent procès de mort. Frapper le moribond furieux, et qu'il s'éteigne!

MOKHTAR: Et après? Le vieux monde n'en finit pas d'empuantir ce qu'on lui substitue. L'odeur est si forte que pour s'en protéger, il faut refaire autant de murs, autant de règles et de ventilations, autant de bureaux fermés, que le mort en contenait lui-même.

CÉPHAS: Notre peuple est abruti comme il faut. Ni les ornements impériaux ne le consolent, ni les chansons qu'on lui coule aux oreilles. La possibilité sexuelle sans limite, excitante au début, le laisse souterrainement désireux de la restauration des lois.

SCENE 2: In the place of truths.

CEPHAS: Workers of the factory, now is the winter of the Other.[4]

The city in the old men's hands is freezing its pipes. Everywhere there's the sound of the rivers' solid surface cracking. The gasoline shortage is keeping all but some very green buses[5] from gliding over the frozen puddles.

If you look through the slit in my eyes, you'll see, superimposed over the world's glaciers, a crowd of people running and shouting.

MOKHTAR: True, the masses are turning toward our impending victory. What are our orders?

CEPHAS: The total disruption of everything is continuing. In the absence of Villembray, the government's efforts are all in vain.

At night, the streets disappear from themselves and are no more than trenches. The police slink around in search of their lost shadows.[6]

The money's so worthless that people warm themselves by the fires they light with it.

Waiting is spreading an empire of necessity over everyone.

Meanwhile, winter has the city in its grip, and we're debating the right moment to force something that has already come to an end by itself to give up.

CAMILLE: It's wrong to wait, in thrall to the present moment. Because it's the long haul that matters.

CEPHAS: I loathe it when things drag on! Anything that lasts only deteriorates. Not the whole body, just the joints, which can snap from a sudden movement.

Our task, informed by an all-consuming obsession, is to turn the long process of dying into destruction. To whack the dying old fool, and to hell with him!

MOKHTAR: And then what? The old world keeps on stinking up whatever it's replaced by. The odor's so strong that to protect yourself from it you have to put back up as many walls, cubicles and air conditioners, and private offices as the corpse itself contained.

CEPHAS: Our people's minds are as deadened as can be. The expensive trappings of Empire don't cheer them up, nor do the songs that are poured into their ears. The unlimited opportunity for sex, although exciting at first, leaves them secretly wishing for the laws to be restored.

Je nais de cette absorption de toute brève débauche. J'ai dansé loin dans la nuit sous la mitraille des couleurs. Je parlais à l'oreille des plus belles femmes, seins nus dans la résille, sans parvenir à entendre ce que je leur disais d'obscène.

Aujourd'hui, toute grâce de la jonction des cœurs, toute humeur et tout génie nous ont été retirés.

Nous n'avons plus pour but que de persévérer dans le déclin, et de le ralentir, jour après jour, par le sentiment de son éternité.

Rien n'a d'autre mérite que d'être publié aux millions d'exemplaires requis, et de disparaître allègrement dans la confusion générale.

Cependant vous et moi, insoucieux du nombre, n'avons respect que de notre vérité et de notre ordre.

Le contenu de toute pensée s'absorbe par nous dans la mise à mort de ce qui en interdit l'étendue.

MOKHTAR : Mais que diras-tu, Céphas, à tous ceux que tu appelles abrutis ?

CÉPHAS : Ils conviendront qu'au jeu du spectacle, celui de la destruction est le plus magnifique. (MME PINTRE *rit*.) Pourquoi ris-tu ?

MME PINTRE : Ils vont t'aimer, Céphas ! Tu seras l'histrion supérieur ! Ta faconde n'est-elle que de jouer la comédie du rien ?

CÉPHAS : L'insurrection est un art. Nous avons conquis ce dont toutes les politiques étaient antérieurement dépourvues.

CAMILLE : Quoi donc ?

CÉPHAS : La précision.

Je vous considère dans nos corps connexes, je vois votre volonté.

Les chefs d'État parlementaires évaluent les pressions et les menaces. Ils consultent l'humeur des syndicats et sont tournés vers la disposition de leurs confrères. Ils se font apporter, pour savoir leur image et calmer leurs doutes, les éditoriaux du matin. Ils prennent soin des éleveurs et des ingénieurs, des médecins et des bonnetiers, des vieillards et des officines pharmaceutiques. Ils passent sur toute la chevelure sociale la gomina des crédits et des assistances. Ils ne décident que contraints et forcés, ils rognent plus qu'ils ne règnent.

I was born from that engrossment in any brief debauchery. I danced far into the night under the troops' shelling. I'd whisper in the ears of the best-looking women, their breasts bare under their mesh camisoles, though I couldn't hear the obscene things I was saying to them.

Today, all the poetry of hearts uniting, all playfulness and spontaneity have been taken away from us.

Our only objective now is to keep on with the decline, and to drag it out, day after day, by making it feel endless.

Nothing has any merit other than being published in the millions of requisite copies, then quickly disappearing in the general confusion.

You and I, however, unconcerned about number, have regard only for our truth and our mission.

The content of all our thought is intent on destroying whatever keeps it from spreading.

MOKHTAR: But what will you say to all the people you call mind-deadened, Cephas?

CEPHAS: They'll agree that when it comes to a show, there's nothing more thrilling than the spectacle of destruction. (MADAME PINTRE *laughs*.) Why are you laughing?

MADAME PINTRE: They're going to love you, Cephas! You'll be such a brilliant buffoon! Is your way with words only good for performing the play of nothingness?

CEPHAS: Insurrection is an art.[7] We've achieved what all prior instances of politics lacked.

CAMILLE: What's that?

CEPHAS: Precision.

I observe you through our connected bodies; I can see your determination.

Parliamentary heads of state assess pressures and threats. They scrutinize the unions' moods and are focused on their colleagues' attitudes. To check up on their image and allay their doubts, they have the morning editorials brought to them. They take care of the cattle breeders and the engineers, the doctors and the haberdashers, the elderly and the drugstores. They spread the gel of funds and aid all over the head of society. They make decisions only under duress; they do more cutting than commanding.

Nous ne sommes pas de cette espèce. Nous en appelons en chacun à une prédiction cachée : celle qui le porte, dans le vide statutaire, à la croix du tout et du rien.

Certes, chez beaucoup, que domine l'anxiété des places assises, il n'y a qu'une température de reptile.

Mais en d'autres, dont le nombre est soudain suffisant, comme la femme arrachée à tout par la vindicte et l'errance d'un amour, se fait le geste du parieur redoutable.

Et nous ne pouvons souffrir que la considération des timides fasse partage ou obstacle.

MME PINTRE: Tu as expliqué parfaitement ce que tu veux. (*Elle rit.*)

CÉPHAS: Pourquoi ris-tu?

MME PINTRE: Et toi, qui décides en chef à partir de la connaissance de ce qui est, pourquoi ignores-tu justement la raison de mon rire?

CÉPHAS: Prends garde! Je peux t'entraîner, riante, échevelante, au point pur du fracas.

MOKHTAR: Certes, Céphas, nous te connaissons depuis longtemps. Nous t'accordons la confiance. Nous t'examinons aussi.

On dit chez moi: l'homme libre est plus proche de celui qui est entré avant-hier par la fenêtre que de celui qui depuis des années a la clef de la porte.

CÉPHAS: Parle de façon moins enveloppée. Nomme carrément Paule, camarade amateur de proverbes.

CAMILLE: Paule est belle, je veux dire . . . Paule est venue parmi nous comme une provocation. Je sais ce qui se brusque, à l'affût de soustraire à mon vœu le temps de l'assaut. Paule fait de notre patience une attente, j'en ai assez de sa caserne sans feu.

MME PINTRE: Rien n'est si asservi que la jeunesse d'une idée ne soit prête à le rompre; rien n'est si solennel que le débat ouvrier ne soit plus certain; rien n'est si certain que la consistance ne soit meilleure. Paule s'aperçoit avec nous qu'un pouvoir, si même il est à prendre, n'est pas toujours le bon objet de notre prise.

MOKHTAR: Et s'ils le veulent, tous? Et si dans l'atelier on nous demande où est l'instant? Et si ce murmure se fait, comme un vent refermé derrière la haie, de ce qui proteste contre notre lenteur?

CAMILLE: Notre jeunesse n'a pas eu tant de victoires, qu'il faille encore lui en retirer une toute cuite.

We're not of that ilk. We appeal to a secret prophecy in everyone: the prophecy that leads them, in the legal vacuum, to the crossroads of all or nothing.

Sure, many people, the ones anxious about not getting a seat, have cold feet.

But in others, and there are suddenly plenty of them, like the woman alienated from everything by a fickle love and bitter resentment, the mindset of the serious gambler is developing.

And we can't allow concern for the faint-hearted to come between us or stand in our way.

MADAME PINTRE: You've explained what you want perfectly. (*She laughs.*)

CEPHAS: Why are you laughing?

MADAME PINTRE: And why don't you, the leader who decides everything based on knowing how things really are, have a clue as to why I'm laughing?

CEPHAS: You better watch out! I can drag you off, laughing and raging, into the eye of the storm.

MOKHTAR: Granted, we've known you for a long time, Cephas. You have our trust. But we study you, too.

Where I come from we say: the free man is more like someone who came in through the window the day before yesterday than like someone who's had the key to the door for years.

CEPHAS: Don't speak so cryptically. Come right out and say Paula, you proverb-loving comrade.

CAMILLE: Paula's beautiful. I mean . . . Paula's come here among us like a provocation. I know I'm being pressured to stop wanting the attack to happen. Paula's turning our patience into an endless waiting game. I've had it with these freezing barracks of hers.

MADAME PINTRE: Nothing is so enslaved that the freshness of an idea can't set it free; nothing is so solemn that factory-based politics[8] isn't surer; nothing is so sure that consistency isn't better. Paula realizes as we do that power, even if it's there for the taking, isn't always the right thing for us to take.

MOKHTAR: But what if that's what they all want? And what if they ask us on the shop floor when the right time is going to be? And what if that muttering starts to grow, like the wind whipping up behind the hedges, out of the protest against our slowness?

CAMILLE: Our young people haven't had so many victories that they should be deprived yet again of such an easy one.

MME PINTRE: N'est-elle, la pensée ouvrière qu'un monde attend depuis deux siècles et dont il doute depuis vingt ans, que ce malade éveillé en sursaut d'un long sommeil par l'effondrement du toit de l'hospice? Si je tourne la tête à gauche vers ce portail, ornementation du fer prévaricateur, je vois que c'est la pâque du rassemblement.

CÉPHAS: Paule n'a-t-elle pas épousé Mokhtar? N'a-t-elle pas eu un fils de lui?

MOKHTAR: Vraiment l'ai-je épousée? Ai-je eu un fils? Je ne m'en souviens plus. Paule n'a pas besoin de moi, car mon exaltation lui paraît petite. Elle n'obéit plus guère, sachez-le. Elle est comme quelqu'un qui longe un mur, et les yeux clos discerne où nul ne peut la suivre le carré bleu d'une ouverture.

Céphas! Rallie-nous!

CÉPHAS: Je suis le plus impersonnel de vous tous, et c'est pourquoi vous n'avez ni à m'aimer ni à me craindre. (*Tourné vers* MME PINTRE:) Pourquoi te sers-tu d'un sourire pour refuser?

MME PINTRE: Et qu'as-tu proposé à quoi il faille que je dise oui ou non? Je suis une grosse femme fatiguée. Le jugement que j'ai sur la catastrophe qui t'énerve est que cela ne change que la couleur du temps, non son poids.

CÉPHAS: N'avez-vous pas, comme les autres, attendu ce moment? N'étiez-vous pas des gens que surélève enfin le ralliement des forces et des nombres?

CAMILLE: Dans la brisure d'une jeunesse, nous nous sentons comme à la veillée d'armes.

Désignés pour le premier coup de feu, nous ne pouvons dormir, cherchant de l'œil dans le noir la flamme en face d'un briquet.

SCÈNE 3: Dans le lieu des réserves de la guerre.

VILLEMBRAY, *de plus en plus dépenaillé, est allongé sur une caisse. À côté de lui,* UN PETIT CHIEN. *Entrent* MAURY *et* MAURY.

JEAN MAURY: Monsieur Villembray?

VILLEMBRAY (*sans bouger ni regarder*): L'humaniste parlementaire me rend visite. De Gaulle! Voici les sectateurs de l'Homme en soi. Salue l'Homme immédiatement.

(LE CHIEN *remue la queue.*)

MADAME PINTRE: Is working-class thought, which the world has been awaiting for two hundred years and having doubts about for the last twenty, just a sick man startled awake from a long sleep by the collapse of the nursing home roof? If I turn my head to the left toward the gate, that ornate construction of plundered iron, I can see that it's the rebirth of the rally.

CEPHAS: Didn't Paula marry Mokhtar? Didn't she have a son by him?

MOKHTAR: Did I really marry her? Did I have a son? I can't remember anymore. Paula doesn't need me, since my fervor seems trivial to her. She hardly listens anymore, I'll have you know. She's like someone who's walking beside a wall, and, with her eyes shut, detects the blue square of a cranny that no one can follow her into.

Cephas! Rally us!

CEPHAS: I'm the most anonymous[9] one of you all, and that's why there's no need for you either to love or to fear me. (*Turning to face* MADAME PINTRE:) Why are you using a smile to object?

MADAME PINTRE: Just what have you suggested that I need to say either yes or no to? I'm a big, weary woman. What annoys you about my take on the disaster is that I think it only changes the mood of the times, not their substance.

CEPHAS: Haven't you waited for this moment, like everyone else? Weren't you one of the people positively elated by the rallying of the forces and numbers?

CAMILLE: To us, in the breach of youth, it feels like the night before a big battle.

Chosen to fire the first shot, we can't sleep and keep peering around in the dark for the flame of a cigarette lighter out there.[10]

SCENE 3: In the place of the war reserves.

An ever-more disheveled VILLEMBRAY *is stretched out on a crate. Next to him is* A LITTLE DOG. *ENTER* MAURY *and* MAURY.

JEAN MAURY: Mr. Villembray?

VILLEMBRAY (*without moving or looking up*): The parliamentary humanist has come to pay me a visit. De Gaulle! Here are the disciples of Man-in-himself. Say hello to Man this instant.

(THE DOG *wags his tail.*)

PIERRE MAURY: Nous venons. . .

VILLEMBRAY: . . . me faire des courbettes. Je connais l'Homme, Messieurs, il ne cesse de se repentir d'avoir été tout à fait inhumain, Messieurs de l'Homme, divertissez-moi de vos plus récentes indignations.

JEAN MAURY (*à* PIERRE MAURY): On s'en va?

VILLEMBRAY: De Gaulle, mon doux fox, si l'Homme, le Français, le capital le plus précieux, fait mine de partir, mors-le!

(DE GAULLE *descend de la caisse.*)

PIERRE MAURY: Attention au clébard, il a l'air mauvais.

VILLEMBRAY: Il est tout à fait féroce. De Gaulle, montre à l'Homme en soi ta férocité. (LE CHIEN *aboie une seule fois.*) De Gaulle économise les preuves de sa fureur. Dès que vous voyez l'Homme, montrez un minuscule bout de votre force, pour n'avoir pas à vous en servir. L'Homme est essentiellement peureux.

PIERRE MAURY: Je me jette à l'eau, je . . .

VILLEMBRAY: Vous allez vous noyer. L'Homme se noie dans son verre à dents.

JEAN MAURY: Vos plaisanteries sont grossières, Monsieur. Nous avons notre dignité . . .

VILLEMBRAY: . . . d'Homme! Absolument! Votre dignité d'Homme!

JEAN MAURY: Et d'élus démocratiques, Monsieur. Nous représentons bien des gens, tenez en compte.

PIERRE MAURY: Je dirai même mieux. Nous représentons les forces vives, la jeunesse, les techniciens de pointe, les femmes libres. Songez-y.

VILLEMBRAY: Si j'y songe! Nous le disons toujours, le chien et moi. Que ferions-nous sans les mandataires de l'humanité générale? N'y a-t-il pas lieu d'honorer en vous la non-force et la non-pensée? Le sympathique glou-glou? Dans vos façons épanouies, la force tranquille et républicaine va son bonhomme de chemin. Je vois derrière vous les millions de rêveurs pleurnichards dont se fait toute omnipotence. Que vaut le cynisme, sans les idiots qu'il subjugue? Y aurait-il la moindre volupté dans la puissance, si ne venaient incessamment s'en plaindre des benêts sentencieux? Le monde n'est pas si drôle. Rien ne soulage l'esprit comme de vous voir galoper derrière les chariots de l'époque, pantalons troussés aux genoux et pipe au bec, pour supplier les conducteurs de respecter les droits et de ne pas écrabouiller dans un tournant l'Homme digne. Car l'Homme digne, le ressourcé, l'équilibré, le conscientisé, l'horticulteur de sa différence invisible, marche à pied, lui, menton relevé sous le soleil et sac au dos.

PIERRE MAURY: We've come . . .

VILLEMBRAY: . . . to bow and scrape before me. I know Man, gentlemen: he never stops blaming himself for having been thoroughly inhuman. Gentlemen of Man, go ahead and entertain me with your latest outrages.

JEAN MAURY (*to* PIERRE MAURY): Should we go?

VILLEMBRAY: De Gaulle, my nice little fox terrier, if Man, the Frenchman, the most precious capital,[11] makes a move to leave, bite him!

(DE GAULLE *comes down off the crate.*)

PIERRE MAURY: Watch out for the mutt; he looks vicious.

VILLEMBRAY: He's absolutely ferocious. De Gaulle, show Man-in-himself how ferocious you are. (THE DOG *barks just once.*) De Gaulle is sparing with the evidence of his fury. As soon as you see Man, show him just a tiny bit of your power, so as not to have to use it. Man is naturally fearful.

PIERRE MAURY: Let me take the plunge, I . . .

VILLEMBRAY: Don't—you'll drown. Man can drown in his own toothbrush glass.

JEAN MAURY: Your jokes[12] are offensive, sir. We have our dignity . . .

VILLEMBRAY: . . . Your human dignity! Absolutely! Your human dignity!

JEAN MAURY: And the dignity of democratically elected representatives, sir. We represent lots of people, keep that in mind.

PIERRE MAURY: Better yet, we represent the movers and shakers in society, youth, cutting-edge technicians, free women. Just think about that.

VILLEMBRAY: I'm thinking about it all right! We're always saying as much, my dog and I. Whatever would we do without the representatives of humanity as a whole? Shouldn't we salute the non-force and non-thought in you? The cheerful gurgling? With your smug attitude, quiet republican force[13] continues on its merry way. I see the millions of whiny fools behind you that all power is based on. What good is cynicism without the idiots it enthralls? Would there be the least bit of pleasure in power if pompous asses weren't endlessly griping about it? The world's hardly a barrel of laughs. Nothing eases the mind more than seeing you sprinting behind our wagons today, with your pants rolled up to your knees and your pipes between your teeth, to beg the drivers to obey the rules of the road and not run over self-respecting Man at some bend in the road. Because self-respecting Man, Man with his recharged batteries, well-adjusted, consciousness-raised Man, Man the caretaker of his miniscule difference, *he* walks, chin up in the sun, his knapsack on his back.

JEAN MAURY (*à* PIERRE MAURY): N'y a-t-il pas là des insultes? Ne devons-nous pas partir?

PIERRE MAURY (*à* JEAN MAURY): Songe à ce qui est en jeu. Villembray est retors. Il nous éprouve. Ne tombons pas dans le panneau. (À VILLEMBRAY:) Monsieur, je suis chargé par le parti socialiste démocratique et la confédération des travailleurs salariés de proposer à votre signature un nouvel appel aux hommes de bonne volonté de ce pays.

VILLEMBRAY: Ah! Ah! Je mâche du persil trempé dans le vinaigre, je me roule par terre dans la niche de Charles de Gaulle, mordant le bois comme lui l'os d'un mouton d'Égypte arraché au sépulcre du Dieu! Je gambade au cerf-volant de la volonté bonne.

(VILLEMBRAY *et* SON CHIEN *sautent très haut, très gracieusement, au-dessus des deux autres, presque jusqu'aux cintres, soustraits à la pesanteur.*)

VILLEMBRAY (*d'en haut*): Dans mes ailes, le vent désentravé de tout ce qui est volontaire! Guili-guili, démocrates! Quittez vos semelles!

(DE GAULLE *aboie furieusement en sautant de plus en plus haut.*)

JEAN MAURY: Le malheureux!

PIERRE MAURY: Claude Villembray a perdu la raison! Allons prévenir les journaux de gauche.

JEAN MAURY: Et ceux de droite. Quel événement! Quel titre!

(LES DEUX MAURY *sortent un appareil photo et essaient de prendre une image de* VILLEMBRAY *et du chien volant. Juste à ce moment,* VILLEMBRAY *et* DE GAULLE *retombent assez lourdement.*)

LES DEUX MAURY (*ensemble*): Raté! Zut!

VILLEMBRAY (*essoufflé au début, et de plus en plus véhément*): Répondez! Pourquoi? Deux gaillards ordinaires ordinairement équipés pour passer ici-bas sans se faire remarquer par quiconque. À quoi vous sert d'imaginer que vous faites de la politique? La course à pied sur les trottoirs en tenue de jogging sur vos cuisses poilues, l'évitement élastique des poubelles, tout s'offre à vos talents.

PIERRE MAURY: L'homme doit se mêler des affaires de la cité. L'homme ne s'épanouit que dans la citoyenneté responsable.

JEAN MAURY (*to* PIERRE MAURY): Aren't those insults? Shouldn't we leave?

PIERRE MAURY (*to* JEAN MAURY): Think about what's at stake. Villembray's a crafty one. He's testing us. Let's not fall for it. (*To* VILLEMBRAY:) Sir, I've been appointed by the Democratic Socialist Party and the Confederation of Salaried Employees to request your signature on a new appeal to people of good will in this country.

VILLEMBRAY: Ha, ha! I'm chewing parsley soaked in vinegar, I'm rolling around in Charles de Gaulle's doghouse, gnawing on the wood the way he does on an Egyptian sheep bone pilfered from the tomb of a god! I'm frolicking around with the kite of Good Will.[14]

(VILLEMBRAY *and his* DOG *jump high up in the air, very gracefully, over the heads of the other two, almost right up to the flies, defying gravity.*)

VILLEMBRAY (*from up above*): The wind in my wings, unfettered from everything deliberate! Hey, you democrats, cootchy-cootchy-coo! Don't be shy; give it a try!

(DE GAULLE *barks furiously, jumping higher and higher.*)

JEAN MAURY: The poor bastard!

PIERRE MAURY: Claude Villembray has lost his mind! Let's go tell the left-wing papers.

JEAN MAURY: And the right-wing ones too. This is some event! Some headlines *this* will make!

(THE MAURYS *take out a camera and try to snap a shot of* VILLEMBRAY *and his flying dog. At that very moment, though,* VILLEMBRAY *and* DE GAULLE *drop back to earth with a thud.*)

THE MAURYS (*in unison*): Missed the shot! Damn it!

VILLEMBRAY (*all out of breath at first, then increasingly vehemently*): Answer me! Why? Two unremarkable guys like you, unremarkably equipped to pass unnoticed by anyone here on earth. What good does it do you to think you're involved in politics? Running on the sidewalk in track suits over your hairy legs, nimbly avoiding trashcans—with talents like yours you could do anything.

PIERRE MAURY: Man should be involved in public affairs. Man is only fulfilled by being a responsible citizen.

VILLEMBRAY: Frères aux cheveux d'Avril, à la barbe frisée! Que voyez-vous qui ne vous soit étranger et brutal? Des ombres musulmanes s'arriment aux chaînes de l'acier. Leur œil âprement vous décortique. Ténacité recluse! Des gamins à couteaux, des jeunes filles échevelées bleu sous le cuir et la fume! Vous rasez les murs à leur seule approche, vous louez une armure et du plomb. Quelques penseurs s'accrochent à ces lambeaux modernes de la haine, dont les propos vous sont angoisse et sauvagerie.

Derrière vous, certes, la foule insipide des bureaux. Le microscopique va-et-vient d'ascenseurs et de cartables, le chef de service flanqué de son sous-chef, le pré-chef en escorte muré de secrétaires. Les écrans allumés de toute l'informatique planétaire! La banque et la poste! L'enseignement et la préfecture! Les ministères et les journaux! Les mairies et les sécurités sociales! Les chèques et les contraventions! Les assurances, les échelons, les suggestions! Horreur! Dix millions de personnes s'écrivent l'une à l'autre sur le formulaire correct. Et tous vivent de quelques arabes enchâssés aux machines.

Qu'avez-vous dans la tête, ô gens que disperse la vanité vitrière des aplombs? Classeurs de porte à porte, cliquetis infernal des claviers! Estampilles, et signatures en cécité!

Maury! Maury! Qui proclame par votre bouche que le rien est quelque chose? Qui exige le droit de l'homme à persévérer librement dans sa parasitaire inexistence? Fuyez, volatiles aux pattes grêles! De Gaulle! Sus aux poules! Sus aux poulets! Sus aux oisons et aux autruches! J'éparpille autour de moi les confettis d'une planète!

(VILLEMBRAY *déchire cent journaux sortis d'on ne sait où et remplit toute la scène de papier.* DE GAULLE *court autour des* DEUX MAURY *avec de petits aboiements suraigus. Tout s'arrête brusquement.* VIL-LEMBRAY *semble éteint les bras ballants. Un silence.*)

JEAN MAURY: Et où mène, je vous prie, cette vaticination?

PIERRE MAURY: Croyez-vous nous faire peur?

JEAN MAURY: Vous n'êtes plus rien, plus rien du tout. Une merde.

PIERRE MAURY: Parfaitement! Vous ne valez pas la crotte de de Gau…, de votre chien.

JEAN MAURY: Vous êtes rétamé, bousillé, archicuit.

VILLEMBRAY: You brothers with your April hair[15] and frizzy beards! Is there anything you see that doesn't seem foreign and brutal to you? Shadowy Muslims are bound with chains of steel. Their eyes scrutinize you mercilessly. Solitary single-mindedness! Kids with knives, girls with messy blue hair, swathed in leather and cigarette smoke! You hug the walls at their mere approach; you rent body armor and ammo. A few thinkers cling to these modern scraps of hatred, whose words fill you with dread and brutality.

Behind you, of course, is the vapid office crowd. The relentless coming and going of elevators and briefcases, the head manager flanked by his assistant manager, the wannabe manager with his secretaries escorting him like bodyguards. The lit-up screens of information technology the world over! The bank and the post office! Education and local government! Ministries and newspapers! City halls and social services bureaus! Checks and traffic tickets! Insurance, ranks, suggestions! The horror! Ten million people writing to each other on the correct forms. And all of them living off a few Arabs embedded in the machinery.

What's wrong with you, O people scattered by the vitreous vacuity of huge office towers? Door-to-door salesmen's binders, the furious clacking of keyboards! Timestamps and blind signatures!

Maury! Maury! Who's proclaiming through you that nothingness is something? Who's demanding people's right to freely pursue their parasitic non-existence? Away with you, you spindly-footed fowls! De Gaulle! Sic the hens! Sic the chickens! Sic the goslings and ostriches! I'm strewing the confetti of the whole wide world all around me!

(VILLEMBRAY *rips to shreds a hundred newspapers that he got from who knows where, covering the whole stage with paper.* DE GAULLE *runs around* THE MAURYS, *yelping shrilly. Suddenly everything comes to a halt.* VILLEMBRAY *just stands there, seeming burned out. A silence ensues.*)

JEAN MAURY: And what might I ask is the point of all this ranting and raving?

PIERRE MAURY: Do you think you're scaring us?

JEAN MAURY: You're nothing anymore, nothing at all. A piece of shit.

PIERRE MAURY: Absolutely! You're not even worth one of De Gau.., one of your dog's turds.

JEAN MAURY: You're through, you've had it, you're all washed up.

PIERRE MAURY: Personne ne parle plus de vous à la télé, et le syndicat ne vous a pas nommé dans ses communications depuis quatorze mois.

JEAN MAURY: Le Parti du Rassemblement vous encule.

PIERRE MAURY: Le Parti Socialiste Démocratique vous fait ça! (*Un bras d'honneur.*)

JEAN MAURY: Un politicien au rancart . . .

PIERRE MAURY: Une guenille parlementaire . . .

JEAN MAURY: Une serpillière ministérielle . . .

PIERRE MAURY: Pas un flic pour vous arrêter au petit jour.

JEAN MAURY: Pas un canard pour insinuer que vous aimez les partouzes.

PIERRE MAURY: Pas un magazine pour vous magaziner.

JEAN MAURY: Même le rétro vous rétrocède.

PIERRE MAURY: Trop décati pour les rétrospectives.

JEAN MAURY: Pas assez inaugural pour les inaugurations.

PIERRE MAURY: Nul au passé, nul au présent, nul au futur.

JEAN MAURY: Et ça nous fait du cirque!

PIERRE MAURY: Et ça nous fait la grosse voix!

JEAN MAURY: Matamore!

PIERRE MAURY: Bellâtre!

JEAN MAURY: Sycophante!

PIERRE MAURY: Totalitaire!

JEAN MAURY: Petit Staline, tiens!

PIERRE MAURY: Bien envoyé, ça. Petit Staline!

(*Ils s'arrêtent, essoufflés.* DE GAULLE *s'endort sur la caisse. Long silence.*)

VILLEMBRAY: À qui ai-je l'honneur?

SCÈNE 4: Dans le lieu des choix.

Une grande table de réunion est posée en travers de la route. Autour de la table CÉPHAS, PAULE *et tous les autres.*

PAULE (*les regardant tour à tour comme si elle avait du mal à les reconnaître*):
    Est-ce là l'embellie? Je vous vois dans la poudre d'or.

PIERRE MAURY: Nobody talks about you on TV anymore, and the union hasn't mentioned you in its press releases for the past fourteen months.

JEAN MAURY: The Unity Party doesn't give a flying fuck about you.

PIERRE MAURY: And here's what the Democratic Socialist Party has to say to you! (*He gives him the finger.*)

JEAN MAURY: A politician who's been put out to pasture . . .

PIERRE MAURY: An old parliament rag . . .

JEAN MAURY: A ministry mop . . .

PIERRE MAURY: No cop would even bother to arrest you in the wee hours of the morning.

JEAN MAURY: No gossip rag would even bother to insinuate that you're fond of orgies.

PIERRE MAURY: No review would even bother to review you.

JEAN MAURY: Even the conservatives don't want to conserve you.

PIERRE MAURY: You're too old-hat for retrospectives.

JEAN MAURY: And not inaugural enough for inaugurations.

PIERRE MAURY: A nobody in the past, a nobody in the present, a nobody in the future.

JEAN MAURY: And he puts on this big act for our benefit!

PIERRE MAURY: And he lectures us!

JEAN MAURY: You blowhard!

PIERRE MAURY: You loudmouth!

JEAN MAURY: You informer!

PIERRE MAURY: You totalitarian!

JEAN MAURY: You two-bit Stalin!

PIERRE MAURY: Two-bit Stalin! That's a good one!

(*They stop, out of breath.* DE GAULLE *falls asleep on the crate. A long silence ensues.*)

VILLEMBRAY: To whom do I have the honor of speaking?

SCENE 4: In the place of choices.

A big conference table is set up crosswise on the road. Around the table are CEPHAS, PAULA, *and* ALL THE OTHERS.

PAULA (*looking at them one by one as though having trouble recognizing them*):
    Is this the calm before the storm? I see you in a golden light.

À quoi sert cette table comme un chariot pour l'exil tiré par un bœuf?
J'imagine une telle lenteur!

CAMILLE: Ne joue pas à la folle. L'affaire est diablement sérieuse.

PAULE: Soit. Je ne me fie plus à ma jeunesse. Mokhtar! Tu l'as emportée
avec toi.

Vection du ciel d'usine! L'étonnement d'ordre des hommes dont
avec toi je me suis couverte est supprimé. Je sors de tes mains subite-
ment vieillie.

CAMILLE: Voyons, ma beauté! J'ai bloqué mon pied dans la porte. Le
néon des musiques a mis sur les murs de la piaule une sacrée bario-
lure! On va tout fiche en l'air.

RENÉ: Tu nous prêches le lent qui n'est que trop de la terre. Le sillon,
il faut faire demi-tour, et puis non. À midi debout sur le tracteur
j'inspecte vers l'Est si la ville va brûler. Céphas, me dis-je, va donner
le canon. Alors, le fusil de chasse, on le décroche du mur. J'y vais d'un
mugi de la corne. Nous voici très bas sous la haie. Paule, tu ne peux
plus différer cette image. Toute somme fixe de la terre prononcée
contre elle.

MME PINTRE: Sinon que toujours fixe après prononciation.

PAULE: Vos raisons, égales. Quel est le village où va ce chemin?

CAMILLE: Antioche.

RENÉ: Gamine! C'est Jérusalem qui compte.

La betterave, ô Paule, le cochon qu'on égorge, la machine pour
traire et le tracteur qui ronronne, l'ensemencement et les engrais, le
soin tardif de la vigne, ne sont pas de ta réflexion, pour que je te voie
tenir en suspens la hache du vouloir.

Puisque Villembray–non, non, je ne rappelle pas qu'il est ton
frère, ces choses, à la campagne, ont trop de poids; puisqu'il a re-
noncé, et que la chance opère, et que Céphas ne dit mot, c'est à nous
d'expliquer l'erreur d'un grandissement inactif.

What's the purpose of this table that's like an ox-drawn wagon for going into exile? I imagine such slowness!

CAMILLE: Stop acting crazy. This is a mighty serious matter.

PAULA: Fine. No more relying on my youth. Mokhtar! You took it away with you.

Vection[16] of the sky above the factory! The wondrous amazement of male authority in which I was cloaked when with you is ended. I've been released from your hands suddenly aged.

CAMILLE: Oh, come on, sweetheart! I've wedged my foot in the door. The neon lights from the dance halls have covered the walls of the place with a whole mess of colors![17] Let's trash it all.

RENÉ: You're preaching a kind of slowness that's all too like farming. With plowing, you always have to turn around and go back—oh, the hell with that. Standing on my tractor at noon, I check over east to see whether the city's going up in flames yet. Cephas, I think to myself, will give the signal. Then we take the hunting rifles down from the wall. I give a blast on the horn. Here we are crouching down low under the hedges. Paula, you can't delay this picture any longer. It's been fined every set amount on earth.

MADAME PINTRE: Except the amount's always set *after* the fine's imposed.

PAULA: Your arguments are the same. What village[18] does this road lead to?

CAMILLE: Antioch.

RENÉ: Silly girl! It's Jerusalem that matters.

The beets, O Paula, the hogs that are slaughtered, the milking machines and humming tractors, the sowing and fertilizing, the long, slow tending of the vines can have no part in your thinking if I can see you hesitating to bring down the axe of will.

Since Villembray—no, don't worry, I'm not reminding everyone that he's your brother; things like that, out here in the country, are too important—since Villembray withdrew, and luck is on our side, and Cephas is keeping quiet, it's up to us to explain the error of stagnant growth.

CAMILLE: Si après une sacrée gueule de bois je passe à la très petite aube devant les vitraux de la Banque, et si j'ai la fronde à la main, le crime n'est-il pas de passer comme un chien vague? L'artifice du verre à son éclat m'illumine! Sauvée de la nuit grise! Nous sommes comme des baladins à la queue sur un fil entre la dispersion ordinaire et le feu mis aux poudres.

PAULE: Vos raisons sont ordinaires.

MOKHTAR: Vu que nous avons su grandir dans l'atelier qui travaille; vu que les chefs, véloces, n'ont pu nous empêcher de passer le mot juste; vu que la fatigue et le tonnerre des presses ne nous ont pas abattus; vu que les forts veulent la force; vu que le salaire est pis que nul; vu que l'homme a des besoins, et que la femme a des désirs; je déclare qu'il est temps.

MME PINTRE: La ville est la forme de l'humanité. Oh! Quelle sera cette industrie de la cité

Quand la circulation du signe ayant recouvré son vrai, l'homme sera mis avec tous les hommes dans une relation visible,

Et par sa place ayant appris ce qui la déplace, il en excédera dans la joie la mesure,

Et dans l'angoisse au courage versée, il tirera sur le réel des traites de lumière,

Sujet d'une science où dissiper son désir.

CÉPHAS: Conclus! Achève!

MOKHTAR: La science naturelle a livré le monde aux argentiers, maintenant la science de l'histoire nous le livre. Autour de l'ouvrier au teint sombre, l'humanité entière est constituée comme un corps. L'architecture de ses membres est tenue de lever comme emblème, à deux mains, la lourde massue pour écraser la mouche de l'État.

Et sur la ruine que j'arpente, prenant avec amour chaque pierre, j'édifie la mosquée de la justice.

PAULE: Bien dit.

MME PINTRE: Paule, mets-toi avec Céphas et nous, afin que nous rassemblions la durée, et pliions l'acte à la consolidation de ce qui devient.

RENÉ: Céphas, mets-toi avec Paule et nous, afin que nous interrompions ce qui est, et que celui qui existe advienne à sa suprématie.

PAULE: Non!

CAMILLE: If, after a really nasty hangover, I walk by the stained-glass windows of the Bank at the crack of dawn and I happen to have a slingshot in my hand, wouldn't it be a crime just to walk by like some stray dog? The explosion of shattering glass lights me up! Saved from the dreary night! We're like street performers lined up on a tightrope between dispersing as usual and setting off a firestorm.

PAULA: Your arguments are banal.

MOKHTAR: Given that we've been able to increase our numbers on the working shop floor; given that the foremen, though quick, haven't been able to keep us from spreading the good word; given that fatigue and the deafening roar of the presses haven't demoralized us; given that the powerful want to use force; given that our wages are worse than nothing; given that men have needs and women have desires,[19] I declare that the time has come.

MADAME PINTRE: The city is the model of humanity. Oh, just think how dynamic the city will be

When, once the circulation of signs has recovered its truth, everyone is placed in a visible relationship with everyone else,

And from their place having learned what can displace it, they joyfully exceed its bounds,

And with their anxiety deposited in courage, they make withdrawals of light from the real,[20]

Subjects of a science in which their desire can be dissolved.[21]

CEPHAS: Conclude! Finish!

MOKHTAR: Natural science handed the world over to the financiers; now the science of history is handing it over to us. Around the dark-skinned worker the whole human race is configured like a body. The architecture of its limbs must lift the heavy club like a symbol and bring it down with both hands on the fly of State.

And on the ruins I'll stride over, lovingly picking up each stone, I'll build the mosque of justice.

PAULA: Well said.

MADAME PINTRE: Paula, join Cephas and us so that we can muster the forces for continuing and bend our action to support what's becoming.

RENÉ: Cephas, join Paula and us so that we can put an end to the way things are and that those who exist can come into their rightful place of superiority.

PAULA: No!

CÉPHAS: Es-tu donc réjouie par le train du monde?

PAULE: Violence, au point de ce désir! Nous n'avons rien pour nous
satisfaire, nous sommes aussi vieux
Nativement que la ville.
Sachez que ce qui nous est offert de feu et d'assaut n'est que
l'exécution par nous
De ce que le train du monde a prononcé quant à son achèvement.
J'ai longtemps transmis la mort, et ce n'est pas même qu'elle se
transmet dans la fureur de vaincre,
Mais l'éradication en nous du sujet qui veut,
Par ce que nous croyons la fortune du temps,
Et qui n'est que ce qu'exige l'endroit.
Confusion de l'espace et de l'heure!
Je constate, j'examine le vermoulu de l'ordre où je prospère. Mais,
Pas plus qu'une baie vitrée sur les mers du sud ne m'enjoint d'en
briser la transparence par l'imagination de posséder ainsi la vague, et
le sel,
Ou qu'une roche en équilibre millénaire sur l'arête d'une souche ne
fait droit au désir de la pousser—et que jaillisse en écume le torrent!
Pas plus la possibilité d'arracher la victoire n'est ce qui prouverait
que j'existe.
La loi de la victoire est trop particulière pour que l'universel sujet y
interrompe une astreinte, c'est lui qui s'y trouve dilapidé.
L'action où j'appelle est à tout instant recevable pour la surface
entière de ce monde. Un infini travail sur soi, partout reproductible.
Le rejet par saint Paul de la vieille loi avait puissance millénaire
d'ouvrir à l'enfant et à l'esclave, au Perse et au Viking, la possibilité
de la grâce et du salut.
Ainsi nous sommes à cette deuxième fondation où l'acte inouï est
de ne pas saisir un pouvoir disponible.
Parce qu'ainsi le monde apprend que la loi est scindée, et que ne
pèse plus sur nous l'obligation de la puissance.
Révolution: honneur nominal des peuples. Mais, dès lors, anticipation des Empires. Disqualifions ce mot, avec courage. Il marque sur
nous la loi périmée, celle où n'est pas mûre encore la subsomption,
par le lien, de notre pensée de l'égal.

CEPHAS: So you're content with the usual order of things?

PAULA: Only rage, with regard to that desire![22] There's nothing to satisfy us here; we've been around for

As long as the city.

Be aware that the opportunity we're being offered for armed combat is merely the way we'll accomplish

What the usual order of things has declared about its own demise.

I've spread death for a long time, and it's not even spread by the lust for victory

But the eradication in us of the subject that wills

By what we think is the luck of the moment

But is merely what the place requires.

A confusion between space and time!

I observe, I study the moldering away of the society I live in. However,

No more does a picture window facing the South Seas compel me to smash its transparency by the fantasy that I could thereby possess the waves and the salt,

Or does a boulder balanced for millennia on the edge of a tree stump sanction the desire to push it off—and let the stream gush forth in foam!—

Than would the chance to seize victory be the proof that I exist.

The law of victory is too specific for the universal subject to put an end to any constraint in it; it's he who'll be destroyed by it.

The action I'm calling for is valid at all times anywhere on the face of this earth. An endless working on oneself, reproducible everywhere.

St. Paul's rejection of the old law had the time-honored power to afford the child and the slave, the Persian and the Viking, the opportunity for grace and salvation.

So now we've come to the second foundational moment, when the unprecedented act consists in *not* seizing a power that's there for the taking.

Because that's how the world will learn that the law's been split in two and we're no longer burdened by having to take power.

Revolution: the nominal pride of people everywhere. But thereafter, the prelude to Empires. Let's rule that word out, valiantly. It brands us with the obsolete law, the law in which the subsumption of our thinking of equality by the social bond is not yet mature.[23]

Comme la circoncision pour saint Paul, la révolution n'est rien, la non-révolution n'est rien. Laissons ces épisodes aux futilités de l'image.

La révolution n'a jamais été dans la révolution.

Au-delà! Au-delà d'un tel orage!

L'autre histoire, prise à rien qu'à son trébuchement nocturne depuis cent ans, trouve ici sa croix. Sommes-nous les derniers guerriers de la vieille époque? La rupture consommatrice des espèces du temps est-elle l'antique guerre civile?

Considérons celui qui au sommet de la colline inspecte la plaine marquée du vol des buses.

Il se demande s'il doit lui aussi fondre vers le village par le droit de la pente et de l'herbe comme sur une proie,

Ou s'asseoir et allumer un feu clair dont jusqu'à l'horizon tous les hommes interprètent l'énigme.

Tel est notre choix. Il vaut pour que personne ne désespère, et que partout on se persuade qu'après les siècles de l'État,

Vient cette pensée que rien n'ordonne à la domination,

Et dont la violence elle-même est la peinture

D'une Nativité.

(*Silence.*)

MME PINTRE: Céphas! Écoute ce qu'on te dit. Ne soyons pas, déjà, les magistratures criminelles qui prononcent l'arrêt sur un corps malade.

CAMILLE: Les jeunes sont à ce point dégoûtés du monde qu'il est requis de le réduire en cendres. Vois, encore, la gaieté et l'aplomb de leur parcours du macadam, mains ballantes et pantalons serrés, l'œil noir sur toutes choses! Qu'avons-nous à leur dire, sinon les ruines qu'ils habitent et adorent?

MME PINTRE: Oublie l'angoisse, ma fille, laisse-toi vaincre par la patience et l'acuité d'un nouveau sens de la bravoure. Écoute ce que dit Paule. Surmonte la limitation de ton rêve. N'en appelle pas à la complaisance de la terreur.

MOKHTAR: Songe à tout le passé qui ici s'ouvre au soleil, et dont il faut tourmenter la corolle avant qu'elle soit fanée. N'aie aucune compassion.

RENÉ: Le meurtre est au principe de la nourriture, la possession est le sens de l'être. Sans le pouvoir, nous n'avons pour nous consoler qu'un regard orgueilleux sur l'humiliation. Que la réalité vienne au regard, comme un cheval au commandement.

Just as circumcision was for St. Paul, revolution is nothing and unrevolution is nothing.[24] Let's relegate those incidents to the realm of trivial images.

Revolution has never been in the revolution.[25]

Beyond! Beyond any such storm!

The alternative history, based on nothing but its stumbling around in the dark for the past hundred years, is finding its cross here. Are we the last warriors of the old era? Is the consummate rupture of all time between the classes the age-old civil war?

Consider the man who from the top of a hill surveys the plain with hawks circling over it.

He wonders whether he, too, should swoop straight down the slope and the grass to the village as he would on a prey,

Or sit down and light a bright fire whose mystery will be interpreted by everyone all the way to the horizon.

That's what *we* choose. Its merit is that no one will lose hope, and that people everywhere will become convinced that, after all these centuries of the State,

There now comes this thought that nothing can subdue,

And whose very intensity is the painting

Of a Nativity.

(*Silence.*)

MADAME PINTRE: Cephas! Listen to what you're being told. Let's not be the criminal courts passing judgment on an ailing body already.

CAMILLE: The young are so disgusted with the world that it's got to be reduced to ashes. Just look, still, at the high-spirited, self-assured way they saunter down the street in their tight pants, swinging their arms and scowling at everything! What do we have to offer them, other than the ruins they live in and love?

MADAME PINTRE: Forget about anxiety, honey, and give yourself up to equanimity and the keenness of a new sense of bravery. Listen to what Paula's saying. Go beyond the bounds of your dream. Don't resort to the complacency of terror.

MOKHTAR: Think about the whole past that's blossoming here in the sun and whose petals have to be pulled out before they wilt. Have no pity.

RENÉ: Murder is the source of food, possession is the meaning of being. Without power, all we have to console ourselves with is a disdainful glance at our humiliation. Reality must come into the glance, like a horse obeying a command.

CAMILLE (*tapant sur la table*): Quelles jérémiades! Assez! Faut-il toujours regarder sur l'épaule du temps,
Et prendre son ticket pour le repas des amis?

MME PINTRE: La décision reste hors lieu. Ô incision de la trame! Durée compatible!

MOKHTAR: La décision saisit l'occurrence. Ô incision de la trame! Instant fécond!

CÉPHAS (*il fixe les autres un par un, les nommant*): Mokhtar! Madame Pintre! Camille! René! Et toi aussi, Paule Villembray, mon égale en toutes choses.

Nous appartient-il de changer la décision? Réfléchissez ce point, qu'une décision véritable est plus importante, et de beaucoup, que celui qui la prend.

Aussi je vous donne également tort, si profonde soit la scission parmi vous.

Car les uns sont comme le chasseur qui délibère à l'affût si tirer l'oiseau qui passe,
—Ah! le sillon bleu sur la dorure des genêts—
Est bien en harmonie avec l'élégance durable de la chasse et l'éthique de vie ou de mort dont elle est l'exercice,
Quand tuer la colombe est cela seul qui prouve. Avant même toute pensée, dans une pure grâce de l'œil, le feu doit avoir complété et fauché la superbe du vol.

Mais les autres sont comme un pêcheur sur sa barque au long des roseaux, dans le matin gris de l'étang. Il a vu l'ombre d'une grande carpe souterraine à peine remuée sur la boue. Saisi d'impatience, il fait aller et venir l'hameçon à grands gestes.

Il oublie que son silence et son immobilité peuvent seuls, prolongeant la science des appâts, susciter la joie suraiguë du bouchon qui d'un seul coup plonge avec la bête.

Une décision, chers camarades, portant sur ce qui est entre nous en litige, est un composé fort étrange. D'un côté elle est rapt de notre geste par un ordre supérieur, un court-circuit de toute méditation; et de l'autre elle convoque ce que nous savons en son entier, par le travers d'un silence et d'un calme où nous surgissons au comble de nous-mêmes. Elle met en jeu toute la consistance que nous avons su maintenir, par le trou qu'y fait ce qui ne dépend plus d'elle, et où se loge, après l'acte, non avant, l'exact sujet d'une promesse.

CAMILLE (*banging on the table*): What moaning and groaning! Enough
is enough! Do we always have to be looking over time's shoulder
And reserving our seats for the class reunion?[26] *repas des amis* . . .

MADAME PINTRE: The decision remains outside of place. O cutting of
the fabric! Compatible consequences![27]

MOKHTAR: The decision seizes the chance. O cutting of the fabric! Fer-
tile moment!

CEPHAS (*staring at each of them in turn and saying their names*):
Mokhtar! Madame Pintre! Camille! René! And you, too, Paula Villembray, my equal in all things.

Is it up to us to change the decision? Consider this: a true decision
is more important, by far, than the person making it.

So I think all of you are wrong, however deep the split between
you.

For some of you are like a hunter in his blind pondering whether
shooting the bird flying by

—Ah, the streak of blue over the golden broom flowers!—

Is really consistent with the enduring elegance of hunting and the
ethics of life and death it exemplifies,

When killing the dove is the only proof there is. Even before any
thought, in the pure grace of the eye, the shot has to have finished off
and cut down the majesty of the bird's flight.

But the others are like a fisherman in his boat, drifting among the
reeds in the misty morning on the pond. He's seen the shadow of
a big carp just barely stirring the mud at the bottom. In the grip of
impatience, he jerks his line around wildly.

He forgets that only his silence and stillness, extending the art
of the lure, can elicit the exquisite joy of seeing the float suddenly
plunge down with the fish that's been hooked.

A decision, dear comrades, as to what's in dispute between us, is
a very strange compound. On the one hand, it's a take-over of our
act by a higher order, a short-circuiting of all reflection, while on the
other hand, it summons up what we know in its entirety, through a
silence and a stillness from which we suddenly emerge at our best. It
jeopardizes all the tenacity we've been able to maintain, on account
of the hole punched in it by what's no longer dependent on it, the
hole in which there dwells—after the act, not before—the true subject
of a promise.

L'heure est venue, Mars entre au Lion.

Et la naissance aussi est un signe, valant contre son propre avis, de femmes telles que vous en voyez une devant vous, Paule. Paule est la plus forte injonction de n'avoir à tenir de ce qu'elle propose nul compte.

PAULE: Que comptes-tu faire?

CÉPHAS: Je ne pense pas, comme vous imaginez qu'on pense. Je n'ai pas apprivoisé mon cœur comme un chat au fil d'une laine. Sur quelle route, sinon celle-ci, qui ne mène à rien qu'à Antioche, village insignifiant, aurions-nous arrêté une armée dont l'état-major discuterait s'il faut livrer bataille?

Rien ne se passe ainsi. J'objecte, Paule, à l'incertitude où ta pensée de ce qui vaut universellement plonge notre aveugle pari. Jetons les dés! Jetons-les, car c'est notre tour. La règle est là. L'économie de la particularité terrorisante, telle que tu la désires, ne conduit qu'à la dissolution du lien. Ce qui est à prendre, il est vrai que nous ne l'avons pas choisi. Mais nul ne peut prétendre remonter de la possibilité du choix à celle où le choix même pourrait être choisi.

Je ne fais pas, moi, la fine bouche devant la révolution. Ce qui advient après elle n'est lisible que pour qui a su fermer les yeux au moment où le tumulte fond sur lui et l'enferme dans les murs étroits de l'action.

Délivrons à l'instant ce qui nous donne chance d'être Un.

Ne mourrons pas sans connaître

Qu'ici, et fût-ce dans le bornage de cet «ici»,

Le plus faible a vaincu.

PAULE: Ce n'est pas le vieux monde dont ton «ici» va interrompre la chanson. Hélas, dans ta bouche, et dans ce qui déjà est accompli, c'est la nouveauté prévisible qui s'achève en la répétition de ce contre quoi elle s'est fondée. Ainsi, tout est fini?

(*Silence.*)

CÉPHAS: À propos: l'insurrection commencera par le jugement populaire et l'exécution de Villembray. Ce dernier fétiche de la ville parlementaire sera condamné à mort. Nul ne s'y trompera. (PAULE *ne fait pas un signe.*) Levons la main, pour que le scribe écrive ceci: près d'un bourg à betteraves, Antioche, le tournant de l'Histoire a été décidé par?

The time has come, Mars is entering Leo.

And birth, too, is a sign, her own opinion to the contrary not-withstanding, of such women as the one you see before you, Paula. Paula herself is the most powerful injunction not to have to take any account of what she's suggesting.

PAULA: What are you thinking of doing?

CEPHAS: I don't think, the way you imagine one thinks. I haven't tamed my heart like a cat with a bit of yarn. On what road, other than this one, leading to nowhere but Antioch, a paltry little village, would we have stopped an army whose high command would be debating whether or not to fight?

Things never happen that way. I object, Paula, to the uncertainty into which your thinking of what's valid for everyone is plunging our blind wager. Let's throw the dice![28] Yes, let's, because it's our turn now. Those are the rules. Doing away with the particularity of terror, as you would have it, only leads to the destruction of the bond. It's true we haven't chosen what's there to be taken. But no one can hope to go back from the opportunity for a choice to the opportunity for the choice itself to be chosen.

I don't turn my nose up at revolution. What happens after it can be understood only by someone who was able to close his eyes right when the turmoil crashed down on him and shut him up within the narrow walls of action.

Let's carry out right now what's giving us a chance to be One.
Let's not die without having experienced
That here, even if only within the bounds of this "here,"
The weaker party was victorious.

PAULA: Your "here" will hardly put a stop to the old world's same old song. Unfortunately, in what you're saying, and in what's already been accomplished, the predictable novelty is ending up repeating what it was originally intended to combat. So, is it all over?

(*Silence.*)

CEPHAS: By the way, the uprising will begin with Villembray's trial and execution by the people. The parliamentary city's latest darling will be condemned to death. No doubt about it. (PAULA *doesn't react.*) Let's have a show of hands, so the scribe can write this down: near Antioch, a little beet-growing burg, the turning point of History was decided by?

(CAMILLE, RENÉ *lèvent la main.* CÉPHAS *aussi, quelques secondes plus tard.*)

MOKHTAR: Je doute, soudain. Je suivrai cependant l'avis de la majorité.

CÉPHAS: Trois voix contre deux et une abstention. Une aussi courte majorité fera très bien dans la légende.

Eh bien, chers camarades, soyons à la fois le bon pêcheur et le bon chasseur. Notre gibier, quoique malade, a encore un sacré coup d'aile, et sait aussi s'enfoncer dans sa boue.

Ah! le monde est comme un lac, surface claire et profondeur de volcan.

Nous pouvons écouter notre souffle.

(PAULE, *comme réveillée, se lève en renversant sa chaise.*)

PAULE: J'empêcherai ce crime. Si l'action est restreinte, qu'elle soit cet empêchement!

(PAULE *sort.*)

CÉPHAS (*levant la main*): Adieu, Paule!

SCÈNE 5: Dans le lieu des réserves de la guerre.

Le port est désert, il fait un temps sombre et pluvieux. VILLEMBRAY *et* PAULE *sont assis sur le quai, les jambes dans le vide.*

VILLEMBRAY: Tu te souviens comme je m'initiais à ta dureté, à la douleur. Je courais sur les dunes, le sable aux genoux, jusqu'à la rage et l'épuisement. Et ma sœur lisait dans le damier de l'ombre, sous les pins. Je vois mon enfance avec toi comme un long exercice, jusqu'à ce jour où tu viens me dire: on veut te tuer, va-t-en. C'est toi qui as couru, Paule, pauvre sœur, et c'est moi qui suis immobile.

PAULE: Je te demande de partir pour eux, autant que pour moi.

L'absence d'une victime peut dérégler tout le sacrifice, toute la cérémonie. Je n'ai pas su les convaincre. Je me faisais à moi-même l'effet d'être timorée. Céphas a été superbe. Mais tu pleures?

VILLEMBRAY: Quelqu'un pleure en moi. Celui d'une patrie manquante.

(CAMILLE *and* RENÉ *raise their hands. So does* CEPHAS, *a few seconds later.*)

MOKHTAR: I'm having misgivings all of a sudden. I'll go along with whatever the majority decides, though.

CEPHAS: Three in favor, two against, and one abstention. Such a narrow majority will be great for the legend.

Well, dear comrades, let's be both good fishermen *and* good hunters. Our prey, albeit weakened, still has a hell of a lot of strength left in its wings, and it can burrow in the mud, too.

Oh, the world is like a lake, transparent on the surface and deep as a volcano!

We can hear our own breathing.

(PAULA, *as if suddenly coming out of a trance, stands up, knocking over her chair in the process.*)

PAULA: I'll prevent this crime from happening. Although action may be restricted,[29] let it be this preventing!

(*EXIT* PAULA.)

CEPHAS (*raising his hand*): Goodbye, Paula!

SCENE 5: In the place of the war reserves.

The harbor is deserted; it is dark and rainy out. VILLEMBRAY *and* PAULA *are sitting on the pier with their legs dangling over the side.*

VILLEMBRAY: Remember how I trained myself to get used to your toughness, to pain. I'd run on the dunes, up to my knees in the sand, till I collapsed from rage and exhaustion. And there my sister would sit reading in the dappled shade, under the pine trees. I see our childhood together as one long drill, right up to today when you've come to tell me: they're planning to kill you, get away from here. This time you're the one who ran, poor Paula, and I'm the one who's sitting still.

PAULA: I'm asking you to leave for *their* sake, as much as for my own. If there's no victim, it can throw off the whole sacrifice, the whole ritual. I couldn't convince them. I struck myself as being faint-hearted. Cephas was superb. Wait—are you crying?

VILLEMBRAY: Someone's crying in me. Someone from a country that's gone missing.

PAULE: Mes camarades vont cependant nous illustrer à la face du monde.

VILLEMBRAY: Ils n'iront guère plus loin que mon cadavre. L'armée tient encore bon. Ils en ont pour vingt ans. Je sens envers ce gâchis une rancune effroyable. On m'a fait du tort personnellement.

PAULE: Comme tes larmes sont inconsolantes!

VILLEMBRAY: Douceur de la remarque! Là où je voulais la fidélité d'une nation, il n'y aura eu de constant que des femmes, dont tu fus dès l'enfance la première, et aujourd'hui la dernière.

PAULE: Cette femme au nom des autres t'enjoint de partir et d'attendre.

VILLEMBRAY: Il m'a manqué une dose de bêtise. Je suis dégoûté du jeu. En politique, il faut garder l'appétit, même quand le plat est répugnant.

PAULE: Le temps presse, Claude.

VILLEMBRAY: Royauté d'un enfant. Je connais bien son usage. Tes camarades jouent la partition classique de la chance à prendre au vol. Comme je les comprends! Et le symbole de mon exécution! Comme c'est ordinaire! Je n'arrive même pas à me réjouir d'être, moi, ce symbole, parce que je sais mieux que quiconque ce qu'il vaut.

Recueille mes dernières paroles.

PAULE: Depuis toujours tu fais des phrases. Maladie masculine de la pose! Enfuis-toi, cours te cacher, là est la raison et la grandeur.

VILLEMBRAY: Vivant ici avec un chien dont je partageais la pitance, j'ai fait une découverte qu'il est juste que j'expie, pour n'avoir pas à la répandre.

PAULE: Tu ne m'en feras pas grâce, ô mon frère, capable de mourir d'un cœur léger pour achever son discours!

VILLEMBRAY: Il n'y a que la logique qui existe, et toute réalité en est une réalisation. Celui qui n'a d'autre règle que d'inférer à partir des axiomes produit, en outre, de la grandeur. C'est sa récompense, mais il ne l'obtient qu'au prix de ne l'avoir jamais désirée. J'appelle cela le principe de l'obtus. Bienheureux en politique l'esprit obtus qui s'acharne à la règle sans s'encombrer du moindre ornement.

PAULA: My comrades are still going to use us as an example for the world to behold.

VILLEMBRAY: They won't get much farther than my dead body. The army's still holding out. It'll take them another twenty years. I feel terribly resentful about this whole waste. I've been personally wronged.

PAULA: What little comfort your tears are to you!

VILLEMBRAY: Now there's a sweet remark! Where I was hoping for a whole nation to be loyal, the only thing that's been faithful has turned out to be women, you being the first, right from childhood, and now the last.

PAULA: Well, *this* woman orders you on behalf of all the rest to go away and wait.

VILLEMBRAY: I lacked a certain amount of stupidity. I'm sick of the whole game. In politics, you have to keep your appetite, even when the dish you're served is disgusting.

PAULA: There's no time to lose, Claude.

VILLEMBRAY: Kingship belongs to the child.[30] I know how that works. Your comrades are singing the old refrain about leaping at the chance. How well I understand them! And the symbol of my execution! How perfectly banal! I can't even manage to be glad that *I'm* the symbol, because I know better than anyone how worthless it is.

Hear my last words.

PAULA: You've always been one for pontificating. The old male syndrome of posturing! Get away from here, run and hide—that's where good sense and greatness lie.

VILLEMBRAY: Living here with a dog whose chow I shared, I made a discovery for which it's right that I atone, so as not to have to spread it.

PAULA: I can see you won't spare me, O brother who can die with a happy heart so long as he can finish what he's saying!

VILLEMBRAY: There's nothing but logic, and all reality is its product. He whose only rule is to infer from axioms produces greatness as well. That's his reward, but he can only get it by never having wanted it. That's what I call the principle of obtuseness. Happy in politics is the obtuse mind that sticks strictly to the rules and doesn't bother about any extraneous details.

Vois-tu, j'avais dessein, dans le commerce des forces, d'injecter sous la surface du cynisme une dose de légende. Il me semblait qu'une nation qui se rêve a plus de chance d'inverser ce qui la pousse au déclin. Je voulais substituer insidieusement l'ascétisme des images à l'économie solide.

Aujourd'hui je vois l'erreur. Se glissait là-dedans la mort obscure.

Plutôt que d'assister à l'enfoncement, au règne du défaut, j'ai désiré sans le savoir que mon pays meure, si je puis dire, par excès.

PAULE: C'est ce que tes assassins lui préparent. Ah! Je vois que tu es leur complice.

VILLEMBRAY: Ma mort est une production mathématique. Je n'y échapperais qu'en revenant au rêve, dont j'ai vu l'inconsistance.

Paule, ma sœur, à ce moment si dépourvu de légende, je veux, comme une amphore d'avant les cendres, te remettre ceci. (VILLEMBRAY *sort de sa poche une grande carte qu'il déplie.*) C'est l'idée d'une guerre que j'avais projetée en secret avec quelques amis de l'état-major, lors de ma seconde présidence. Nous devions vaincre en trois jours, dans la surprise la plus complète. Nous détenions à la fin trois provinces supplémentaires. Et nous les aurions gardées. Il suffit d'oser et de faire vite. C'est tout ce que j'ai ramené des greniers de l'État.

Aux heures de fatigue et de confusion, lisant ces flèches, ces impacts,

Où l'autrefois de la puissance se condensait comme un livre d'enfant,

J'entrais dans la considération nostalgique.

Je te donne, Paule, cet objet,

Pour que tu aies avec toi le comble de l'absurde,

Et qu'ainsi tu sois dotée d'un instrument de mesure

Quant à ce qui possède, dans l'action, sens et durée.

Si tu sais placer ce parchemin dans l'angle d'une flamme,

Tu y verras apparaître et mystérieusement s'ouvrir entre tes doigts

Une fleur sanglante contenue dans les dix-sept arêtes d'un polygone régulier. (*Il lui donne la carte.*) Maintenant, c'est à moi de te dire de partir. Je sais que tu es convaincue.

(PAULE *serre son frère contre elle longuement, puis s'écarte.*)

You see, in the dealings between the various forces, I intended to inject a bit of myth under the surface of cynicism. I thought that a nation that could dream itself up would have a better chance of reversing what's hastening its decline. I wanted to secretly replace a robust economy with the austerity of images.

Now I see my mistake. The darkness of death slipped in.

Rather than witness its gradual deterioration, the reign of scarcity, I unwittingly wanted my country to die, so to speak, through excess.

PAULA: That's what your killers have in store for it. Oh, I see you're their partner in crime!

VILLEMBRAY: My death is a mathematical given. The only way I could avoid it is if I went back to dreaming, and I've already seen the futility of that.

Paula, my sister, in these times so lacking in myth, I want to give you this, like an urn before it's been filled with ashes. (*From his pocket* VILLEMBRAY *takes out a large map and unfolds it.*) This is the plan of a war that I'd secretly mapped out with some friends from the high command, during my second term as chief of staff. We were to win in three days, with a big surprise attack. We were to have captured three additional provinces by the end. And we would've held on to them too. You just have to be daring and act quickly. This is all I brought back from the coffers of the State.

In moments of weariness and confusion, as I looked over these arrows, these strikes,

In which the bygone days of power were condensed like a children's book,

I would slip into a nostalgic reverie.

I'm giving you this, Paula,

So that you might have the epitome of absurdity with you

And so be equipped with a device for measuring

What's meaningful and enduring in action.

If you're able to place this scroll at the tip of a flame,

A blood-red flower contained within the seventeen sides of a regular polygon

Will appear to you and blossom mysteriously between your fingers. (*He gives her the map.*) Now it's my turn to tell *you* to leave. I know you've been won over.

(PAULA *hugs her brother tightly for a long time then moves away.*)

PAULE: J'ai froid! Voilà le vent qui se lève! Ce ciel gris!

(PAULE *sort. Un temps pendant lequel* VILLEMBRAY *range ses affaires dans une caisse. Puis il lance des cailloux dans l'eau.* CÉPHAS, MOKHTAR *et* RENÉ *entrent en tenue militaire, armés.*)

RENÉ: Villembray! Vous êtes jugé.

VILLEMBRAY (*se met à quatre pattes*): Tuez-moi comme un chien, Messieurs.

CÉPHAS: Peu importe!

(*Ils tuent* VILLEMBRAY.)

PAULA: I'm so cold! The wind's coming up! What a gray sky!

(*EXIT* PAULA. *Some time goes by during which* VILLEMBRAY *puts his things in a crate. Then he tosses pebbles into the water. ENTER* CEPHAS, MOKHTAR, *and* RENÉ, *in military fatigues and carrying guns.*)

RENÉ: Villembray! You've been sentenced to death.

VILLEMBRAY (*gets down on all fours*): Go ahead and kill me like a dog, gentlemen.

CEPHAS: What does it matter!

(*They kill* VILLEMBRAY.)

ACTE TROISIÈME

Le concile de Nicée

SCÈNE 1: Dans le lieu des fondations.

Au crépuscule, dans les ruines, en tenue militaire, MOKHTAR, CAMILLE, RENÉ *veillent autour des feux. Tous les personnages ont vieilli d'une bonne quinzaine d'années.* DAVID *est beaucoup plus jeune que les autres. Il se tient un peu à l'écart.*

MOKHTAR: Encore une nuit où le ciel, par absorption dans un miroir du
   sol gelé, est suspendu au-dessus de nos feux
         Comme une banquise d'étoiles.
CAMILLE: Quel foutu temps pour garder des cailloux! Et pas un chien.
   Qui donc s'amuserait à passer l'ordre des rouges d'éviter les décombres de la ville?
         Tous sont dispersés vers leur fumier natal.
         Si quelqu'un vient gratter par ici, au mur!
         Ça nous donnerait de l'emploi.
RENÉ: Telle fut la fin. Le dirigeant suprême Céphas, qui possède notre
   cœur par le truchement de son obstination, nous a menés quinze ans
   dans le dédale des circonstances. Et aujourd'hui, comme un barrage
   qui cède à la hauteur des neiges, tout s'est écroulé. L'État, ramené à
   l'aune d'un village puant dans un creux, est enseveli sous la ruine et la
   boue.
DAVID (*de loin*): Les gens errent sur les routes, ou ont été répartis également dans les provinces. Il s'agit avant tout de se nourrir.
RENÉ: Quinze ans de haine instruite! La terre se venge des cités. La production de ce qui se mange redevenue la charge de tous. La monnaie
   brûlée en tas dans de furtives cérémonies.

ACT III

The Council of Nicea[1]

SCENE 1: In the place of foundations.

In the ruins at dusk, MOKHTAR, CAMILLE, *and* RENÉ, *in military fatigues, are standing guard around the fires. All the characters are a good fifteen years older.* DAVID *is much younger than everyone else. He is standing a little apart.*

MOKHTAR: Another night when the sky, by absorption into the mirror of the frozen ground, is suspended over our campfires
    Like an ice floe of stars.

CAMILLE: What lousy weather for standing guard over rubble! And not a soul around. Who'd risk ignoring the Reds' order to keep away from the ruins of the city?
    They've all gone back to the sticks where they came from.
    If anyone comes snooping around here, put 'em up against the wall and shoot 'em!
    That'd give us something to do.

RENÉ: Such was the end. Cephas, the supreme leader, who has a hold on our hearts because of his stubborn determination, led us through the maze of events for fifteen years. And now, like a dam giving way at snow level, it has all collapsed. The State, reduced to the status of a grubby little village in the boondocks, is buried beneath the mud and rubble.

DAVID (*from a distance*): People wander the roads, or have been evenly spread out among the provinces. Everyone's chief concern is finding enough to eat.

RENÉ: Fifteen years of informed hatred! The land is taking its revenge on the cities. Producing food to eat everyone's responsibility again. Money burned by the pile in secret rituals.

Je regarde le chaos d'un œil clair.

Comme le granit violet des îles sur une mer d'encre, je vois
Survivre, à l'exclusion de tout, l'ordre campagnard sous la vigilance des armes.

Dans les vallées circule à nouveau, parmi les carcasses des tracteurs, le bœuf gascon sous le joug.

MOKHTAR : L'usine repart à zéro. Quatre professionnels dans un hangar au toit crevé rafistolent une fraiseuse. L'électricité crachote d'un générateur avec le bruit du bourdon. Nul ne sait ce qu'il convient de produire, mais qu'importe! Le savoir-faire ouvrier est nu comme la main sur un tournevis.

CAMILLE : Les enfants de tous âges et de toutes provenances sont rassemblés en cercle autour d'un conteur. Du vieux monde on leur enseigne la légende, et de ce qui accouche dans le sang et le cri, on leur promet l'éclat. À la fin vient la roulotte fumante où cuit, à doses égales, la farine de maïs. La parenté n'est plus qu'un fantôme. L'enfance engendre son propre village ambulant.

MOKHTAR : L'humanité, au jour de son effort ultime, traverse son désastre.

DAVID : Vous le dites. Organisée par son nom, la victoire calcine d'un seul coup dix mille ans. Le monde est cassé en deux. Toutefois, il s'agit de reconstruire implacablement, sans rien laisser au hasard ou à l'engrais de quelques-uns. Dans la loi refaite sur les décombres, chacun compte autant, et par conséquent très peu.

RENÉ : L'égalité devant la vie mesurable à tout instant à l'égalité devant la mort. La justice de la loi mise au niveau de la justice de l'être.

MOKHTAR : L'œil du vieillard voit les choses dans la confusion de la distance. Il me semble que tout a été râclé, comme avec un râteau, pêle-mêle les feuilles, les fleurs, la vidange et les cailloux. Mais trop de morts et trop d'indifférence entament l'idée, à la longue. Notre chef Céphas le sait. Le matin de cette nuit veut qu'on plante,

Sur le sol rempli de fumier,

La tendresse d'un saule, où attacher avec malice nos chevaux squelettiques.

Car il ne se peut que toujours la seule façon pour l'homme de régner sur lui-même soit d'abattre ce qui bronche.

I observe the chaos with a clear eye.

I see rural society, like the purple granite of islands in a jet-black sea,

Surviving, to the exclusion of all else, under the watchful eye of armed soldiers.

In the valleys, amid the tractor hulks, the Gascon ox in the yoke is plodding once again.

MOKHTAR: The factories are starting up again from scratch. Four pros in a shed with a busted roof try to patch up a milling machine. Electricity sputters out of a generator with the sound of a bumblebee. Nobody has a clue what ought to be manufactured, but what does it matter! Worker expertise is as bare as a hand on a screwdriver.

CAMILLE: Children of all ages from all over are gathered in a circle around a storyteller. They're taught the legend of the old world and are promised the glory of what's born in blood and strife. Afterwards comes the steaming lunch truck, where cornmeal, in individual portions, is cooking. Family ties are but a ghost of their former selves. Children are creating a traveling village of their own.

MOKHTAR: Humanity, on the day of its final effort, is going through its collapse.

DAVID: You said it! As determined by its name, victory is reducing ten thousand years to ashes in one fell swoop. The world is broken in two. Yet the point is to rebuild relentlessly and not leave anything to chance or to the enrichment of a few. In the law reconstituted on the ruins, everyone counts the same, and therefore very little.

RENÉ: Equality before life constantly equivalent to equality before death. The justice of the law put on a par with the justice of the individual.

MOKHTAR: An old man's eye sees things confusedly, as though from a distance. To me it looks as though everything's been scraped together helter-skelter, as with a rake: leaves, flowers, drains, and stones. But too many deaths and too much apathy undermine the idea, in the long run. Our leader Cephas knows this. The morning after a night like this is meant for planting,

In the ground spread with manure,

Something fragile like a willow, to which we can deftly hitch our scrawny horses.

For it can't be that the only way ever for people to govern themselves is to kill anything that resists.

CAMILLE: Le monde est noir comme un four où cuit un pain mauvais. Aussi taper sur le voleur et sur le débrouillard est la seule satisfaction. Aurions-nous dévasté la terre pour y voir se pavaner à nouveau des messieurs à cartable? Le chiendent doit être arraché pour toujours. Les morts sont invisibles, à l'échelle de ce qui se passe ici. Le général qui se met, la tête dans les mains, à compter les blessures au plus fort du feu est parfaitement foutu. Un univers entièrement refait, ou rien. Céphas l'a dit, dès l'incident d'Antioche: les dés, cette fois, sont jetés. Dans la mise du jeu, rien d'autre que le Tout.

RENÉ: Au loin les volcans fument dans la limpidité de l'air salin.

DAVID (*sur le ton du commandement*): Dites avec moi le salut.

Je salue la page blanche tachée de sang où il nous revient d'écrire le poème du siècle!

Je salue la nuit du gel et l'effroi du feu, le désespoir énergique, la dispersion et le rassemblement!

CAMILLE: Je salue le chaos et la nuit! Je salue la mort, où se fait la passe de la vie! Je salue la garantie de nos armes et les gravats fumants où gisent les lois!

MOKHTAR: Mais il n'est pas vrai qu'il n'y ait rien, car il y a suréminemment

Nous! Et c'est trop peut-être pour nous

Que d'être sur la peur des foules le seul signe du vrai.

Car cette vérité n'est que dans le lieu de sa force, et il n'est pas acquis que de cette force elle fasse lien.

L'eau claire coule au fond des égouts éventrés. Le tapis gluant des algues couvre le bassin des préfectures en ruine.

Cependant le calme et l'œuvre de pensée déclinent dans ce peuple, où règnent trop de jeunes gens dans l'orgueil du fusil.

La jeunesse est la vertu de la destruction. Que vaut-elle, dans la tyrannie de la durée?

Je m'interroge, chers camarades, comme un vieux dont la confiance est mémorable.

Nuit! Tu mets en suspens le désordre, par le pur gel de l'ombre. Enseigne-nous l'outre-victoire, la forme de l'Un, l'aube étrangère, l'achèvement, par la guerre, de la guerre.

CAMILLE: The world is as black as an oven in which some foul bread is baking. So beating up on crooks and hustlers is our only source of satisfaction. Did we lay waste the earth just to see another bunch of suits strutting around again? The weeds have got to be pulled up for good. The dead are invisible compared with what's going on here. A general who sits there with his head in his hands counting the wounded in the heat of battle is totally screwed. A world changed from top to bottom or nothing at all. Cephas said it, right from the incident at Antioch: this time, the dice have been rolled. We're betting the Whole Pot and nothing less.

RENÉ: In the distance, smoke is rising from the volcanoes in the limpid salt air.

DAVID (*in the tone of an order*): Recite the prayer with me.

Hail, the blood-stained blank page on which it's up to us to write the poem of the century![2]

Hail, freezing night and terrifying fire, heroic despair, scattering and regrouping!

CAMILLE: Hail, chaos and night! Hail, death, through which life is transmitted! Hail, the security our weapons provide and the smoking rubble where the laws lie dying!

MOKHTAR: But it's not true that there's nothing, since there's supremely Us! And yet it may be too hard for us

To be the sole sign of the true standing above the fear of the masses.

Because that truth is only in the place of its force, and there's no guarantee that from that force it can create a social bond.

Clear water is flowing at the bottom of the bombed-out sewers. A slimy bloom of algae is covering the water in the fountains of the abandoned government buildings.

Meanwhile, peace of mind and the work of thought are deteriorating in our people, with too many gun-proud young men in their midst.

Youth is the force of destruction. But is it any good under the tyranny of the long haul?

I wonder about this, dear comrades, like an old man whose confidence is legendary.

Night! You keep chaos in abeyance simply by freezing the dark. Teach us the other side of victory, the form of the One, the unfamiliar dawn, the end of war through war.[3]

SCÈNE 2: Dans le lieu des fondations.

En pleine nuit. DAVID *et* CAMILLE *veillent.* MOKHTAR *et* RENÉ *sont endormis, roulés dans des couvertures. Entre* CÉPHAS.

DAVID: Le voici. Évite de le fixer des yeux. Il n'aime pas qu'on le regarde.

CAMILLE: Tu le connais trop bien, David.

CÉPHAS: Je vous salue.

CAMILLE: Salut, Céphas.

(*Silence.*)

CÉPHAS: Bon. Quoi de nouveau? (CÉPHAS *regarde au loin comme s'il voyait dans la nuit. Puis il rit silencieusement. Se retournant tout à coup:*) Pourquoi me regardez-vous ainsi?

CAMILLE: Nous ne vous regardons pas.

DAVID: C'est vous! Comme la chouette-effraie cherche un rat, vous fixez d'un regard d'aile blanche l'invisibilité des orties.

CÉPHAS: Je suis satisfait. Voyez, d'une satisfaction qui est comme un point sans étendue de mon âme.

La jeunesse est finie, remercions-en l'histoire. J'étais un homme d'héritage, et la pensée n'avait plus cours.

Dans ce lieu méprisable et déclinant, j'ai soutenu, avec bien peu, que la grandeur passait par le trésor des ruines.

J'ai délivré le feu intérieur.

J'ai su circonvenir la menace. J'avais en moi une placidité suspecte, sachez-le. Le goût des plaisirs noirs . . .

Mais la pensée à elle seule est implacable. Il suffit de s'y confier.

Oui, je vois dans l'ombre! Je vois qu'il n'y a rien. À cause de cela, mon cœur se soulève comme la main levée pour bénir.

Cette heure est absolument nulle.

DAVID: Toutes sortes de décisions attendent.

CÉPHAS: Succulence du froid!

DAVID: Donne ton plan pour la reconstruction. Le débat est général. Les souffrances, gigantesques.

CÉPHAS: Laisse-moi, jeune homme. Je vois dans l'ombre, et mon regard porte si loin sans que rien n'y fasse obstacle

SCENE 2: In the place of foundations.

In the middle of the night. CAMILLE *and* DAVID *are on watch.* MOKHTAR *and* RENÉ, *wrapped in blankets, are asleep. ENTER* CEPHAS.

DAVID: Here he is. Be careful not to stare at him. He doesn't like to be looked at.

CAMILLE: You know him so well, David.

CEPHAS: Greetings.

CAMILLE: Hi, Cephas.

(*Silence.*)

CEPHAS: All right then. What's new? (CEPHAS *stares into the distance as if he could see in the dark. Then he laughs to himself. Suddenly wheeling around to face them:*) Why are you staring at me like that?

CAMILLE: We're not staring at you.

DAVID: *You're* the one who's staring! Like a screech owl hunting a rat, you fix your white-winged gaze upon the invisible thing in the nettles.

CEPHAS: I'm content, see, with a contentment that's like an extension-less point in my soul.

Youth is over; let's thank history for that. I was a man of the past, and thinking was obsolete.

In this despicable, deteriorating place, I argued, without much to go on, that the road to greatness went through the treasure of the ruins.

I set the inner fire free.

I was able to avert the threat. I had a suspicious calmness about me, if you must know. A taste for dark pleasures . . .

But thinking, by itself, is relentless. You just have to trust in it.

Yes, I can see in the dark! I can see that there's nothing there. And because of that, my heart leaps up like a hand raised in blessing.

These times are utterly worthless.

DAVID: All sorts of decisions lie ahead.

CEPHAS: How exquisite the cold is!

DAVID: Give us your plan for reconstruction. The discussion's wide open; people's suffering, enormous.

CEPHAS: Let me alone, young man. I can see in the dark, and my eyes penetrate so far without encountering any obstacle

Que je ne puis combler par ma joie le vide qui la cause.

L'homme a détruit son propre lieu. Il est rendu à l'errance, et s'aperçoit, stupéfait, que les liens dont se faisait son idée de la vie sont tous rompus.

DAVID: Toutefois si détruire interrompt le lien, ce qui fait alors politique en est en un seul point l'insoutenable intensité. Nous avons charge de la loi.

(*Silence.*)

CÉPHAS: Quand j'ai été blessé. Nous marchions plein nord, le long de la mer. La nuit, j'étais assis sur mon brancard, les sentinelles m'apparaissaient comme des masses de plomb. Je voyais que le sable craquait sous la lune, et l'écume brillait, mêlée à la glace. La retraite amassait en nous son incertitude.

J'étais tourmenté par trop de détails, comme l'est un chef de guerre, qui a autant de mal à remembrer sa pensée qu'un homme au bord de la noyade.

Une voix est entendue de la mer, comme confisquée par le froid. Durcie, amoindrie, coupante. La voix de Paule? Est-ce elle-même? Est-ce le remuement marin des funérailles? Ce n'était que mon nom, tel un galet roulé par le reflux de cette voix. Paule, ou l'océan, ont dit: « Céphas! » une première fois.

Et je voulais gravir un tank rouillé pour chasser les hommes devant moi,

Éventrer la fourmilière du givre!

J'étais cloué sur le métal du sable, frissonnant comme un phoque écorché.

De nouveau: « Céphas! » Une troisième fois :

« Céphas! » Tel un mot fait avec une femme sous-marine.

Qu'avez-vous à me dire, où l'analyse en son silence éclaire, comme au couteau,

L'interruption du rêve?

Que dis-tu, David?

DAVID: Je m'impatiente. Que signifie, toi, l'anonyme, de nous bassiner d'une angoisse?

CÉPHAS: La fin. Je m'étendrai dans la cendre des États. Je m'en irai avec les vieux textes.

Adieu, je pars, j'abandonne.

That my joy isn't adequate to fill the void that's causing it.

Man has destroyed his own place. He's back to wandering, and suddenly realizes, in utter amazement, that the bonds that constituted his conception of life are all broken.

DAVID: Yet if destruction undoes the bonds, then what constitutes politics is, in one regard alone, that destruction's unbearable intensity. We're responsible for the law.

(*Silence.*)

CEPHAS: When I was wounded. We were walking due north, along the sea. At night, I was sitting on my stretcher, and the sentries looked like blocks of lead to me. I could tell that the sand was crackling in the moonlight, and the foam, mixed with ice, was glittering. The retreat was building up its uncertainty in us.

I was tormented by too many details, like a war commander, who has as hard a time gathering his thoughts as a man on the verge of drowning.

A voice was heard from the sea, as if spirited away by the cold. Glacial, terse, biting. Paula's voice? Was it really she? Or was it the oceanic rumbling of a funeral? It was only my name, like a pebble washed out to sea on the tide of that voice. Paula, or the ocean, said: "Cephas!" a first time.

And I wanted to climb up on a rusted tank to drive the men before me,

To eviscerate the anthill of the frost!

I was pinned down on the metal of the sand, shivering like a flayed seal.

Again: "Cephas!" Then for a third time:

"Cephas!" Like a word formed by an underwater woman.

What have you to say to me now, when analysis in its silence starkly illuminates

The end of the dream?

What do *you* think, David?

DAVID: I'm getting impatient. What's the meaning—you, the anonymous one—of boring us stiff with some anxiety or other of yours?

CEPHAS: The end. I'll go lie down in the ashes of States. I'll take the old laws away with me.

Goodbye, I'm leaving, I'm throwing in the towel.

CAMILLE: Comment! Céphas! Vous n'allez pas laisser les choses en rade! Vous n'allez pas décapiter l'entreprise au milieu du désastre et de la nécessité!

DAVID: Sans explication! Sans critique! Tourner le dos quand il faut ramasser les cailloux!

CÉPHAS: Ce pour quoi j'étais lié à vous dans la juridiction du commandement, nous l'avons accompli. Le coup d'accélérateur sur le déclin de ce pays, par nous ramené à sa terrorisante origine, nous l'avons donné.

Au-delà de la victoire, il n'y a que la défaite. Non, non! pas la défaite dans le soudain et le renversement! La défaite lente, irrémissible, de qui doit composer avec ce qui est.

Pas la défaite inutile et pleine de gloire, pas la catastrophe légendaire! La défaite au contraire utile et féconde, la défaite qui ramène la paix du travail et restaure la puissance de l'État.

Je vous laisse la grandeur de ce genre de défaite, non par orgueil ou désintérêt de sa patience, mais parce que j'y suis inapte.

J'encombre aujourd'hui, par l'ordre de ma pensée du désordre, l'impératif de l'édification.

DAVID: Où regardes-tu encore?

CÉPHAS: David! Fils de Paule! Tu exiges les décisions que le chaos appelle. Tu veux, sans le savoir, que la terreur abstraite d'un gouvernement achève la terreur vitale de la révolution.

Tu as raison.

Je ne vaux pas mieux pour cette occurrence que Villembray au début de notre équipée ne valait pour le salut des vieillards. Villembray que nous avons tué, parce qu'ainsi sonnait le tocsin de l'irréversible.

Comme lui je me retire en un lieu désossé de la carcasse des jours. Comme lui, peut-être, vous aurez à m'abattre. C'est ce que je ferais, à votre place. Ce sera le tocsin du retour dans les villes.

Toutefois, que le mensonge soit tenu dans la clarté! De ce que nous avons détruit sous nos pieds,

Que le décombre enchâssé dans la restauration conserve sur vous son empire, et que la puanteur

Subsiste!

CAMILLE: Céphas, ne partez pas.

DAVID: Reste. Sois l'inquiétude, si le pouvoir t'offense.

CAMILLE: What?! Cephas! You can't leave things in the lurch! You can't cut off the head of our undertaking right in the midst of disaster and destitution!

DAVID: With no explanation! With no critique! Turning your back when the rubble has to be cleared away!

CEPHAS: We've achieved what I joined you for in the command jurisdiction. We've given a jump start to the decline of this country, reduced by us to its terrifying embryonic origins.

Beyond victory there's only defeat. No, no—not the sudden reversal kind of defeat! The slow, irreversible kind, the defeat of those who have to come to terms with the way things are.

Not the useless, glory-filled defeat, not the debacle that's the stuff of legend! But the useful, fruitful defeat, the defeat that brings back labor peace and restores the State's power.

I'll leave the grandeur of that kind of defeat to you, not out of pride or indifference to its progress, but because I'm simply not cut out for it.

Owing to my way of thinking about the chaos, I'm getting in the way now of the obligation to rebuild.

DAVID: Now where are you looking?

CEPHAS: David! Son of Paula! You're insisting on the decisions called for by the chaos. You unwittingly want the abstract terror of a government to bring the vital terror of the revolution to an end.

You're right.

I'm of no more use in a situation like this than Villembray was for saving the old men back at the beginning of our venture. Villembray, whom we murdered, because that was how the bell of inevitability was tolling.

Like him, I'll retreat to a bare spot on the carcass of time. And just as you did with him, you may have to kill me. That's what I'd do, if I were you. It would be the bell announcing the return to the cities.

Yet let the lie be held up to the light! Of all we've trampled underfoot,

May the remains embedded in the restoration preserve their hold over you, and may the stench

Endure!

CAMILLE: Cephas, don't leave.

DAVID: Stay. Be our uneasiness, if power offends you.

CÉPHAS: Au commencement, j'ai aimé être un chef. Ce n'étaient pas là des choses méprisables:

La circulaire, brève comme un télégramme amoureux, qui met debout à l'autre extrémité du pays des lycéens en rupture d'école, ou fomente à l'encan des banlieues un hourvari d'atelier.

L'ovation à la tribune dans l'été de la foule, entre les drapeaux rouges et les portraits.

Ou la halte au feu des armes, dans l'hiver caravanier.

Mais tout cela a eu son comble, et seule subsiste la crainte du regard.

C'est pourquoi je sortirai du cercle, franchissant la craie de la gloire.

Prends-le, David. Je te le donne. (*Il décroche le revolver qu'il porte à la ceinture, et le donne à* DAVID.) Adieu! Avec rien de l'Histoire je ne veux plus d'appartenance.

Comme le poète que l'événement-foudre ne saurait détourner du rythme où s'échoue la présence, je ne supporterai plus la décision.

J'aspire à l'immobile.

Je ne resterai pas dans la communauté de la nuit. Là où mon nom fut prononcé trois fois,

C'est là que j'irai. Dunes saisies par la neige!

L'océan charrie dans le brouillard le destin des méduses.

Je m'accroupirai dans les ruines d'un fortin, quand les guerres oubliées ne sont plus, entre les tiges de ferraille,

Qu'une flaque d'eau douce où urinent les chèvres.

(CÉPHAS *s'éloigne.*)

DAVID: Céphas!

CAMILLE: Partirez-vous sans testament? Tout seul, vous livrez-vous ainsi?

(CÉPHAS *sort.*)

DAVID: Il est parti.

(CAMILLE *et* DAVID *restent longtemps immobiles.*)

CEPHAS: In the beginning, I liked being a leader. Some things were not to be sneezed at:

The flyer, brief as a lover's telegram, rousing high school drop-outs clear across the country, or stirring up a big shop-floor commotion out in the *banlieues*.

The applause for the leaders on the grandstand, amid the red flags and the portraits, in the summer heat of the crowds.

Or the ceasefire, in the winter chill of the army vans.

But all of that finally peaked, and the only thing left is the fear of being looked at.

That's why I'll step over the chalk outline of fame and leave the circle.

Take this, David. I'm giving it to you. (*He removes the revolver attached to his belt and hands it to* DAVID.) Goodbye! With no part of History do I want any further belonging.

Like the poet who can't be distracted by the sudden great event from the rhythm in which presence turns up, I'll no longer abide making decisions.

I long for immobility.

I won't remain in the community of night. Where my name was spoken three times

Is where I'll go. Dunes covered in snow!

The waves carry the fate of the jellyfish off into the fog.

I'll lie low in an abandoned bunker, when the long-forgotten wars are no more, between the rusty iron rods,

Than a puddle of fresh water where the goats come to pee.

(CEPHAS *starts to walk away.*)

DAVID: Cephas!

CAMILLE: Are you going to leave without writing a will? Are you going to give yourself up, all alone like this?

(*EXIT* CEPHAS.)

DAVID: He's gone.

(CAMILLE *and* DAVID *stand there motionless for a long time.*)

SCÈNE 3: Dans le lieu des fondations.

Vers quatre heures du matin. Autour d'une table, lourdement vêtus, à cause du froid, MOKHTAR, CAMILLE, RENÉ *et* DAVID. *Sur la table, des bougies font l'unique lumière.*

CAMILLE: Annonçons que Céphas est mort.

MOKHTAR: Annonçons que le secrétariat, sur la recommandation testamentaire de notre grand dirigeant Céphas, a élu David. Provisoirement.

RENÉ: Jusqu'au congrès.

CAMILLE: Le congrès! À la saint-glin-glin, le congrès.

RENÉ: Le principe n'a pas plus droit de s'interrompre que l'enchaînement des saisons. Il convient de fabriquer le document nécessaire. La mort de Céphas ne peut qu'être établie dans la douleur d'un deuil national. Il aura griffonné le message qui recommande David. Nous produirons le papier.

CAMILLE (*ricanant*): Bien entendu. Dans le genre: « Si c'est toi qui es aux affaires, je suis tranquille. » Prenons surtout les sûretés militaires. La quatrième région n'est pas acquise d'avance.

DAVID: Pourquoi moi? Mokhtar ferait l'unanimité, par l'expérience, la pondération.

RENÉ: Le père plutôt que le fils. C'est régulier.

CAMILLE (*brutalement*): Le temps n'est pas encore venu qu'un arabe commande à ce peuple.

DAVID: Je suis à demi arabe, Camille.

MOKHTAR: Camille a raison. Je vous prie de le noter: la preuve est faite qu'au prix de tant de violences, nous n'avons pas changé le monde autant que nous le prétendons. Plus tard, l'arabe intégral! Prudence. Une moitié suffit. Mais je suis bien d'accord.

DAVID: Nous pouvons passer outre, s'il le faut, par la force.

RENÉ: Force sur force, le monde va plier, puis rompre. Les cadavres de notre guerre civile reconnaîtront à sa racine la canine d'argent du vieux chef.

DAVID: Paix! La décision fut déjà prise il y a longtemps. Je suis préparé par l'ignorance à savoir ce que je vaux. Dans l'enfance j'ai été touché conjointement

SCENE 3: In the place of foundations.

Around 4 A.M. Sitting around a table are MOKHTAR, CAMILLE, RENÉ, *and* DAVID, *all dressed in heavy clothing on account of the cold. The only light is provided by a few candles on the table.*

CAMILLE: Let's announce that Cephas is dead.

MOKHTAR: Let's announce that the central committee, in accordance with our great leader Cephas's will, has elected David. For the time being.

RENÉ: Until the Party congress.

CAMILLE: The Party congress! I wouldn't hold my breath!

RENÉ: The basic principle can no more be suspended than can the changing of the seasons. The necessary document's got to be forged. Cephas's death can only be officially confirmed through the grief of national mourning. We'll say he scribbled the message recommending David. We'll come up with the scrap of paper he supposedly wrote it on.

CAMILLE (*snickering*): Of course. Something along the lines of: "If you're the one in charge, I can rest easy." But let's make sure we take the necessary military precautions. The fourth region isn't a done deal.

DAVID: Why me, though? Mokhtar, with all his experience and sound judgment, would get everyone's vote.

RENÉ: The father rather than the son. That's only normal.

CAMILLE (*sharply*): It's not yet time for an Arab to lead our people.

DAVID: I'm half-Arab, Camille.

MOKHTAR: Camille's right. May I remind you that even after so much bloodshed it's clear we haven't changed the world as much as we might claim. A full-blooded Arab only later on! We've got to be cautious. A half will do for now. I couldn't agree more.

DAVID: We can disregard that, if need be, by using force.

RENÉ: Use force over and over and the world will eventually give out, then break apart. Our civil war dead will recognize the old commander by his silver eye tooth.

DAVID: Quiet! The decision was already made a long time ago. My lack of experience has prepared me to know my own worth. As a child, I was influenced by both

Par la parole de ma mère, Paule, telle un avertissement sibyllin,
Et par la droiture de mon père, Mokhtar, que j'ai suivi dans la
guerre comme on fait d'une étoile sur le pont d'un navire.
La prédisposition vieillit ma jeunesse, et me rend acceptable à tous.
Le gouvernement du désastre n'est pas trop pour y établir à nous
tous la signification.
Je serai parmi vous, entre l'aspiration à la paix et la volonté de
détruire,
Le point focal et l'intelligence d'un recours.
Mais tout d'abord, car un doute me poursuit: par quel arrêt com-
mencer ici, dès Céphas disparu,
L'endiguement du tumulte?

RENÉ: Il s'agit de la reconstruction nationale.

DAVID: Et quel est le début d'un tel apaisement?

MOKHTAR: Le retour dans les villes. L'administration régulière. La
légalité des tribunaux. Le contrôle des commissions d'épuration. Le
désarmement des milices locales. L'unicité de la police, soumise à
notre autorité exclusive. L'amnistie pour les fautes secondaires. La
recomposition des échanges et de la monnaie. La relance du système
scolaire. Un plan pour l'industrie. La réhabilitation des ingénieurs,
peut-être.

(*Silence.*)

RENÉ: Que reste-t-il de notre œuvre? Le monde va-t-il renaître dans sa
permanence et sa sécurité? Où donc la disparition de l'État? Que
devient l'égalité violente?

CAMILLE: Les canailles et les profiteurs vont surgir de leurs trous. Priv-
ilèges, affairistes, bureaucrates en tout genre, pots de vin et voitures
noires. La jeunesse va pourrir sur pied dans le scepticisme.

(*Silence.*)

RENÉ: Quel est donc, David, ton sentiment propre?

MOKHTAR: Qu'as-tu à proposer d'autre?

DAVID: Rien. Qu'auraient donc à faire ceux qui dirigent, parvenus au
comble du ravage, que d'assurer la lente renaissance d'une société
civile, et de l'État qui correspond à l'exigence

The word of my mother, Paula, like a cryptic warning,
And the integrity of my father, Mokhtar, whom I followed into
war the way you follow a star from the bridge of a ship. This family
background has matured me and makes me acceptable to everyone.
    Managing the disaster is not too hard to do to determine its mean-
ing for us all.
    Between your desire for peace and your determination to destroy,
I'll be
    The focal point for you and someone to turn to as a resource.
    But first of all, because a doubt's been nagging at me: with what
official decree, once Cephas has been declared dead, should we begin
    Containing the turmoil?

RENÉ: That would be national reconstruction.

DAVID: So how do we begin calming things down that way?

MOKHTAR: By having people return to the cities. Having a legitimate
    government. Re-establishing the legality of the courts. Overseeing
    purge commissions. Disarming the local militias. Unifying the police,
    under our exclusive authority. Granting amnesty for minor crimes.
    Restructuring trade and the currency. Getting the school system back
    up and running. Devising a plan for industry. Rehabilitating the engi-
    neers, perhaps.

(Silence.)

RENÉ: What'll be left of our enterprise, then? Won't the world just come
    back the way it was before, with all its stability and security? Then
    what about the abolition of the State? And what'll become of forcible
    equality?

CAMILLE: The crooks and profiteers will come rushing back out of their
    hiding places. Special favors, wheeler-dealers, bureaucrats of every
    stripe, kick-backs, and big black cars. The younger generation will
    waste away in nihilism.

(Silence.)

RENÉ: So what's *your* feeling about it, David?

MOKHTAR: Do you have anything other to suggest?

DAVID: No, nothing. What else would there be for those in charge to do,
    once at the peak of the devastation, except ensure the gradual rebirth
    of civil society and the State that corresponds to the demand

D'une activité productive? (*Silence.*) Mokhtar! Est-ce là toute la leçon que tu as tirée de ces années extravagantes? Et du siècle entier?
Que cherchait notre esprit dans l'obstination à mettre à la mise
Plus que notre vie même?
Quoi! Toujours cette idée de la reconstruction d'un État?
L'exigence populaire de la vie et de la survie
Toujours aux rets de la capacité économique et de la loi qui la règle? Mieux valait le suspens meurtrier où Céphas nous a tenus!
Car l'ordre n'est pas la fin que se propose la foule devenue le sujet de la politique qu'elle devient.

CAMILLE: Tu as raison. La fin est dans l'absoluité du désordre.

DAVID: Pas davantage. René, Camille! Imaginez-vous que se soutienne dans la durée
Que la mort soit l'étalon de l'égalité entre les hommes?
Et par quelle terreur dépourvue du sacré de l'histoire pensez-vous contraindre la lassitude d'un peuple à vouloir faire une loi féroce de l'absence de toute loi?
À quel despote remettrez-vous le soin
De faire régner partout le caprice et la peur, pour que ce pays tire de lui-même,
sous la chiourme, de quoi se prévaloir d'une puissance dévoratrice?
Mais c'est ici que je ne sais plus. L'État est haïssable, et l'anarchie plus encore. La politique est au rouet de n'avoir pour but ni l'ordre, qui l'administre, ni le désordre, qui la corrompt.

SCÈNE 4: Dans le lieu des fondations.

À l'aube, très grise. RENÉ *se lève.* DAVID, MOKHTAR *et* CAMILLE *entrent brusquement.*

CAMILLE: Attention. Quelqu'un arrive. Une drôle de poupée.
(*Entre* PAULE *presque méconnaissable, habillée avec une magnifique élégance, maquillée, à peine vieillie.*)

For productive activity? (*Silence.*) Mokhtar! Is that the whole extent of the lesson you've learned from these wild and crazy years? And from the entire century? What were we hoping to achieve with our stubborn persistence in putting

More than our very lives at stake?

What?! Still the same old idea of rebuilding a State? The people's demand for life and livelihood

Still caught in the trap of economic capacity and the laws regulating it? Better the deadly suspense we were held in by Cephas!

Because law and order can't be the aim of the masses once they've become the subjects of the politics they're in the process of becoming.

CAMILLE: You're right. The aim is absolute disorder.

DAVID: No, not any more so. René, Camille! Do you really think that, over the long term,

Death can be maintained as the standard of equality among people?

And with what terror lacking the sanctity of history do you intend to force a weary people to consent to turn the absence of all law into a cruel law?

To what dictator will you assign the task

Of imposing tyranny and fear throughout the land so that this country, under the jackboot, will draw from itself the means to embrace an all-consuming power?

But here's where I just don't know. The State is hateful, but anarchy is even more so. Politics goes around in circles, because neither order, which governs it, nor disorder, which corrupts it, can be its aim.

SCENE 4: In the place of foundations.

Dawn, very gray. RENÉ *is getting up.* DAVID, MOKHTAR, *and* CAMILLE *suddenly rush in.*

CAMILLE: Careful, someone's coming. Some weird chick.

(*ENTER an almost unrecognizable* PAULA, *beautifully dressed in elegant clothes, made up, and looking scarcely any older than she was before.*)

PAULE: David!

DAVID: C'est mon nom.

PAULE: Te voilà dans ta dignité, fils de la séparation.

DAVID: Ne suis-je pas sous les armes? Peut-on m'appeler « fils » sans précaution?

PAULE: Ta naissance n'a pas été ce qui fusionne deux en un. Mokhtar et moi, nous étant en toi délivrés de ce que nous avions en commun, nous sommes séparés.

DAVID: Tu es donc ma mère, Paule, parmi nous surnommée durement « la Sainte »!

PAULE: La Sainte! N'avez-vous pas brûlé les calendriers de la superstition?

MOKHTAR: Le nom de Paule, quoique sainte, n'est pas fait parmi nous pour la cendre des églises.

Aucune femme n'est comparable à celle-là que nous avons rencontrée comme la torche suspendue au tournant de la route,

Et qui s'est séparée comme elle était venue, éteignant d'un souffle son propre feu.

Visitation de l'Idée pure! Infécondité de la comète, quand le ciel s'embrase et pervertit la nuit!

RENÉ: Explique-nous, Paule, cette absence, et quel dessein te fit refuser de partager la victoire.

PAULE: Laissons cela. Le hasard d'un meurtre m'a rompue vive. Je n'ai pas à m'en vanter. L'écroulement d'un monde livré à la pourriture et aux chiens: Céphas avait raison, le jour d'Antioche. Je ne proposais que de vous retarder. Et de quel droit? Il n'est au pouvoir de personne de réfuter le principe, « ce qui naît mérite de périr ».

Je rêvais d'une autre figure de la mort. Inventée par nous. Relevant le défi de l'horreur.

Pour ce qui est de la haine et de la destruction, vous vous êtes livrés sans retenue à l'art classique. Je n'avais rien à vous dire qui vaille la certitude éduquée du stratège.

Aussi je me suis tue. J'ai accepté que s'accomplisse, une dernière fois, le rite de la révolution. Je veux dire: de la révolution classique, au comble de son style.

MOKHTAR: Femme du vieil amour! Où as-tu passé tout ce temps?

PAULA: David!

DAVID: That's my name.

PAULA: There you are in all your dignity, child of separation.

DAVID: I'm a soldier, aren't I? No one should casually refer to me as a "child."

PAULA: Your birth wasn't something that melds two into one. Since, through you, Mokhtar and I were relieved of what we had in common, we went our separate ways.

DAVID: Oh, so you're my mother, Paula, ironically nicknamed "The Saint" around here!

PAULA: The Saint! I thought you'd burned the old calendars of religious superstition.

MOKHTAR: Around here, the name Paula, even though she's a saint, isn't meant for the ashes of the churches.

No woman can compare with her, whom we came upon like a torch burning on high at a bend in the road,

And who parted from us the way she'd come, snuffing out her own flame with a single breath.

Visitation of the pure Idea! Sterility of the comet, when the sky is set ablaze and desecrates the night!

RENÉ: Tell us why you went away, Paula, and what reason made you refuse to share in our victory.

PAULA: Let's leave that aside. A murder unexpectedly tore me apart. It's nothing to be proud of. A world given over to corruption and gone to the dogs collapsed: Cephas was right, that day at Antioch. What I was suggesting would only have slowed you down. And what right did I have anyway? No one can refute the principle "All that comes into being deserves to perish."[4]

I was dreaming of a different form of death. One devised by us. Taking up the challenge of the horror.

As far as hatred and destruction are concerned, you plunged head-long into the classic art. Nothing I could have told you would have been a match for the knowledgeable certainty of the commander.

So I kept quiet. I accepted that, for one last time, the ritual of revolution should be performed. I mean: classical revolution, at the height of its style.[5]

MOKHTAR: Woman of the old love! Where did you spend all this time?

PAULE: J'ai disparu. Dans l'étude, dans l'attention à écouter. J'intervenais anonyme. Dans les gravats individuels de votre victoire. Je viens reconstituer la certitude au pli de son défaut.

CAMILLE: Et quel est, dis-moi, ce déguisement de bourgeoise?

PAULE: Je suis nue. Je suis nue entre toutes les femmes.

RENÉ: Nue et pauvre peut-être? La robe pourpre de l'évêque fait donc le moine?

DAVID: Laissez-la dire.

CAMILLE: Le chiendent remplit les salons, les champignons noirs pullulent sur les bureaux des sociétés que notre fureur éventre. Les femmes de ces messieurs charrient le purin pour l'ensemencement des patates.

Et te voici comme la dernière à fouiller dans la malle d'un convoi d'égéries!

PAULE: Et qui a dit que la laideur, le cheveu plat, la femme éteinte au kaki de la guerre, la jupe de laine noire étaient requis, pour la promesse et l'enchantement de notre politique? Êtes-vous sur le fluo, le néon,

La seiche et son jet d'encre?

Écoutez-moi plutôt, du point où ma beauté calculatrice vous met en défaillance.

MOKHTAR: Garde-toi, ô mon aimée, de nous promettre le bonheur. Il nous faut la solidité du présent. La principale qualité de ces ruines est qu'elles sont composées de vraies pierres. C'est à les reprendre une par une, dans le dénombrement de leur poids, que nous passerons sur l'autre rive.

PAULE: Mokhtar! Inoublié Mokhtar! Ne sois pas aussi obstiné dans la paix et la procédure que tu le fus dans l'emballement de l'insurrection.

Le soleil se lève, et tu croiserais en vain ton fer avec les rayons impassibles.

Écoute-moi dire une vérité. Le froid cède avec l'heure. Je dois m'emparer de votre étonnement.

Voyez autour de vous la terre nettoyée et assombrie. Toutes choses sont dévoilées. L'os du monde est à nu.

À quoi serviriez-vous s'il vous fallait, vous, proclamer la trêve et le pacte? Dans l'usage où vous avez été de la guerre, vous ne pourriez que mettre derrière chaque homme et chaque femme, et chaque enfant,

PAULA: I disappeared. Into learning, into listening carefully. I participated anonymously. In each little bit of rubble of your victory. I've come to re-establish certainty where it's lacking.

CAMILLE: So tell me, what's with the fancy get-up?

PAULA: I'm naked. I'm naked among women.[6]

RENÉ: Naked and poor, no doubt? So do designer clothes make the woman?[7]

DAVID: Let her explain.

CAMILLE: Weeds are invading upper-class living rooms, toadstools are sprouting on the desks of the companies trashed by our rage. The executives' wives are hauling the manure for sowing potatoes.

Yet here *you* are looking every bit as though you'd just rummaged through the wardrobe of a cavalcade of fashion icons!

PAULA: Who ever said that looking ugly, wearing your hair pulled back, hiding your femininity under military fatigues or wearing a shapeless dress were required for our politics to be one of hope and joy? Do fluorescent and neon colors

Get your goat?

Listen to me instead, based on the heart failure my consciously calculated good looks are giving you.

MOKHTAR: Be careful, O my beloved, not to promise us happiness. We need the solidity of the present. The chief virtue of these ruins is that they're made up of real stones. It's by picking them up one by one, re-cording each one's weight, that we'll make it over to the other shore.

PAULA: Mokhtar! Unforgotten Mokhtar! Don't be as stubborn in peace and all its red tape as you were in the heat of the uprising.

The sun's coming up and you'd get nowhere crossing swords with its impassive rays.

Let me say something true. The cold is giving way even as we speak. I've got to seize hold of your astonishment.

Look at the cleansed and darkened earth all around you. All things are revealed. The world's bones have been laid bare.

What good would you be if *you* had to announce a truce and a peace treaty? So accustomed to war have you become that you could do nothing but put an officer of the declared peace

Le sergent de la paix proclamée. La guerre ne serait pas finie, non. Elle serait congelée dans tout le corps social, et pour toujours.

Il vous est impossible d'ordonner votre pouvoir à sa disparition. Vous n'avez d'autre fidélité, et c'est justice, que celle de la terreur. Je ne puis vous le reprocher. Dans les circonstances qui firent de vous des héros, la terreur est le moyen simple, la claire mesure de ce que vaut la vie. Peut-on tolérer la marche en arrière, la restauration? Après tant d'épreuves? Mieux vaut tuer.

Toutefois l'obligation des fusillades et des camps de concentration vous interdit à jamais de vous représenter à vous-mêmes comme des libérateurs. La chose est mal engagée dans son principe. Il n'y a plus dans ce pays une seule voix significative, que la mienne.

CAMILLE: Quel orgueil absurde! Quels sont tes titres et tes exploits, pour parler si haut?

PAULE: Camille! Déjà pour toi la parole ne vaut que de qui en détient l'exercice.

Je vous dis ceci: Abandonnez le pouvoir! Laissez les choses s'ordonner sans vous. Les brigands que la situation exige naîtront tout seuls, et sans retard, de cette terre dévastée. Refondez votre groupe dans cette renonciation. Disparaissez dans le peuple, qui d'avance poursuit de sa haine ce que vous alliez entreprendre. Un pas de plus vers la coercition de l'État, et l'Histoire ne retiendra de vous qu'un sanglant effort national ramené, quant à la justice, au quelconque ou au pire.

CAMILLE: Tu nous vois comme des corbeaux, prêts à lâcher la proie pour l'ombre.

PAULE: Et quelle ombre, je te prie, Camille, sinon celle que vous allez jeter sur votre intention elle-même?

L'erreur où vous êtes est ancienne, et c'est ce qui permet de la nommer: crime. Car, une première fois, elle n'a été que la somme des exigences de l'instant. Une seconde fois, passe encore, l'erreur insiste, le dogme protège le vouloir. Une troisième fois n'appelle aucun pardon.

Notre génération connaît la secrète noirceur du rouge. Il nous appartient, par une décision sans précédent, de ne pas laisser sans effet cette connaissance.

RENÉ: Nous ne trahirons pas Céphas, la décision d'Antioche, prise contre toi.

Behind every man, woman, and child. The war wouldn't be over, not by a long shot. It would be frozen in society as a whole, forever.

It's impossible for you to order your power to disappear. Your only loyalty, and that's only fair, is to terror. I can't blame you for that. In the circumstances that made heroes of you, terror is the easy way, the clear measure of life's worth. Could you stand going backwards, restoration? After all you've been though? No, better to kill.

Yet the need for firing squads and concentration camps forever precludes you from regarding yourselves as liberators. It's doomed from the start. There's not a single voice that matters anymore in this country, except for mine.

CAMILLE: What ridiculous conceit! What great things have *you* accomplished that entitle you to speak with such authority?

PAULA: Camille! Already words only matter for you if they come from someone with the right to say them.

What I'm saying to all of you is this: Give up power! Let things run their course without you. The bandits the situation calls for will spring up all by themselves, soon enough, from this ravaged earth. Start your group over on the basis of that renunciation. Scatter among the people, whose hatred is already pursuing what you yourselves were going to attack. Take one more step toward State coercion and History will remember you as no more than a bloody national struggle reduced, where justice is concerned, to mediocrity or even worse.

CAMILLE: You see us as crows, ready to drop the prey for the shadow.[8]

PAULA: And what may I ask would that shadow be, Camille, if not the one you're going to cast on your cause itself?

The error you've fallen into is a very old one, and that's what makes it possible to identify it: crime.

The first time around, it was merely the sum of the demands of the moment. The second time—but let it pass—the error persisted, your intention was shielded by your ideology. The third time, though, it's unforgivable.

Our generation knows the secret blackness in the red. It's up to us, by making an unprecedented decision, not to let that knowledge go to waste.

RENÉ: We won't betray Cephas and the decision we made at Antioch, against you.

PAULE: Céphas savait ce que je dis. Je le comprends mieux que vous tous. Il vous dirigeait au-delà de la répétition. Ne sachant l'interrompre, du moins s'entêtait-il à l'exagérer. Céphas représentait la révolution pure. Cependant, il n'y a aujourd'hui, où toute révolution classique conduit à l'Empire, d'autre pureté néo-classique que la mort. La grandeur de Céphas est d'avoir abdiqué quand la mort devait prendre la forme de l'État. À défaut de trouver l'interruption de tous, il s'est interrompu lui-même. Tout ceci s'achève dans le désert d'un seul.

CAMILLE: Diras-tu qu'au moment de la victoire, il faut tout recommencer à zéro?

PAULE: Quel mot emploies-tu, « zéro »? N'est-ce pas le nombre que tu accordes, dans l'arrogance militaire, à la pensée de millions de gens? Et n'est-ce pas de là qu'il convient de repartir? La politique est à réinventer dans ce qui lui soumet la guerre, et non l'inverse.

CAMILLE: Tu essaieras en vain de me troubler. Celle qui pendant quinze ans a vu la mort dans la distance de son souffle, et qui survit à un monde écroulé

Possède une âme victorieuse, et ne cédera pas sur l'administration du présent.

RENÉ: Nous ne rendrons pas les terres aux gens des offices du blé.

MOKHTAR: Ni les machines, ou ce qu'il en reste.

DAVID: Je ne serai pas celui qui ne prend la charge que pour la déposer. Non, mère, il y a dans ton discours quelque chose de flou et de décourageant. Je ne laisserai pas s'étaler cette capitulation.

PAULE: Je veux te voir seul.

SCÈNE 5: Dans le lieu des fondations.

Il est dix heures du matin. Une sorte de tente a été dressée aux abords des ruines. Il y a un soleil pâle. PAULE *et* DAVID *achèvent de déjeuner.*

PAULE: Comment s'appelait cet endroit?

DAVID: C'était une sorte de ville nouvelle, inachevée. Toutes les tours ont été détruites à la dynamite.

PAULA: Cephas knew what I'm talking about. I understand him better than all the rest of you. He was trying to take you beyond repetition. As he couldn't put a stop to it, he at least kept on trying to amplify it. Cephas stood for revolution in its purest form. Today, however, when every classical revolution leads only to Empire, there's no neo-classical purity save death. Cephas's greatness is to have stepped down when death was about to be embodied in the State. Since he couldn't find a way of stopping everyone else, he stopped himself. It all ends in the absence of a single person.

CAMILLE: So you'd say that just when victory is achieved everything has to be started all over again from square one? *"Zero" or this doesn't make sense*

PAULA: "Square one," is *that* what you call it? Isn't that the paltry number that, with typical military condescension, you're assigning to the thought of millions of people? But isn't it precisely from there that we ought to start over? Politics has got to be reinvented through what war presents it with, not the other way around.[9]

CAMILLE: You won't get anywhere trying to unnerve me. As someone who for the past fifteen years has seen death no further than a breath away and has outlived a world that collapsed,
I possess a triumphant spirit, and I won't back down on governing the present.

RENÉ: We won't give the land back to the people from the grain agencies.

MOKHTAR: Or the machines either, whatever's left of them.

DAVID: I won't be someone who takes up the burden only to lay it back down. No, Mother, there's something unclear and discouraging in what you're saying. I won't allow that sort of surrender to spread any further.

PAULA: I want to see you alone.

SCENE 5: In the place of foundations.

It is 10 A.M. A tent of sorts has been pitched on the outskirts of the ruins. There is a pale sun in the sky. PAULA *and* DAVID *are finishing their breakfast.*

PAULA: What was this place called?

DAVID: It was a sort of new town, never completed. All the high-rises were dynamited.

PAULE: Mais le nom?

DAVID: Nicée. Comme Nice, avec un accent et un « e » supplémentaire.

PAULE: Comme le fameux concile, où quelques voix de majorité ont choisi pour les siècles que le Fils soit consubstantiel au Père, et non co-semblable.

DAVID: Qu'est-ce que j'ai à faire de ces foutaises?

PAULE: Rien. Ton royaume est de ce monde. Si monde il y a.

DAVID: C'est très curieux de se dire: voilà ma mère. Elle est en face de moi.

PAULE: Le culte de la mère, chez les hommes, est une saloperie. C'est la couverture du mépris des femmes.

DAVID: Je n'ai pas eu le temps de régler ton culte.

(*Silence.*)

PAULE: Tu n'as pas l'air assez arabe. Tu aurais dû emprunter plus à ton père.

DAVID: Pour être à mon tour consubstantiel, peut-être. Je n'y suis pour rien.

PAULE: On est responsable de son visage. Tu dois être raciste dans le fond.

DAVID: Je ne trouve pas ça drôle.

PAULE: Moi non plus. Te savoir le chef de tout ce qui se passe ici de monstrueux n'est pas drôle.

DAVID: Fais attention! Tu n'as aucune impunité. Je te ferai arrêter, s'il le faut.

PAULE: Mais comment donc! Des mères dénoncées par le fils, ou fusillées devant lui, j'ai vu ça, en province.

DAVID: Et qu'importe, après tout? Le désordre s'accomplit, le sang coule. Qui s'en souviendra? Aucun d'entre nous ne veut ces atrocités particulières. Elles sont comme un prélèvement forcé sur le réel. Il s'agit maintenant de restaurer les lois.

PAULE: « Restaurer », tu le dis. Ton excuse est lamentable. On se souviendra fort bien des massacres, si ce qui vient après est la répétition de ce qu'il y avait avant. Si vous n'êtes pas des criminels, vous êtes des imbéciles.

DAVID (*se jetant sur elle*): Ferme-la! Qu'est-ce que tu viens faire ici? Vieille peau parfumée! Nous en avons assez sur les bras. Tais-toi! Retourne dans ton trou!

(*Ils se battent. Mais étrangement, c'est* PAULE *qui se dégage d'un coup, et* DAVID *qui recule, plié en deux.*)

PAULA: But what was the name of it?

DAVID: Nicea. Like "Nice," but pronounced differently and with an "a" at the end.

PAULA: Oh, like the famous council, where a slim majority decided for the ages that the Son was consubstantial with the Father, not just of a similar substance.[10]

DAVID: Why should I care about bullshit like that?

PAULA: You shouldn't. Your kingdom is of this world. If there *is* a world.

DAVID: It's really strange to say to yourself: there's my mother. That's her sitting right across from me.

PAULA: Mother worship, in men, is crap. It's just a cover for their contempt for women.

DAVID: Sorry, I didn't have time to arrange for you to be worshipped. (*Silence.*)

PAULA: You don't look enough like an Arab. You should have gotten more of your father's genes.

DAVID: So that I could be consubstantial with him, too, no doubt. Well, I had nothing to do with it.

PAULA: We're responsible for how our own faces look. You must be a racist deep down.

DAVID: I don't think that's funny.

PAULA: Neither do I. Knowing you're the one in charge of all the horrific things going on here is hardly funny.

DAVID: Careful! You have no impunity. I'll have you arrested, if need be.

PAULA: But of course! Mothers denounced by their own sons, or shot by a firing squad right in front of them: I saw things like that, in the provinces.

DAVID: Well, what does it matter, after all? Chaos is spreading, blood is flowing. You think anyone will remember? None of us wants these particular atrocities to happen. They're like a compulsory tax on the real. We need to restore the rule of law now.

PAULA: "Restore"—there, you said it. What a pathetic excuse! People will remember the bloodbath all right, if what comes afterward is a repeat of what there was before. If you aren't all criminals then you're idiots.

DAVID (*lunging at her*): Shut your mouth! Why have you come here? You gussied-up old bag! We have enough on our plates as it is. Shut up! Go crawl back under your rock!

(*They wrestle. But oddly enough, it's* PAULA *who suddenly breaks free and* DAVID *who backs away, bent over in pain.*)

PAULE (*essoufflée*): Ah! la mère n'a pas perdu le coup pour rosser son fils.

DAVID: Eh! pour venir embrasser sa maman, il ne faut pas oublier la coquille sur les couilles.

PAULE: Tu n'as pas trop mal? Respire à fond.

DAVID: Il est clair que je ne suis pas un arabe. Je devrais te faire lapider.

PAULE: C'est vrai. Tu pourrais ajouter l'Iran au Cambodge.

DAVID: Tu veux un deuxième round?

PAULE: Assez d'enfantillages. Le prologue est fini.

DAVID: Que demandes-tu exactement?

PAULE: Je te l'ai dit. Que vous abandonniez le pouvoir.

DAVID: Mais quel est cet acharnement à exercer la fonction maternelle dans la direction contre-révolutionnaire?

PAULE: La contre-révolution, c'est vous. Vous exténuez jusqu'aux traces de la volonté de justice. Votre politique est vulgaire.

DAVID: Et toi tu es tout à fait distinguée.

PAULE: Écoute-moi. Laisse-moi prendre le ton masculin. Notre hypothèse, n'est-ce pas, n'a pas été dans son principe que nous allions résoudre le problème du bon gouvernement. Nous ne nous mêlions pas des spéculations des philosophes sur l'État idéal. Nous disions que le monde pouvait supporter la trajectoire d'une politique résiliable, d'une politique destinée à en finir avec la politique. C'est-à-dire avec la domination. Tu es bien d'accord.

DAVID: Je te suis, professeur.

PAULE: Il est arrivé que la réalisation historique de cette hypothèse s'est elle-même engloutie dans l'État. L'organisation libératrice a partout fusionné avec l'État. Il faut dire qu'elle s'était, dans la clandestinité et la guerre, entièrement ordonnée à sa conquête.

Ainsi la volonté émancipatrice s'est-elle soustraite à sa propre origine. Elle doit être *restituée*.

DAVID: Que veux-tu dire?

PAULE: Je veux dire *substituée*.

Aucune politique juste ne peut aujourd'hui soutenir qu'elle continue le travail antérieur. Il nous est imparti de desceller une fois pour toutes la conscience, qui organise la justice, l'égalité, la fin des États ou des trafics impériaux, de ce socle résiduel où le souci du pouvoir capte à lui seul toutes les énergies.

PAULA (*out of breath*): Ah, your old mother hasn't lost her touch for giving her son a good wallop!

DAVID: Wow, better not forget to wear a crotch cup when you go to give
your mom a kiss!

PAULA: You're not hurt too badly, are you? Take a deep breath.

DAVID: I'm obviously not an Arab. I should have you stoned.

PAULA: Right. Then you could add Iran to Cambodia.

DAVID: Wanna go a second round?

PAULA: Enough of this silliness. The prologue's over.

DAVID: What exactly do you want?

PAULA: I already told you. For all of you to give up power.

DAVID: What is this relentless insistence of yours on using your maternal
role in a counter-revolutionary direction?

PAULA: *You're* the counter-revolution. You're all wiping out every last
trace of the desire for justice. Your politics are vulgar.

DAVID: Yeah, and *you're* absolutely genteel.

PAULA: Listen to me. Let me speak like a man. Our basic hypothesis—
right?—wasn't that we were going to solve the problem of what a
good government should be. We didn't get involved in philosophers'
speculations about the ideal State. We said that the world could toler-
ate the trajectory of a politics to be terminated later on, a politics
that would put an end to politics. To domination, in other words.
You agree, right?

DAVID: I'm listening, professor.

PAULA: What happened was that the historical realization of that hypothesis itself got swallowed up in the State. The liberationist organization everywhere merged with the State. The fact is that when it was
underground, during the war, it became entirely focused on conquer-
ing the State.

Thus, the desire for emancipation became deflected from its own
origins. It needs to be *reinstated*.

DAVID: What do you mean?

PAULA: I mean *put back in place*.

No correct politics today can claim to be carrying on the earlier
work. Our task is to detach consciousness, which ensures justice,
equality, the end of States or the illicit dealings of Empire, once and
for all from this residual base wherein the lust for power alone absorbs all our energies.

Quelle immense portée peut avoir, faite par vous, la proclamation d'une fidélité dont la forme pratique serait que vous repreniez le chemin de la conscience collective et de sa mise en sujet! Vous laisseriez l'État à qui en aime les pompes, et la meurtrière bêtise.

DAVID: Il y a derrière nous, comme un impératif supérieur à notre volonté, le sacrifice de milliers de gens, dont notre victoire est le seul sens. Allons-nous, pour une abdication sublime, réunir dans l'été de l'absurde un peuple entier de morts?

PAULE: On nous a déjà fait le coup du parti des fusillés. À quoi rime de placer le sens politique sous la juridiction des morts? C'est de bien mauvais augure. Et je te fais remarquer qu'aujourd'hui des gens meurent en foule, non pour la victoire, mais à cause de la victoire. Tu seras forcé, quel que soit ton choix, de sélectionner parmi les cadavres ceux qui te justifient.

DAVID: Où mène ce chantage moral? La pitié ne sert à rien. Dans la dévastation, l'ordre est de reconstruire. S'il faut emprunter au passé, nous le ferons sans crainte. Qui peut s'imaginer qu'après une telle secousse, le vieil état des choses va resurgir comme si de rien n'était? Le monde est changé pour toujours. Il suffit de s'y confier. Ma très chère mère, tu viens un peu trop du bas des choses. Tu es éloignée de la décision.

PAULE: Vieille ficelle, David! Je te propose justement la seule décision possible. Tout le reste n'est que la gestion des contraintes, par les moyens brutaux qui sont à votre disposition. Bien entendu, vous allez faire du nouveau! Vous allez peindre en gris la surface du soleil.

DAVID: Dis-moi précisément qui tu es. Condamnes-tu ce que nous avons fait? Es-tu avec les blancs, avec la racaille qui se terre? Je retrouve toute ma froideur, je te préviens.

PAULE: Vous avez fait une besogne inéluctable. La petite bête impériale est abattue, elle gît dans l'entre-deux de ces collines. Vous avez été les sacrificateurs. Par vous, le premier cycle de l'histoire de la justice vient à son achèvement. C'est pourquoi vous pouvez prononcer le commencement de sa seconde puissance.

DAVID: Ce n'est certes pas la puissance que tu proposes. Y renoncer, plutôt, et pour longtemps.

What a tremendous impact it could have if you were to announce a fidelity that would take the practical form of your returning to the path of the consciousness of the masses and its subjectivation! You'd leave the State to those who like all its pomp and circumstance, and its murderous stupidity.

DAVID: Behind us, like an imperative surpassing our own will, is the sacrifice of thousands of people, to which our victory alone gives meaning. Just for the sake of some sublime abdication are we going to gather together a whole nation of the dead in loonyville?

PAULA: We've already had "the Party of the executed"[11] number pulled on us. What sense is there in putting the meaning of politics under the authority of the dead?[12] That really bodes ill. And let me point out that masses of people are dying today not *for* victory but *on account of* it. No matter what choice you make, you'll be forced to pick from among the corpses the ones that vindicate you.

DAVID: What's the point of moral blackmail like this? Compassion's of no use. In the face of devastation, the priority is to rebuild. If we have to borrow from the past, we'll have no qualms about it. After an upheaval like this, who could possibly imagine that the old state of affairs will revive as though nothing at all had happened? The world's changed for good. You just have to trust in that. Mother dearest, you're coming at things a little too pessimistically. You're far-removed from the decision.

PAULA: That's an old one, David! I'm actually suggesting the only possible decision to you. Everything else is just about handling resistance, by the brutal means you have at your disposal. Sure, you're going to create something new! You're going to paint the sun's surface gray.[13]

DAVID: Exactly who *are* you? Are you condemning what we've done? Are you with the Whites, with the scum who are in hiding? I'm warning you, I'm starting to feel all my detachment from you again.

PAULA: You did the dirty work that had to be done. The little imperial beast's been slain. It's lying in the hollow between these hills.[14] You were the ones who performed the sacrifice. Thanks to you, the first phase of the history of justice has come to an end. That's why you can announce that the second phase of its power is beginning now.

DAVID: It's anything but power you're proposing—more like giving it up, and for a long time.

PAULE (*sort un grand papier, et le déplie*): Regarde cette carte militaire. Mon frère Claude Villembray me l'a donnée, juste avant que nous le mettions à mort. Là est le rêve, là est l'enfance. Il aurait bien voulu conquérir la terre, comme n'importe quel vieux roi. Allez-vous continuer, interminablement, cette puérile passion? La grandeur particulière de l'espèce humaine n'est pas la puissance. Le bipède sans plumes doit se saisir de lui-même, et contre toute vraisemblance, contre toutes les lois de la nature, et contre toutes les lois de l'histoire, suivre le chemin tortueux qui mène à ce que n'importe qui soit l'égal de tous. Non seulement dans le droit mais dans la vérité matérielle.

DAVID: Comme tu es exaltée!

PAULE: Tu te trompes. Je t'exhorte au contraire à abandonner toute exaltation. La décision que tu dois prendre est froide. Elle est, pour qui s'abandonne à la passion des images, incompréhensible. Laisse choir l'obsession de la conquête et de la totalité. Tiens le fil de la multiplicité.

(*Un long silence.*)

DAVID: Mais dis-moi, Paule, comment ne pas tout disperser et désunir dans le geste inouï que tu proposes?

PAULE: Ne crois pas que j'apporte une recette. Puisque si longtemps l'impasse a été que la politique n'avait son centre et sa représentation que dans l'État, je vous dis de forcer cette impasse, et d'établir que la vérité politique circule durablement dans un peuple adossé aux lieux d'usine, s'abritant de l'État par sa fermeté intérieure.

Elle est comme un événement, tout aussi irreprésentable que l'est, au théâtre, le labeur dont résulte que l'action, devant nous, est mystérieusement unique.

DAVID (*désemparé*): Mais par où commencer ce dont tu dis qu'il n'a aucun commencement?

PAULE: Trouvez ceux qui importent. Soyez au fil de leur parole. Organisez leur consistance, dans la visée de l'égal. Qu'il y ait dans les usines des noyaux de la conviction politique. Dans les cités et les campagnes, des comités de la volonté populaire. Qu'ils transforment ce qui est, et s'élèvent à la généralité des situations. Qu'ils s'opposent à l'État et aux margoulins de la propriété dans la mesure exacte de leur force immanente, et de la pensée qu'ils exercent.

PAULA (*taking out a big piece of paper and unfolding it*): Look at this military map. My brother Claude Villembray gave it to me, right before we executed him. The dream, the childish fantasy—it's all in there. He would've really liked to conquer the whole earth, just like any old king. Are you going to go on endlessly pursuing such an infantile ambition? The unique greatness of the human race doesn't lie in power. The featherless biped must get a hold of himself, and against all the odds, all the laws of nature, and all the laws of history, follow the winding road that leads to the idea that anyone is the equal of anyone else. Not just in law but in material truth.

DAVID: Wow, how passionate you are!

PAULA: You're wrong about that. On the contrary, I'm urging you to give up all passion. The decision you've got to make has to be an unemotional one. To anyone who gives in to the passion for images it's incomprehensible. Let go of your obsession with conquest and totality. Take hold of the thread of multiplicity.

(*A long silence.*)

DAVID: But tell me, Paula, how can we prevent everything from breaking apart and scattering to the winds with the extraordinary act you're suggesting?[15]

PAULA: Don't think I've got an easy answer. Since the deadlock has so long been that politics was only centered in and represented by the State, I'm telling you to push through that deadlock and ensure that political truth is steadfastly at work in a people sustained by the places of the factory,[16] protected from the State by their own inner resolve.

Politics is like an event, as unrepresentable as all the hard work in the theater that ends up making the play we see before us a mysterious, one-time thing.[17]

DAVID (*at a loss*): But where can we begin something you say has no beginning?

PAULA: Find the people who matter. Stay connected to what they say. Organize their consistency, with equality as the goal. Let there be core groups of political conviction in the factories. And committees of popular will in the cities and the countryside. Let them change the way things are and rise to the generality of situations. Let them oppose the State and the private property sharks in direct proportion to their inherent strength and the thinking that they practice.

DAVID: Cela ne fait aucune stratégie.

PAULE: La politique à venir n'est d'abord que de donner forme et racine à sa propre formulation. La politique est d'unir autour d'une vision politique, soustraite à l'emprise mentale de l'État. Ne me demande rien de plus que ce cercle, qui est le cercle de toute pensée initiale. Nous fondons une époque sur une tautologie. C'est bien naturel. Parménide a fondé la philosophie pour deux mille ans à seulement proclamer, avec la clarté requise, que l'être est, et que le non-être n'est pas.

DAVID: La politique est de faire être la politique, pour que l'État ne soit plus.

(*Silence.*)

PAULE: Fils! mon fils! veux-tu te confier à cette pensée où récidive, après une première histoire errante, la vieille hypothèse, l'ancienne interprétation?

DAVID: La tête me tourne. Je vois clairement l'indécidable.

PAULE: Une politique, une seule.

DAVID: Je m'y confie.

PAULE: J'ai confiance qu'une politique est par moi-même réelle, soustraite à la capture de l'État, irreprésentable et incessamment décodée.

J'ai confiance que suivre dans l'intelligence du vouloir ce qui est là désigné oriente lentement la force d'un Sujet à s'excepter

Du règne de la domination.

Je sais que ce trajet est dans l'unicité de sa consistance, et dans l'acharnement de sa subtilité.

J'ai confiance dans l'infinie libération, non comme chimère, ou paravent du despote, mais comme figure et combinaison active, ici et maintenant, de ce par quoi l'homme est en capacité d'autre chose

Que de l'économie hiérarchique des fourmis.

DAVID (*d'une voix blanche*): Tout cela. Tout cela.

PAULE: Engage le fer, mon fils, pour ta confiance régénérée. Que la lutte millénaire pour le pouvoir se change ici en la lutte millénaire pour son abaissement. Son achèvement.

DAVID: Ô décision souveraine! Honneur de l'hiver immodéré!

Cependant je promeus la patience. Mais toi, mère, où est ta place, maintenant?

PAULE: Ce que je pouvais faire, on peut dire, oui, on peut vraiment dire, que je l'ai fait.

(*Ils s'étreignent.*)

DAVID: That's no strategy at all.

PAULA: The politics of the future initially only involves giving shape and substance to its own formulation. Politics is about uniting people around a political vision, free from the mind control exerted by the State. Don't ask anything more of me than that circle, which is the circle of any thinking at its inception. We're founding a new era on a tautology. That's only natural. Parmenides laid the foundation for philosophy for two thousand years merely by declaring, with the requisite clarity, that Being is, and that not-Being is not.

DAVID: Politics is about making politics exist, so that the State should no longer exist.

(*Silence.*)

PAULA: Son! My son! Will you have confidence[18] in that thought, to which the old hypothesis, the previous interpretation, is now returning, after its initial meandering history?

DAVID: My head is spinning. I can see the undecidable clearly.

PAULA: One politics, and only one.

DAVID: I have confidence in that.

PAULA: I have confidence that a politics is real through myself, free from the State's grasp, unrepresentable, and endlessly decoded.

I have confidence that following what's indicated in the intelligence of the will gradually leads a Subject's inner resolve to except itself
From the rule of domination.

I know that that path lies in the uniqueness of its tenacity and in the relentless subtlety of its thought.

I have confidence in infinite liberation, not as a pipe dream, or a dictator's smokescreen, but as a figure and a working model, here and now, of what makes human beings capable of something other
Than just the highly organized social structure of ants.

DAVID (*tonelessly*): All of that. All of that.

PAULA: Take up the sword, my son, for your renewed confidence. May the never-ending struggle for power here turn into the never-ending struggle for its downfall. For its destruction.

DAVID: O sovereign decision! Pride of the intemperate winter!

Yet I'll promote patience.[19] But what about you, Mother? What will your role be, now?

PAULA: What I could do, you can say, yes, you can really say, I've done.

(*They embrace each other.*)

SCÈNE 6: Dans le lieu des fondations.

Il est midi. MOKHTAR, RENÉ, CAMILLE *sont assis dans un coin.* DAVID *est au milieu.*

DAVID (*vers les autres*): Et peu importe où est Paule. Considérez qu'elle n'a été qu'un songe. Une visitation.

RENÉ: Je ne suis pas convaincu.

CAMILLE: Moi non plus, et de loin.

DAVID: Nous avons tout le temps.

CAMILLE:

> La vérité toute nue,
> Je vais vous la dire.
> On s'f'ra hacher menu
> Sitôt dit j'expire.

MOKHTAR: Nous saurons nous défendre.

RENÉ: Donc, déjà le fusil?

DAVID: Ce n'est pas une philosophie de moutons. Nous montrerons les dents, chaque fois qu'on voudra nous faire taire. (*À l'autre extrémité, entre* MME PINTRE, *extrêmement vieillie.*) Voyez, le retour des autres. Madame Pintre.

RENÉ: Symbole du retour en arrière.

MOKHTAR: Symbole d'une unité refaite en altitude. Conjonction de lumière du soleil et de la lune. Minuit diffuse dans Midi.

CAMILLE: Conjonction qui fait une éclipse, où tout vire au noir.

DAVID: Mais c'est le noir aussi, sur la scène, qui prononce qu'un acte succède à un autre.

RENÉ: Et la pièce en est-elle moins une?

MME PINTRE: Il y a eu un soir, l'éclaircie, et puis l'orage.

> Tous les arbres se sont couchés, avec leurs chevelures
> Lisses.
> La machine des cieux restait en court-circuit.

SCENE 6: In the place of foundations.

It is noon. MOKHTAR, RENÉ, *and* CAMILLE *are sitting off in a corner.* DAVID *is in the middle.*

DAVID (*to the others*): So it doesn't matter where Paula is. Imagine she was just a dream. A visitation.[20]
RENÉ: I'm not convinced.
CAMILLE: Me neither, not by a long shot.
DAVID: We've got plenty of time.
CAMILLE:

> The naked truth:
> You wanna know?
> We're dead meat, guys.
> Not long to go!

MOKHTAR: We'll be able to defend ourselves.
RENÉ: So, it's back to guns already?
DAVID: This isn't a philosophy for sheep. We'll bare our teeth every time they try to silence us.[21] (*From the opposite side of the stage, ENTER* MADAME PINTRE, *tremendously aged.*) Look, the others are back. Here's Madame Pintre.
RENÉ: The symbol of going back in time.
MOKHTAR: The symbol of a unity reconstructed on high. The conjunction of the light of the sun and the moon. Midnight diffused in Noon.
CAMILLE: A conjunction that causes an eclipse, where everything goes dark.
DAVID: But it's also darkness, on the stage, that signals that one act is coming after another.
RENÉ: And it's no less a play for that, is it?
MADAME PINTRE: One evening, there was a break in the clouds, and then came the storm.

> All the trees were bent over, with their foliage
> All sleek.
> The machinery of the heavens was shorted out.

Le service d'entretien, de vieux gars à casquette, tapaient la belote sur une souche. Un grand sapin leur est tombé sur la gueule. Ils ont été, les pauvres, écrabouillés.

Ils n'y croyaient plus, il faut dire, ils étaient devenus les métaphysiciens de l'alcool.

On a amené des camions de squelettes pour replanter les arbres. De très jeunes gens très sombres les gardaient au bout du fusil. Ça n'a rien donné. On enfonçait dans la mousse jusqu'aux chevilles. On avait des escargots dans les chaussettes.

Alors tout est reparti, pagaïe et soleil. Il vaut mieux serrer l'orage dans un sac.

L'événement n'est autre que l'éclaircie. Les couleurs sont si pures que l'œil est multiplié.

On a chassé les loups. Mais, ce faisant, il n'y a plus d'écureuils.

DAVID: Nymphe de la forêt humaine! Ô magicienne! L'homme n'est pas fait pour tourner son visage vers le sang. Je mettrai le mors à la jeunesse. Je ne laisserai personne lécher les bottes du plus humble.

RENÉ: Il est vrai que le temps a passé. L'or de la nuit n'a plus le sigle du poinçon.

CAMILLE: Faut-il s'avancer dans une ombre sans marque? Plus aucun souffle n'agite sur la mer l'œil jaune des balises. Le chemin du port est oublié.

TOUS ENSEMBLE: Éclipse de tout sujet.

RENÉ: Mais c'est le sujet, même.

CAMILLE: Plus rien! Plus rien, que l'ordre mis à feu.

MOKHTAR: L'arabe vous le dit: au désert, il faut la pensée la plus fine, véritablement la subtilité du philosophe, pour trouver

Quoi?

La rosée, le renard, et

La piste.

(*Tous sortent, sauf* DAVID.)

DAVID (*seul*): Et maintenant, déclin du siècle, voyons ce que tu as à nous dire.

(DAVID *sort*.)

The maintenance men, some old guys in workmen's caps, were playing pinochle on a tree stump. A big fir tree came crashing down on them. The poor guys were crushed to death.

They didn't think it could ever happen to them, actually—they'd become the metaphysicians of alcohol.

A few truckloads of skeletons were brought in to replant the trees. A bunch of very sullen young kids stood guard over them with rifles. But it was a bust. They were sinking up to their ankles in the moss. They had snails in their socks.

So it all started over again, the chaos and the sun. It'd be easier to squeeze the storm into a bag.

The event is nothing other than the break in the clouds.[22] The colors are so pure that your vision is greatly magnified.

The wolves have been driven out. But now there are no more squirrels.

DAVID: Nymph of the human forest! O sorceress! Human beings aren't meant to turn their faces toward blood. I'll keep the younger generation in check. I won't let anyone suck up to the least members of society.[23]

RENÉ: It's true that time has gone by. The gold of night has no hallmark anymore.

CAMILLE: Do we have to make our way in the dark with nothing to guide us? There's not a breath of wind on the water stirring the yellow eyes of the buoys. The way to port has been forgotten.

ALL IN UNISON: The eclipse of every subject.

RENÉ: But that's the very subject.

CAMILLE: There's nothing's left! Nothing except law and order shot to hell.

MOKHTAR: Take it from the Arab: in the desert, you need to have the subtlest thought, truly the finesse of a philosopher, to find
What?
The dew, the fox, and
The trail.

(EXEUNT everyone except DAVID.)

DAVID (alone): And now, century at its close, let's see what you have to say.

(EXIT DAVID.)

NOTES

TRANSLATOR'S PREFACE

1. *Thinking French Translation* (New York: Routledge, 2002), 163.
2. The phrase describes *L'Écharpe rouge* in Olivier Neveux's *Théâtres en Lutte: Le théâtre militant en France des années 1960 jusqu'à aujourd'hui* (Paris: La Decouverte, 2007), 194, but applies as well to *The Incident*.

INTRODUCTION

1. At this point, there have been three public readings or semi-staged productions of scenes from *The Incident at Antioch*, besides Vitez's performance: in February 2009, at the University of Glasgow; in May 2011 at the UCLA Program for Experimental Critical Theory (the Hammer Museum, Los Angeles); and in June 2011 at HAU 1 in Berlin (sponsored by the Zentrum für Literatur- und Kulturforschung).
2. See 1 Corinthians 12:12: "For as the body is one, and hath many members, and all the members of that one body, being many, are one body: so also is Christ."
3. While for Hegel the Owl of Minerva takes wing at dusk, for Nietzsche philosophy thrives in the bright light of noon. Badiou discusses Claudel's 1906 play *Partage de midi* in relation to Nietzsche and Hegel in his unpublished 1994—95 seminar on Lacan.
4. In a draft of a letter to Cohen found in Gödel's *Nachlass*, dated June 5, 1963. Quoted in Solomon Feferman, "The Gödel Editorial Project: a Synopsis," 11.

5. Paul Cohen, "The Discovery of Forcing," p. 1091. Also see Mary Tiles, *The Philosophy of Set Theory* for a lucid discussion of Cohen's ideas, and Thomas Jech, "What is . . . Forcing?" for an extremely succinct account. Cohen's classic work in this area is *Set Theory and the Continuum Hypothesis*.

6. Unlike the strength of logical implication, where "if p then -q" means that p and q are mutually exclusive (if one is true, the other must be false), the statement "p forces -q" means, in Badiou's explanation, "there exists no condition that is stronger than p and that forces q. . . . The statement q finds itself, so to speak, freed with regard to the conditions that are stronger than p" (*Theory of the Subject*, 271–72).

7. In *Theory of the Subject*, Badiou links this retroactive or future perfect temporality with the relationship of Jesus and Saint Paul: "Christianity, too, begins two times: with Christ and with Saint Paul. Note that the certainty of the first beginning is attached to the truth of the second. Without the founding militant activity of Saint Paul. Without the idea—against Peter—of universalizing the message, of leaving the Law, of exceeding the Jewish universe, what would have become of this millenary power, from which alone we can read a beginning in the tangled history of that sectarian leader liquidated by the Palestinian establishment under the protection of the neutrality of the Roman State?" (125).

8. Traditionally, the Rabbis have been very suspicious of the *dechikat ha'ketz* ("forcing the end"), the idea of hastening the coming of the Messiah and the redemption he heralded. It is not so much that they doubted that it could be done, but on the contrary, they feared that it might be possible, but contrary to God's will. I discuss this concept in "Forcing the Messiah: Paul, Rosenzweig, and Badiou" in *Rosenzweig-Jahrbuch* 4 (2010).

9. We can find a parallel discovery of such "weak forcing" in Walter Benjamin's account of a "weak messianic power" in his famous theses on "The Concept of History," which Giorgio Agamben has argued is a covert commentary on Saint Paul.

10. See Badiou, "Rhapsody for the Theatre," 213. It is worth noting that Lacan too finds perhaps unexpected resources in Claudel, devoting considerable time in his 1961 seminar on transference to a discussion of the *Coûfontaine* trilogy.

11. A passage from this letter, discussing Pottecher's visit to Bayreuth, is reproduced in Jacques Petit's excellent critical edition of *La Ville* (26). As in the case of Badiou, Wagner is one of Claudel's important influences, and although Claudel's early enthusiasm was later tempered by strong criticism, traces of Wagnerian poetics and aesthetics remain in his work.

12. Susan Spitzer has pointed out that Cephas refers to another personal motivation for his revolutionary rage in Act I, scene 1: "My father . . . kept his wife in a state of mute anarchy. And I, his son, am making that silence speak the old language of strife."

13. In a rather coy account of this in *Being and Event*, Badiou comments, "Due to a predilection whose origin I will leave the reader to determine, I will choose the symbol ♀ for this inscription. This symbol will be read 'generic multiple'" (356). One suspects a Lacanian provenance for this choice, because for Lacan woman is "not-all," an infinite and open set, not determined by a universal quantifier, as is the case with men.

ACT I

Alain Badiou's comments to me about some of the lines noted below have been prefaced with **AB**. Only the titles and relevant page numbers of the works cited herein are referenced parenthetically; additional information can be found in the bibliography.

1. See Kenneth Reinhard's introduction for a description of the Biblical incident at Antioch and its far-reaching implications. In his 2010 book *The Communist Hypothesis*, Badiou sheds light on *The Incident*'s political message in a discussion of the situation in France following the "Red Years" of the 1960s and 70s. Noting a twin failure–the betrayal of their ideals by former Maoists and other militants who rallied to the bloodless socialism of Mitterrand in the 80s and to the "delights" of parliamentary power, on the one hand, and the still-fresh memory of the "ultra-left" failure of terror (certain aspects of the Chinese Cultural Revolution, the Khmer Rouge, and the Shining Path in Peru), on the other, he remarked, "This in fact seems to be unavoidable at times when the political dynamic of revolutions can no longer invent its becoming or assert itself for what it is" (19). *The Incident at Antioch*, he went on to say, is devoted to this problem of the need to combat both the right and the ultra-left simultaneously, since neither peaceful continuation nor ultimate sacrifice can lead to a just society. Only universality, represented in the play by Paula, will allow us to live under the rule of equality.

2. Christ's name for the apostle Peter, derived from the Aramaic *kêfâ*, meaning "rock."

3. The French term, increasingly used in English, was retained here to refer to the towns ringing Paris that are associated for the most part with large working-class and immigrant populations, unemployment, and crime. In Act I, scene 3, Paula recites the names of a dozen Paris *banlieues*, calling them "the guardians of the place of the true."

4. War reserves are defined as "Stocks of materiel amassed in peacetime to meet the increase in military requirements consequent upon an outbreak of war." (*Dictionary of Military and Associated Terms*. US Department of Defense, 2005) The literally translated phrase "place of the war reserves" has the advantage of maintaining homogeneity with the four other fable-like "places" in which the play is set.

5. On the road to Damascus to arrest followers of Jesus, the zealous Pharisee Saul of Tarsus had the conversion experience described in several New Testament accounts. See the introduction for a fuller description.

6. In an interview with Peter Hallward, Badiou remarked, "Emancipatory politics always consists in making seem possible precisely that which, from within the situation, is declared to be impossible" (*Ethics*, 121). Or, as he put it elsewhere, "The possibility of the impossible is the basis of politics" (*Can Politics Be Thought?*, 78).

7. This is an allusion to a well-known line in Racine's tragedy *Bérénice*, Act I, scene 4: *Dans l'orient désert quel devint mon ennui!* ("How my anguish grew in the desert of the East!" in David Gervais's translation). Badiou's "desert of the West" bears a close resemblance to "the desert of the Real," Slavoj Žižek's name for the "capitalist utilitarian de-spiritualized universe" that features in his book *Welcome to the Desert of the Real*.

8. AB: "The current symbolic organization, in other words, is worthless." Democracy, in particular, is the "emblem" targeted by Badiou: "Despite all that is devaluing the word *democracy* day after day and in front of our eyes," he wrote in "The Democratic Emblem," "there is no doubt that this word remains the dominant emblem of contemporary political society. An emblem is the untouchable in a symbolic system, a third rail" (*Democracy in What State?*, 6).

9. The religious phraseology prevalent in *The Incident* links the play to its Biblical context. Note that Cephas's language overall in this speech has an archaic flavor.

10. Line hunters walk in small groups, with about 10 yards between them, to flush out quail, doves, and other prey.

11. AB: "As you contemplate summer from the window, you have an experience of nothingness. You're tormented by the force of nothingness, nothingness visible."

12. AB: "This image can be compared with that of a primly dressed woman suddenly removing all her clothes."

13. The condition that is meant here is that of people whose minds have been deadened or numbed by the capitalo-parliamentarian order.

14. AB: "This image conveys the idea of someone locked into their own narrow way of seeing things." A sharp contrast with Cephas, in this scene at least, is provided by the related character Avare in Claudel's *The City*, whose own alienation from the friends with whom he is dining he seeks to cure through *isolation*: "and the desire came over me to set alight the four corners of this place of lies: That I might be alone."

15. AB: "The absence here is an active, positive one: it's the absence or the subtraction from ordinary law, it's everything striving to be absent from that law. It's a revolutionary language that makes it possible to think the real situation based on the fact that people are subtracting themselves from ordinary law. Anonymity is something positive, the life of anonymous power; you've become an anonymous part of it all."

16. **AB:** "*Filiation* implies heredity. You can name what you are and are becoming inasmuch as you are the children, or heirs, of a century and a half of innocence, i.e., the working class from about 1800 to 1980."

17. Capturing the moon's reflection in a washbasin or a bowl is part of an old Chinese ceremony honoring the moon. Here the image is related to an illusory politics or struggle in the past. **AB:** "The washbasin was painted red to trick people into thinking that it was really the revolution that was involved." Not surprisingly, the color red, with its connotation of revolution, is evoked several times in the play, notably in connection with a red scarf (see note 27 below).

18. Paula's assertion of women's equality here is strictly in keeping with Badiou's aversion to identity politics. What matters is only that men and women should *both* be able to participate in a truth process. To that extent, Paula's declaration echoes St. Paul's in Galatians 3:28: "There is neither Jew nor Greek, there is neither slave nor free, there is neither male nor female." See also Badiou's remarks about women and politics in the Glasgow interview included in this book. The play's conversion of Paul into Paula moreover raises the question of the author's identification with her as a symbol of the feminine, or "that which, when it ceases to be the domestic organization of security and fear, goes furthest in the termination of all cowardice" (*The Century*, 26). A vivacious female character who challenges Socrates at every turn features prominently as well in Badiou's recent *La République de Platon* (English translation forthcoming from Columbia University Press). Amantha, as she is called, carries the "spectral" aspect or subtext of the work. "That it should be a female character once again vindicates Hegel, who saw in women 'the community's irony'" (Plato seminar, June 9, 2010). Characterizing Claudel's character Lâla similarly, Badiou in his preface nonetheless distinguishes Paula's voice as one of "emancipatory truth," not irony.

19. **AB:** "The images here are intentionally surrealistic: two ideas of grandeur."

20. Paula's inner conflict regarding the undecidability of the event names the play's key issue of subjectivation. "The fact that the event is undecidable," Badiou has written, "imposes the constraint that the subject of the event must appear. Such a subject is constituted by a sentence in the form of a wager: this sentence is as follows. 'This has taken place, which I can neither calculate nor demonstrate, but to which I shall be faithful.' A subject begins with what fixes an undecidable event because it takes a chance of deciding it" ("On the Truth Process"). In Act III, David's "conversion" to Paula's thinking of politics begins with his saying "I can see the undecidable clearly."

21. **AB:** "In the term *errance* there is the idea of instability." The unsettling nature of Paula's revelation of women's equality will provoke anxiety in the women and trigger a desire to maintain the status quo. Anxiety, one of four affects that, for Badiou, signal the incorporation of a human animal into a

subjective truth process, is associated with "the desire for a continuity, for a monotonous shelter" (*Logics of Worlds*, 86).

22. These lyrics from *The Internationale* would be immediately recognizable to a French reader or audience.

23. While "superfluous" might have served to translate "*inutiles*" in this particular instance, "useless" seemed more appropriate in that uselessness is a key trope in the play, a condition bemoaned by both Paula and her brother at various moments.

24. Badiou agreed that a play more familiar to Anglophone audiences than Racine's tragedy *Britannicus* should be substituted here, with the caveat that it contain, like the French work, a political theme.

25. "The Arabian sands" here stands in for what might otherwise have been for Anglophone audiences a baffling reference to the Syrtes, a remote, barren region of Libya. Badiou may have had in mind the melancholy atmosphere permeating Julien Gracq's novel *Le Rivage des Syrtes* (*The Opposing Shore*).

26. The word "present" is in itself ambiguous: It may be an existential reference or a reference to the gift—her scarf—that Paula is about to throw in the water. **AB:** "The ship metaphorically sings a song of praise the way that poets once celebrated warriors' high deeds."

27. The eponymous red scarf of Badiou's 1979 "*romanopéra*," *L'Écharpe rouge* is reprised here in Paula's scarf as well as in the one Camille wears, which the revolutionaries will later wrap around themselves in scene 4. The allusion is to the red scarves worn by the Paris Communards. The fiery revolutionary Louise Michel (1830–1905) brought her own red scarf with her to New Caledonia, where she had been deported after the crushing of the Commune, and tore it in half to give to two of the insurgents of the local Kanak uprising against the French in 1878, with which she deeply sympathized. I am indebted to Isabelle Vodoz for alerting me to this reference to Louise Michel, who is, moreover, the first of the women mentioned in Paula's litany of extraordinary women in Act I, scene 4.

28. Badiou told me he was thinking of actors here, who sometimes warm up for a performance by reciting tongue-twisters.

29. **AB:** "Mokhtar is in fact an assembly-line worker who paints cars."

30. **AB:** "This is a kind of song: Although you, the worker, may come from darkness, try to be the light, even for what the factory makes of your labor. Don't forget that, as a worker, you're not forced to identify with the factory or your labor (hell), or even with the aspect of it that's *not* hell (i.e., the parasols). 'Hell' and 'parasols' are two different aspects of the factory, but the worker has no part in either of them because they're *imposed* on him in either case."

31. The use of the word "penultimate," Badiou confirmed to me, intentionally evokes "Le Démon de l'analogie," a well-known poem by Mallarmé containing the line "La Pénultième est morte" (The Penultimate is dead).

32. AB: "I'm coming to *you* to get my conviction, I'm not coming to give you mine."

33. These are all poor, working-class suburbs of Paris.

34. AB: "The factory as the fundamental place of politics. But whether the factory's function is to appear or disappear is an unresolved issue."

35. Mokhtar is expressing the solidarity of the revolutionaries with three other uprisings or revolutions: that of June 1848 in France, the Paris Commune of March 1871, and the October Revolution of 1917 in Russia.

36. AB: "That name is 'revolution' or 'communism.'" This sentence might reasonably have been translated as "Hail on behalf of those who seek the meaning of your endurance," but I opted, at the risk of a certain inelegance, to preserve the repetition of *nom* since the play lays great emphasis on names and naming. It should be noted that the title of Badiou's book *De quoi Sarkozy est-il le nom?* was rendered in English as *The Meaning of Sarkozy,* a translation that came in for some criticism at the time the book was published.

37. This is the rendering of the sentence that Badiou preferred. *Maître* (master, teacher, mentor) and particularly the term *maître à penser* implied here, is often left in French since its translation poses problems in English.

38. An echo of Heidegger, who described *Dasein*'s thrownness in the world as a dispersion of being, may be heard here.

39. AB: "Formalization, in other words."

40. A syllabary is a phonetic writing system consisting of symbols representing syllables. Lacan notably used the term in his text "On an ex post facto syllabary," in which he claimed that there has never been any thought other than symbolic thought (*Écrits*, 608). Ken Reinhard deserves thanks for pointing out this connection to me.

41. In his Plato seminar on June 16, 2010, Badiou read aloud this passage from the play (Paula's "conversion") to demonstrate what he called "the eventual impact of the Idea" (*la frappe événementielle de l'Idée*). Paula's posture, on the ground with arms outstretched, was inspired, he remarked, by the well-known Caravaggio portrait of Saint Paul's conversion.

42. AB: "At the very moment that chance strikes me, I unconsciously know what chance knows."

43. AB: "The obstacle that gives way is the obstacle to her conversion. Both the obstacle *and* the shrinking of desire collapse." In the Plato seminar mentioned above, Badiou noted: "Something like the subject she might become is starting to appear."

44. AB: "She had not only what was purely sensible but what was multiple as well. The sensible is being used here as the opposite of the intelligible. 'I had neither the intelligible nor the One.' 'Scattered' implies: the multiple, diversity, the dispersed multiple, the idea of dissemination."

45. AB: "It's almost as though she were complaining; it's almost a sort of violence she feels has been done her: 'Who is forcing (that is, violating) me?

Who is telling me now that there's a kind of strategic direction, an order, a plan of action that has to be followed? I sense, I'm being told, that there's a direction that needs to be found.'"

46. The helmet and the owl are symbols of Athena, whom Badiou, in his Plato seminar, described as "the allegory of thought inseparable from combat."

47. AB: "She's saying, 'The process of my conversion has been taking far too long: I need the word, the name that encapsulates the process.'"

48. AB: "'So, without any emotion, I define a founding thought in order to escape from the process that has been taking too long. *I* emerge from emotion, from simple passivity, whereas *you* are the process that has been taking too long.' She is saying, 'I am what I am.' 'It is I who am here.'" This paroxystic declaration of subjectivity bears an obvious resemblance to Saint Paul's conversion. As Tracy McNulty has observed, Paul's discourse "ties salvation to the event wherein the subject is called forth as a subject: 'by the grace of God I am who I am (I Cor 15:10)' (18) [The embedded page references in this quotation are to *Saint Paul: The Foundation of Universalism*]. Badiou notes that after the conversion event of Damascus, Paul turns away from 'any authority except that of the Voice that personally called him to become a subject' (19)" (*Philosophy and Its Conditions*, 195).

49. AB: "This is the definition of formalization."

50. AB: "'There were chance encounters, and when I was young they were all I needed to be happy, to hold my own in life.' Youth was all about chance encounters. But what's needed now is formalization: language. With this conversion, that aspect of her youth is over: 'Now I'm faced with the difficult labor of formalization, language.' Determination or will vs. randomness."

51. "Throughout the whole passage," Badiou remarked in his Plato seminar, "the subject is under the control of a hitherto unknown real." See Kenneth Reinhard's interpretation of this passage in his introduction.

52. AB: "Giving up any idea of the Divine, giving up the 'trappings' of God: that's what makes her spring back up—not for a new faith, a new prayer, but for a new beginning (a new axiom of life). It's by giving up all those trappings that God represents, i.e., by becoming an atheist, that she's reborn for a new rational beginning."

53. AB: "This text they quote is formalization transformed into recitation." With this line begins an extended quotation, adapted from Marx and Engels' *The German Ideology*. In the standard English translation, the line reads: "The division between the personal and the class individual, the accidental nature of the conditions of life for the individual, appears only with the emergence of the class, which is itself a product of the bourgeoisie" (84). The quotation represents the beginning of the process of incorporation into a body-of-truth that follows the evental impact of the Idea (Plato seminar, June 16, 2010). For purposes of comparison, the relevant

lines from the standard English translation of *The German Ideology* (84–85) are given in italics in the notes below.

54. *"This accidental character is only engendered and developed by competition and the struggle of individuals among themselves. Individuals seem freer under the dominance of the bourgeoisie than before, because their conditions of life seem accidental . . ."*

55. *". . . in reality, of course, they are less free, because they are more subjected to the violence of things."*

56. *"The contradiction between the individuality of each separate proletarian and labour, the condition of life forced upon him, becomes evident to him himself, for he is sacrificed from youth upwards and, within his own class, has no chance of arriving at the conditions which would place him in the other class."*

57. *". . . the proletarians, if they are to assert themselves as individuals, will have to abolish the very condition of their existence hitherto. . ."*

58. *". . . (which has, moreover, been that of all society up to the present), namely, labour."*

59. *"Thus they find themselves directly opposed to the form in which, hitherto, the individuals, of which society consists, have given themselves collective expression . . ."*

60. *". . . that is, the State. In order, therefore, to assert themselves as individuals, they must overthrow the State."*

61. AB: "The first words of the new language."

62. Of the names cited here by Paula, I have given brief biographical notes only for those that might be unfamiliar to some readers:

   Louise Michel: A revolutionary, active in the Paris Commune of 1871, who was frequently imprisoned for her radical opposition to the State.

   Hypatia: A fourth-century Neo-platonist philosopher and the first notable woman mathematician.

   Elisabeth Dmitrieff: A Russian-born feminist and Communard who organized the Women's Union for the Defense of Paris and for Aid to the Wounded.

   Sappho: A great lyric poet of Antiquity whose subjects were passion and love, often for women.

   Marie Curie: A Polish-born French physicist and chemist (1867–1934) who was a pioneer in the field of radioactivity. She won two Nobel Prizes and was also the first woman professor at the University of Paris.

   Camille Claudel: A talented sculptor, the sister of Paul Claudel, who died in 1943 in a mental asylum where she had been interned for thirty years.

   Sophie Germain: A French mathematician, physicist, and philosopher, born in 1776, whose work on Fermat's Last Theorem provided a foundation for mathematicians exploring the subject for two centuries thereafter.

   Emmy Nœther: A German mathematician (1882–1935) known for her groundbreaking contributions to abstract algebra and theoretical physics.

Vera Zassulitch: A Russian Marxist who, along with Plekhanov, founded the Emancipation of Labor, the first Marxist group in the Russian workers movement.

Louise Labé: One of the few female French Renaissance poets.

Bettina von Arnim: A multitalented German writer, publisher, composer, and social activist (1785–1859).

Djuna Barnes: The American author of *Nightwood,* who played an important part in the development of early twentieth-century modernist writing.

Madame de La Fayette: A seventeenth-century French author whose masterpiece *La Princesse de Clèves* was one of the first novels in Western literature.

Madame du Châtelet: An eighteenth-century mathematician, physicist, and author whose translation of Newton's *Principia Mathematica* is still considered the standard translation in French.

Catherine the Second: Catherine the Great of Russia (1729–1796).

Saint Teresa of Ávila: A prominent sixteenth-century Spanish mystic, Carmelite nun, and writer of the Counter Reformation.

Zenobia: A Syrian queen (240–after 274) who led a famous revolt against the Roman Empire.

Alexandra Kollontaï: A Russian revolutionary feminist, best known for founding the Women's Department, an organization that worked to improve the conditions of women's lives in the Soviet Union.

Theodora of Byzantium: The wife of Emperor Justinian I and perhaps the most powerful woman in the history of the Byzantine Empire.

Anna Seghers: A notable German intellectual and active antifascist who chronicled many of the twentieth century's major events in her writing.

Zivia Lubetkin: One of the leaders of the Warsaw Ghetto Uprising in 1944 and the only woman on the High Command of the Jewish resistance group ŻOB.

Lady Murasaki: The author (c.973–c.1020) of the classic work of Japanese literature *The Tale of Genji,* regarded as the first modern novel in world literature.

Jiang Qing: The wife of Mao Zedong and a prominent Chinese Communist Party figure who played a major role in the Cultural Revolution. She was subsequently imprisoned as a founding member of the "Gang of Four" that was branded as counter-revolutionary by Mao's successors.

Rosa Luxembourg: A Marxist theorist, philosopher, economist, and activist who was among the founders of the antiwar Spartacus League, which later became the Communist Party of Germany. After the Spartacist uprising in 1919 was crushed she was executed.

63. Virginia Woolf and Catherine Mansfield, Badiou told me.

64. AB: "When formalization has been achieved."

65. AB: "'Do Athena's life journey over! Renounce your renunciation!' What is meant here is Athena's life conceived of as all the different things she did

is this supposed to be a novel idea?

throughout it, i.e., a woman's life not just as the itinerary of love, or of being a wife, but the possibility of *thinking* for women. Athena is the symbol of the woman who assumes responsibility for thinking. She's the woman who seems to be most in competition with men: she was born from the head of Zeus, etc."

66. This is an allusion to the end of Goethe's *Faust, Part Two*. A literal translation of the Mystic Chorus's lines reads: "Everything transient/Is but a symbol;/The Unattainable/Here is realized;/The Indescribable/Here is accomplished;/The Eternal Feminine/Draws us upward."

67. Concerning the use of this phrase both here and in Act III, see the introduction.

ACT II

1. In Greek mythology, the Danaides, the fifty daughters of Danaus, married the fifty sons of Aegyptus, whom they murdered on their wedding night. They were punished in Hades by having to carry water in jugs with holes, so that the water always leaked out.

2. AB: "This is the state of mind of the obscure subject. It is a way of thinking that lacks clarity, an obscure disposition of the mind, a sort of disturbance that precedes violence." See *Logics of Worlds* for a fuller discussion of the obscure subject.

3. The ox was originally *chewing on* a yellow cork, but Badiou decided to change the line to accord with Villembray's fishing activity. The image, reminiscent of the peaceful bull Ferdinand, the eponymous character of the 1936 children's book who prefers sitting beneath a cork tree smelling the flowers to bullfighting, had probably been in the back of Badiou's mind, he confirmed to me, since he'd read the book as a child.

4. This line is an obvious echo of Richard III's "Now is the winter of our discontent," which is usually translated in French as *Voici l'hiver de notre mécontentement.* "The Other" here may be the Lacanian "big Other."

5. Badiou told me he imagined these buses as the old green ones that used to run in Paris.

6. The French combines literal and figurative meanings, in that *raser les murs* can mean both "hug the walls" and "slink around, keep a low profile," while *à la recherche de son ombre* can mean both "looking for one's lost shadow" (à la Peter Pan) and something like "seeking one's lost identity, or purpose, in life."

7. In *Germany: Revolution and Counter Revolution*, Engels, in collaboration with Marx, wrote: "Now, insurrection is an art quite as much as war or any other, and subject to certain rules of proceeding, which, when neglected, will produce the ruin of the party neglecting them" (100). Lenin

used the phrase in "The Lessons of the Moscow Uprising" (1906) and elsewhere.

8. "Factory-based politics" is a form of collective action in the factory, based on what the workers, organized in small groups, or *noyaux*, think and on their relationship with one other.

9. **AB:** "Cephas is being conceited here. It's as if he were saying: 'I, more than any of the rest of you, am the representative of the Idea.'"

10. The implication is that, in the dark, an enemy soldier can be spotted when he lights a cigarette.

11. "Man, the most precious capital" was a slogan in the Soviet constitution of 1936 and the title of a speech given by Stalin that same year.

12. The joke has to do with the play on the expression *se noyer dans un verre d'eau* ("to drown in a glass of water"), which means "to be easily overwhelmed; to make a mountain out of a molehill." Villembray, emphasizing the literalness of the expression, has also made the glass insultingly smaller.

13. "The quiet force" (*la force tranquille*) was a reassuring slogan used by the Socialist candidate François Mitterrand during his third run for president of France in 1981.

14. *La volonté bonne* is the French translation of Kant's notion of the good will. It plays off *la bonne volonté* mentioned a moment before in Pierre Maury's phrase "*gens de bonne volonté*" ("people of good will"). The placement of the adjective in French allows for a distinction that cannot be perceived in English other than by capitalizing Good Will.

15. **AB:** "Long, floaty hair"

16. Vection is the sensation of movement of the body in space produced purely by visual stimulation.

17. **AB:** "This is an expression of exaltation: 'I've wedged my foot in the door and no one will be able to shut it now!' It's also an allusion to all the colorful political posters that cover the walls during the uprising."

18. With a population of over a half million people, Antioch was actually the third-largest city in the Roman Empire, after Rome and Alexandria. Indeed, Badiou mentions these facts in his *Saint Paul* book. But, in the play, Antioch is always referred to as a "village." Later in this scene Cephas calls it a "paltry little village" and "a little beet-growing burg."

19. **AB:** "'Needs' and 'desires' in the sense that Lacan uses such terms."

20. **AB:** "That is, withdrawals of light from the future." Anxiety, as noted earlier, is one of the four fundamental affects that "signal the incorporation of a human animal into a subjective truth-process" (*Logics of Worlds*, 86); courage is another, and is the flip side of anxiety. In *Theory of the Subject*, courage is characterized as a "putting-to-work" of anxiety, notes Adrian Johnston, "with the latter depicted (using Lacan's vocabulary) as an effect of the disruption of the Symbolic by the Real" ("Courage Before the Event: The Force of Affects," 128).

21. **AB:** "This has to do with something that, when achieved, preserves no trace of their desire. Your very desire will disappear in a science of this sort, unlike, for example, the desire of a male artist for the naked woman he's painting, which will remain even after he has completed the painting."

22. **AB:** "'Right where a desire for things to continue as usual might have been, I can find nothing but rage in myself.'"

23. **AB:** "Our thinking of equality is not yet subsumed/dominated by a thinking of, or by the reality of, the relationship among people. Revolutions have been thus far unable to create a truly new relationship among people; hence true equality has not yet existed. There have been breaks with the past, certainly, but not true relationship."

24. The allusion here is to Paul's statement in 1 Corinthians 7:19: "Circumcision is nothing, and uncircumcision is nothing, but the keeping of the commandments of God."

25. In an interview with Steven Sackur on the BBC, Badiou elaborated on this idea: "I don't know what can be a revolution in France today. It was unclear in 1968. The word 'revolution' was here, but the revolution itself was not here, not at all. Nobody knows what is the signification of the word 'revolution' today. We have to begin by something else, not 'revolution,' and so on, but by an abstract Idea first, an abstract conviction concerning communism as such, [which] is the possibility of something else than the world as it is. And when we speak of the possibility of something else than the world as it is, we are in the philosophical field."

26. **AB:** "This image signifies the need to have assurances about the future."

27. **AB:** "This has to do with how the sheer brutality of the event can be simultaneously a construction. The decision cuts into the fabric of time. The *durée* here stands for all the consequences of the decision. It is being asked to be compatible with, to be able to withstand, the tear in the fabric."

28. The importance of the wager in Badiou's thought cannot be overestimated. Since the event from which a truth proceeds is undecidable, a decision must be made in the form of a wager. Mallarmé's famous "dice throw," one of the persistent references in Badiou's work, represents the moment of decision that defines the situation, which will be forever altered after the throw of the dice. "A subject," Badiou writes, "is a throw of the dice which does not abolish chance but accomplishes it as the verification of the axiom which founds it" (*Conditions*, 124).

29. "*L'action restreinte*" is an essay in Mallarmé's *Divagations* from which Badiou draws his notion of a "militancy" of restricted (or restrained) action: "Restricted action is the ineluctable contemporary form of the little political truth of which we are capable" (*Logics of Worlds*, 528).

30. Heraclitus, fragment XCIV, D52: "Lifetime is a child at play, moving pieces in a game. Kingship belongs to the child."

ACT III

1. See the Introduction. In the last act of Claudel's *La Ville*, the poet-turned-bishop Cœuvre recites, in substance, the Nicene Creed's orthodox profession of faith; in Act III, scene 5 of Badiou's play Paula articulates an atheistic "creed."

2. Cf. Mao Zedong: "On a blank sheet of paper free from any mark, the freshest and most beautiful characters can be written, the freshest and most beautiful pictures can be painted" ("Introducing a Co-operative").

3. AB: "This has to do with the theme of the social bond, the relationship with others, with not destroying everything."

4. This is a translation of the Anaximander fragment, notably quoted from Goethe's *Faust Part I*, scene 3 by Hegel in *The Dialectics of Nature* (20). Engels, Nietzsche, Freud, and Heidegger, among others, also discussed the fragment in their works. Badiou's own fondness for it is clear. He quotes the phrase in at least three other places: in "Politique et vérité," in *Ahmed philosophe*, and in *La République de Platon*.

5. The model of Cephas's insurrection is that of the Leninist avant-garde party, which Badiou regards as being saturated today. "With regard to the question of the State and power, of the duration of the power of the State, the model of the Party-State ended up showing serious limitations, whether it be what the Trotskyists called the tendency to bureaucratization, what the anarchists identified with State terrorism or the Maoists with revisionism. . . . From the point of view of taking power, the Party was victorious. But not from the perspective of exercising power" ("We Need a Popular Discipline," 649). What is needed for emancipatory politics is the popular discipline, the capacity of the masses to act together, that Paula will propose instead below.

6. Paula's use of the phrase "*entre toutes les femmes*" ("among women") echoes the description of Mary, who is said in the New Testament to be *bénie entre toutes les femmes* ("blessed among women"). The religious tonality of descriptions of Paula is evident, too, in her characterization as a "visitation." See note 20.

7. A well-known French proverb *L'habit ne fait pas le moine* ("The habit doesn't make the monk.") is usually translated as "You can't judge a book by its cover." But the proverb also exists in a positive formulation, *L'habit fait le moine,* or "Clothes make the man," and it is on this one that Badiou is playing. Mokhtar's question, translated literally, would read "So the bishop's purple robe does in fact make the monk?"

8. In Lafontaine's *Fables*, it's actually the *dog* who drops his prey on seeing his reflection in the water ("The Dog and his Shadow"). In "The Fox and the Crow," on the other hand, the crow drops the morsel from his beak when the fox flatters him about his singing.

9. This notion that what is required for a correct politics is a commitment to what happens, as opposed to any imposition of our own will on it, is expanded upon in *The Century*. As Peter Hallward puts it, "It is only by remaining aloof from all that is likely to happen (all that is predictable, established, settled, comfortable) that it is possible to throw oneself entirely into what actually does happen" (*Badiou: A Subject to Truth*, 40).

10. The Nicene Creed proclaimed that the Son was "one in being with the Father," expressed by the Greek word *homoousius*, meaning "consubstantial," or "of one substance."

11. After World War II, when many of its resistance fighters had been executed by German firing squads, the French Communist Party called itself "*Le Parti des fusillés*" ("the Party of the executed").

12. This notion was already present in Sartre's play *Les Mains sales*, where the young Communist Hugo reproaches the leader Hoederer for betraying those who died for the ideas promulgated by the Party. Hoederer replies: "I don't give a damn for the dead. They died for the party, and the party can decide as it sees fit about them. I pursue a policy of the living for the living" (217). The play is discussed in *Logics of Worlds*.

13. Badiou thinks that negation, in its destructive and properly negative dimension, must be surpassed today: "Contrary to Hegel, for whom the negation of the negation produces a new affirmation, I think we must assert that today negativity, properly speaking, does not create anything new. It destroys the old, of course, but does not give rise to a new creation" ("We Need a Popular Discipline," 652).

14. The Beast of the Apocalypse, described in Revelations, is said to represent imperial Rome, whose seven hills are recalled in the Beast's seven heads.

15. This concern about the destruction of the social bond is elaborated on in *Metapolitics*: "We have too often wished that justice would act as the foundation for the consistency of the social bond, when it can only name the most extreme moments of inconsistency; *for the effect of the egalitarian axiom is to undo bonds*, to desocialize thought, and to affirm the rights of the infinite and the immortal against finitude, against being-for-death" (104, my emphasis).

16. Every event has a site to which it is attached, a place or point "in which the historicity of the situation is concentrated" (*Being and Event*, 178–79). In "The Factory as Event Site," Badiou called the factory "the event-site par excellence" (172).

17. See the Introduction for a fuller account of this notion.

18. Badiou distinguishes sharply between belief and confidence, as Peter Hallward has observed. Confidence, as opposed to mere belief, is a *subjective* attribute, indifferent (as belief is not) to all contrary evidence (*Badiou: A Subject to Truth*, 39). As Badiou expressed it in *Theory of the Subject*, "As far as I am concerned, I have confidence in the people and in the working class in direct proportion to my lack of belief in them" (322).

19. David's resolution recalls Mao's championing of patience as the cardinal virtue during the revolutionary war in China. Courage, however, is the chief virtue required of us today, Badiou claims ("The Courage of the Present").

20. Already in scene 4 of this act, Mokhtar had declared "Visitation of the pure Idea!" with regard to Paula.

21. David's response to René's anxious query introduces a new conception of the use of violence, one that appears, as Badiou described it elsewhere, "in the form of a protective force, capable of defending something created through a movement of subtraction." ("We Need a Popular Discipline," 652)

22. This definition of the event as something less than miraculous, as a naturally occurring phenomenon, expresses Badiou's conviction that the event is "nothing but a part of a given situation, nothing but *a fragment of Being*" (*Theoretical Writings*, 97).

23. **AB:** "That is, suck up to them just because, before, it was the big shots whom people sucked up to." Like Paula's earlier advice about sticking close to the people, this recalls Lenin: "Do not flatter the masses and do not break away from them" (quoted in Kostantinov et al, *The Fundamentals of Marxist-Leninist Philosophy*, 573).

A DISCUSSION OF AND AROUND
THE INCIDENT AT ANTIOCH

AN INTERVIEW WITH ALAIN BADIOU

Ward Blanton and Susan Spitzer[1]

SUSAN SPITZER: In your introduction to your 1997 book *Saint Paul: The Foundations of Universalism*, you stated: "Fifteen years ago I wrote a play whose heroine was named Paula."[2] This would suggest that the play was written in 1982, the same year that *Theory of the Subject* came out. Can you situate the play for us and comment on the difference in perspective between *Theory of the Subject* and *The Incident at Antioch*.

ALAIN BADIOU: There are actually three drafts of the play. The first was finished in 1982, the second in 1984, and the third—written just for the first public reading of the play in Lyon, France, by the great French director, Antoine Vitez, who was also a friend of mine—in 1989. I should point out that, now, twenty years later, we are having only the second public reading of this play. So it's genuinely an emotional moment for me, and I'm really grateful for the organization of all this, and also for being able to hear my play in English, which is a wonderful surprise.

Now, just a very brief remark about the difference between the first draft, from 1982, and the second, from 1984. First of all, I think the second draft refers less explicitly to the French situation. It's much more metaphorical, if you like, and it also refers much less explicitly to Marxism and the whole political conception of the '60s and the '70s in France. It's more general, more universal—more poetic, perhaps, too. That's the first difference. The second difference involves the play's construction, which is simpler. The first version had lots of characters, a great number of voices, and so on. So, simplification and generalization: that's the difference between 1982 and 1984. We were at the beginning of a new political sequence, I think, and so the transformation of the play is also in keeping with the movement of that new situation—a new situation that we can regard as a bad situation, unfortunately. It was not real progress, but it *was* the birth of something new.

Concerning *Theory of the Subject,* which came out in 1982: it was my first important philosophical work, before *Being and Event* and before *Logics of Worlds,* but it's composed of seminars from the '70s, so the content of the book does not reflect the beginning of the '80s at all. The seminar took place between 1974 and 1978, something like that. And so it's a book of the '70s really, a book of the first sequence and not, like the play, the beginning of the new sequence. It does not really have the same political background or the same ideological battle. So, in fact, in order to go from *Theory of the Subject,* which is really a revolutionary philosophical book, to the play, we have to go from 1978 to 1984, six years, in other words. But during those six years the situation became very different, there was a very important transformation of the situation: from the "Red Years," so to speak—the end of the '60s, May '68, and so on—to the "Black Years," something very different. That's why, to conclude my answer to your question, we have to regard the play as much more like a meditation about the end of the preceding years rather than as something that's part of the first sequence. And that's why there's something creative and affirmative in the play, but why—as you have it here, perhaps— there's something that's also melancholic.

Certainly the play is a search for a new politics, but it's also the embodiment of the idea that something is finished. The last century, if you like, is finished, really, in the political field, so we need to do something really new, but we don't know precisely what. And this is exactly what Paula expresses at the end of the play. I can suggest some principles: for example, politics without the obsession of power, political activity that's not obsessed with power, but Paula doesn't know what the details of this politics will be. . . . So there's a combination of radicalism with respect to the question—we must find a new mode of political action— and something like nostalgia, or melancholy, with respect to the end of the previous sequence.

ss: In 1979 your play *The Red Scarf*, which also deals with a revolutionary movement, was published. Indeed, some of the issues raised in it,
especially the internal struggles of the revolutionaries, seem to prefigure
those in *The Incident*. What is the connection between the two plays? And
what, more generally speaking, is the relationship between your theater
and your more properly theoretical works?

AB: *The Red Scarf* was finished for all intents and purposes in 1975. It's
a play of the '70s, so the answer's the same. *The Incident* is a play of the
'80s and the earlier play is a play of the '70s. *The Red Scarf* is much more
affirmative, much more in terms of classical Marxism; it's much more of
a revolutionary play in an epic sense. The plays have two points in common, the main difference between them being a political one. *The Red
Scarf* is really a play of the history, the narrative of a victorious revolution. It was possible to think of the victorious revolution at the beginning
of the '70s, but it was absolutely impossible to think of something like
that in the middle of the '80s. So it's really a transformation.

But the two points the plays have in common are as follows. First of
all, like *The Incident*, *The Red Scarf* is also based on a play by Claudel
(*The Satin Slipper*). Secondly, the *subject* of the play is the relationship
between personal subjectivity and a revolutionary movement. There are
big differences between the two plays as regards the presentation of revolutionary movement, but in any case the problem in both plays is: *What
exactly is the construction of subjectivity in a political context?* What is,
so to speak, something like the new political subject? In the earlier play,
the new political subject is very close to the classical revolutionary subject, with organization, heroism, sacrifice, and so on, while in the later
play this form of subjectivity is problematic. So, first, we have different
possibilities and something like a question: The new political subject is
unclear. In *The Red Scarf* there are also many discussions among the revolutionaries, and so on, but there is ultimately something like a political
line. We can describe the later play as a play in which the question of
the true line, the correct line, becomes obscure. Probably all of this can
be summed up by saying that in the earlier play, *The Red Scarf*, the central problem is the revolutionary organization, the Party in its classical
sense, in its Leninist sense, the Party, which is, if you like, the Church of
the revolution, the established Church of the revolution. In the later play,

naturally, the question is also the question of the Church but in a *negative* sense. So we go from the foundation of the Church as the representation of the working class, of the revolutionary movement, and so on, to the question of the Church as maybe not only a new means for revolution but a new *obstacle*, a new difficulty.

For the last part of your question, the relationship between my theater and all my philosophical activity, a couple of short answers. First, when I was a very young man I was a Sartrean philosopher. Jean-Paul Sartre was really my master. As you know, Sartre wrote many plays, so maybe it's really only a question of my imitation of the master. Sartre wrote a few novels, and so did I; Sartre was a politically engaged philosopher, and so am I; and so on. The difference lies in our philosophical concepts, which are very, very different. So everything is different between us but not the forms, the image of what a true philosopher is. This is in the tradition of our eighteenth century in France. Throughout the entire eighteenth century in France we called some writers, like Voltaire, Rousseau, Diderot, et al., "philosophers." In fact, many writers were philosophers but they were more fundamentally *writers*; they wrote novels, plays, and so on, exactly like Sartre. So I can say something like: Sartre and I are the last two eighteenth-century philosophers!

ss: *The Incident at Antioch* is based on Claudel's play *The City*. Your decision to stay very close to this play, even to the point of including quite a number of lines written by Claudel in what we might today call a kind of musical sampling, leads me to ask about the deep connection between the two works and what made you decide to write a play unabashedly based on another. And now we know that *The Red Scarf* was also based on Claudel's writings.

ab: It's really a problem because Claudel was a really reactionary writer. So it's another form of imitation, the imitation of someone who was very different from me. He was a Catholic, he was a reactionary, he was also a very "official" man, in the *Académie*, in the Ministry of Foreign Affairs, and so on, something completely different from me. Maybe there are three answers to your question. First, a tradition: We know that in our classical French theater—Racine, Corneille, Molière, and so on—there have always been imitations of plays of the past, usually Greek or Latin plays, but there are sometimes imitations that are very *precise*, imitations that go into the details, so to speak. My attempt is to do the same thing today; that is, to take a play that already exists and to write something based on that play but to take it in another direction. I did that first with Claudel twice, with *The Red Scarf* and *The Incident,* but I also did it with one of Molière's plays, *Les Fourberies de Scapin,* which is a comedy, and therefore very different, in the style of the two Maurys in *The Incident.* It's something like a classical gesture: OK, there are many excellent plays, classical plays, so I can write the same play but do so in another direction.

The second reason is that, specifically in Claudel, we have the question of the relationship between subjective determination and something like a general movement or a general ideological framework. This is at the very heart of Claudel's plays. Naturally, for Claudel, it's the question of religious faith, not at all the question of political adventure. But perhaps in French theater, not classical French theater, Claudel was the most important writer, I think, who organized plays around this question: the becoming of subjectivity across ideological and religious questions. So it's still the question of how we can do something that's greater than ourselves, that's more important than what we can ordinarily do. This is closely related to my theory of the subject because what I name as subject is not the individual but what the individual is capable of, hence the new possibility that can open the individual up to a new subjectivity. So this problem of the creation of the new form of the subject is naturally Claudel's question, in a religious framework: how can we become a new religious man or woman? That's Claudel's question. And it's very important that, in Claudel, we find the idea that it's really a *movement,* it's not something natural, it's not something that's a necessity, it's really a struggle, a struggle to *accept* the new possibility. Opposed to the acceptance of the new possibility there's the whole conservative dimension of the individual. The individual is also like an animal; he or she wants to go on with his or her usual life.

For Claudel the question is about accepting grace, actually, because grace is a *proposition,* it's not a determination, in Claudel's Catholic vision, which is not a Calvinist one. The vision of Claudel's grace is a pure proposition. We have to do something with this proposition. We can refuse the proposition, we can continue in the same way as before. And in my vision, too, for the political subject, for example, but similarly for the subject of love, or the artist, there's something like a proposition. There's an event, an encounter, something that's *outside* the individual and that's like a proposition. And we can accept the proposition, or we can refuse the proposition; we can be faithful to the proposition of the event, or we can on the contrary continue in the same way. This is the problem of *all* Claudel's plays, including the problem of accepting love, for example, and it's my problem as well. And that's why I chose to rewrite Claudel's plays, in a revolutionary, not a Catholic, framework but one with the same problematic vision of what a subject is.

The third and final answer has to do with the question of how it's possible to write about problems like this, which are in some sense abstract or theoretical, how it's possible to write something that's really a *play*, that's really a piece of writing, not a proof, not an abstract text. In Claudel there can be found some poetical means concerning this very difficult question, how we can write something about the destiny of individuals, the becoming-subject of individuals in a new framework, without being completely abstract. So the answer is of a poetical nature, not a theoretical one. And in Claudel we have a new language, truly a new language in French, a language with new images and with an immanent relationship between abstraction and images, something like a new metaphorical way to examine the most important problem of human life. So, first of all, there's tradition, my Classical nature, if you like—I am not a *moderne*. Second of all, a shared question, the same question, in a sense. And third of all, a poetic aspect, a new relationship between poetic language and abstraction.

WARD BLANTON: I want to pick up on this question of transforming Claudel, on the one hand, and also this issue of the Party and the connection to questions of the Church. I'm interested in the way also in which you radically subvert Claudel, in a certain sense. For example, as sites from which to think, or as theater aesthetics, I can hardly imagine a sharper contrast between your Paula, who, among other things, is a figure of ungrounded split subjectivity, a political herald of the renunciation of power, and the triumphalist Christianity of the church bishop in the third act of Claudel's play *The City*. And, for those who haven't read it, in the end, in the third act, the young Claudel allows, as one character says, "the truth and reality of that which is, to replace the place of dreams," with ecclesiastical reality essentially replacing the city of dreaming, misguided revolutionaries in the ruined city. So in all of this, Claudel's final act is almost the antithesis of the call of Paula at the end of *The Incident at Antioch,* and how should we understand this? For example, have you confronted Claudel's triumphalist Christendom with a kind of hyper-Protestant, or perhaps even atheistic, Paula?

AB: It's a difficult question, but I'll try and answer. You know my play is very close to Claudel in its construction, in its generality, but its true origin is not in fact Claudel. Its true origin is much more Paul, the Apostle Paul. The play is something like a new dialectics between the Catholic interpretation of Paul and Paul himself, between a Catholic interpretation of Paul along the lines of the construction of the Church (because Paul is often said to be the first clear proposition of the construction of the Church) and another possible interpretation of Paul, which is not at all Paul as the foundation of the Church but Paul as the foundation of a new conception of universality, of universalism, and the Church is only something like a technical restriction, a technical organization of this new possibility concerning universalism. So in Claudel's play we have something like the old Paul—that is, as you say, the victory of the Church, because at the end of the play there's the priest who comes and says "the Truth." There's a conflict between that sort of image of Paul and another image, which is that of Paula—not Paul but *Paula*—who is completely different from that.

Finally, the play is the presentation of a fundamental conflict, which is not at all the same as in Claudel, because in Claudel the most important conflict is between nihilism and the Church. Ultimately, if we are not organized in the Church (or maybe in the Party as well), we are reduced to pure individualism, and individualism is ultimately always of a nihilist nature: that's the Claudelian affirmation. The individual alone is not able to be free, to be a real human being, so salvation can only be through the Church. That's what's said at the end of *The City.* My idea was completely different and maybe even the opposite of that, because at the end of *The Incident,* Paula says that it's impossible to reduce emancipation, or revolutionary vision, to something like a Church or a Party or a State. It's always through the fundamental critiques of any stable institution that the possibility of the novelty of thinking, of existence, and so on is created. And so Claudel's play is a play that says we *must* exist in the Church to be saved, while my play says we are saved, or we are free, only when we go beyond that sort of closure, beyond the Church, therefore, but also beyond revolutionary organization.

And so the difficulty is not the same in Claudel and in my play. For Claudel, the difficulty has to do with how we can go to the Church, *why* the Church is really the organization of man's salvation, while for me the difficulty has to do with how we can go *beyond* that sort of institution. In Claudel's case, the difficulty is how to go from disorder to order—that's the movement of his play—from a terrible disorder, violence, and nihilism, to a new order, which is in fact the old order of the Church. And in my plays, the movement is how to go from order to disorder, how to find a *new* disorder, if you like. Because it's always when the most important question is a question of an order, of the State, of an institution, that we have violence. So it can also be said that the question of violence is a subject for Claudel and for me as well. For Claudel, violence is a result of disorder, while I propose to say that, finally, violence is the result of *order*, not disorder. But the play organizes an understanding of the *difficulties* of this movement. In Claudel we have the difficulty of the movement from disorder to order, and in my play the difficulty is that of the movement from order to disorder. So it can be said that my play is the New Testament, Paul revisited in Claudelian form, because the apostle is not in Claudel's play at all. And maybe, as you suggest, my play is a Protestant play in a Catholic form.

ss: To return to your *Saint Paul* book, in the introduction you had this to say about Paula, the heroine in *The Incident*: "The change of sex probably prevented too explicit an identification."[3] Why did you make a woman the protagonist? And can you elaborate a bit on what you meant about needing to prevent too explicit an identification with Paul?

ab: To go from Claudel's Paul to *my* Paul, it's simpler to go from Paul to Paula, because it was absolutely impossible for Claudel that the apostle could be a woman. So that's a clear difference. In fact, the change of sex, from Paul to Paula, is a metaphorical gesture, a poetical gesture, because the old vision of the difference between the sexes casts religious or philosophical theory and political action in masculine terms, always, whereas my gesture, Paula, not Paul, signifies that this vision—in which we have, on the masculine side, globally, not only philosophy, not only religious direction, but political action and political forms of power as well—I think that vision is a thing of the past. There have been struggles, and we have to continue, but this is fundamentally a thing of the past.

And so the problem is much more: Isn't the feminine an essential part of a new politics today if a new politics is not based on power? If we have the idea of a new politics that's not based on power but that finds a new way of action to seize power at any price, I suppose that, in that case, women are of a new importance. For the time being, I have no real proof of this point, because we've seen many women who have a great taste for power, so I have no proof, but it's something like an intuition, which is naturally related to the great feminist movements of the past decades.

And I think that Paula, too, has no proof of this point. She says only that she is Paula, so she says that we have to find something in the political field that's not absolutely organized around power. She doesn't say that it's a question involving women, but my intuition is that it is, that there's a new relationship between sexual difference and the political field, not when the political field is organized around power but when we have something *beyond* the question of power—related to the question of power, perhaps, but finally beyond the question of power. And that was after all the vision of Marx himself, of Communism, which is the vision of the end of the State; with communism we have no State at all in the end. But if we have that sort of political vision, certainly the subject of politics is not the State; it is not, precisely, a subject *for* power. So the political subject, if you like, is not a politician if we define a politician, which is possible, as somebody who wants a share of power. That's the simplest definition of the politician. So the political subject is not a politician. If his own subjectivity is not organized by the question of power, that's a big change, which can sometimes be tested out as a change in the political process, and this change is perhaps related to the question of the difference between the sexes. That's my hypothesis—without any proof.

WB: I want to put a question now of Paul as a figure of critique of a particular sort of religion, to think of Paul also in your work as a form of critique of religion wholesale. I'll start by flagging up one of your great philosophical interlocutors and say that, since Hegel, of course, but also closer to our own time, with theologians like Mark C. Taylor or philosophers like Jean-Luc Nancy, Derrida, and others, some aspect of early Christianity has been taken up as an indication of religion's negation, religion's destruction or its overcoming, and of course the classic example is the early theological writings of Hegel, where God dies in early Christianity and is reborn rather as community spirit. Paul has been in this tradition, ironically but nevertheless a profound source of critique against religious establishments and their traditions. In your own book about Paul, you urge audiences not to allow Paul to be subsumed within an economy of thought that is religious or theological. A politically useful Paulinism, it would seem, needs to remain atheistic in a fairly precise sense. Can you say what it is about the religious or theological appropriation of Paul that one must reject? And what is it that we must save Paul *from* in order to preserve this name as a bearer of a significant political legacy?

AB: I don't write, I don't say exactly that to have a positive view of Paul, to interpret Paul in another manner, we must suppress all religious aspects of Paul. That's not exactly my thinking. That's clearly impossible because, for Paul, the original event, the birth of the truth, is of a religious nature, of a supernatural nature, because that event is the resurrection of Christ. So I have to assume, I must assume that in Paul the beginning of the whole process is directly of a religious nature, not reducible to any human activity. What I say is that we can find in Paul a very complete theory of the construction of a new truth. Why the theory of the construction of a new truth? The beginning of a truth is not a structure or a fact but an *event*. So it's something that's not predictable, something that can't be calculated, something that's not reducible to necessity. At the beginning of all new creation we have something like that, which I name an event. After that, we have a subjective process, the process of creation, of construction, which is defined by faithfulness to the event itself. Or, if you like, the subjective construction involves organizing the consequences of the event in the world, the ordinary world. The event is like a rupture and afterwards we have to organize the consequences of that rupture, and that is the subjective process of the creation of a new truth. And, finally, the result is a new form of universality.

So this can be summarized in a very simple manner: The beginning of the construction of a new truth is an event; the subjective process of that sort of construction is the organization of the consequences of the event; and the product, the final product, is something that's universal in a precise sense, which I won't explain right now, but we can really define in what sense the result is universal. These same three points are explained in a very pure way by Paul. First, an event: the resurrection of Christ. Then a subjective process: faith, faith in that sort of event. And then the organization of the consequences of the event, which is a subjective construction, that is, a debate, maybe an objective one, in the form of the Church. So it's the big discussion in the field of Christianity. And the universality of the results, which is very fundamental in Paul, that is, the new faith is for everybody: it's not for Jews, it's not for Romans, it's not for Greeks, it's not for males, it's not for females, it's really for everybody, i.e., the advance embodied in Paul's very famous sentence: "There is neither Jew nor Greek, there is neither slave nor free, there is neither male nor female." All categories, social differences are dissolved from the point of view of the construction of the truth.

So we can understand this theory as a particular new religious thought, certainly we can. But we also can understand this theory as an *abstract formalization* of what the process of the truth is, with religious words naturally, but the general formalization is good enough for *any* truth. And it's not a contradiction, because when you interpret all that as a new religious construction you *assume* the formalization itself. You assume, in fact, that the new religious conviction involves an event at the beginning, a subjective process with faith at the heart of the process itself, and a universal result. And so it's not a contradiction but a clear difference of interpretation that we have a common path, we assume we have something in common with the religious interpretation that is a formalization. And so it's the same idea, the same abstract or formal idea concerning what a new truth is. It's not the opposition between the Catholic interpretation and the Protestant interpretation; it's the difference between an interpretation that assumes the signification of the words themselves, "the resurrection," "God," "the son," and so on, and an interpretation that's at a purely formal level, which says that Paul is not only the apostle of a new religion but is also the philosopher of the new formal conception of what a universal truth is.

WB: One final question about political Paulinism. I mentioned earlier these lines in my introduction to this conference, lines that have been haunting me from your essay *Rhapsody for the Theatre*:[4] namely, that "events always involve the surprising emergence of a strange grouping of characters" and also that genuine political theater always stages something like "a heresy in action." So for the readers of this text, or for the audience of this text's future performance, what do you hope the performance of Paulinism can incite today?

AB: That's a political question, directly: What is the new grouping of to-day? I can say something about that concerning the situation in France perhaps, the political situation in a more limited sense. You know, I think that our societies, the societies of the Western world, the rich societies are becoming increasingly poor today. They're exposed to disaster. But in their general existence, I think there are four groups—I don't use the word "class" because it's too classical here—four components, if you like, of our societies, which can support some possibilities of revolt. There are four groups that are able, in some circumstances, to play a role in the direc-tion of real change, the form of a movement of revolt. First, the educated youth, the students, in universities, on campuses, in high schools, and so on. Second, the youth in the *banlieues,* the poor suburbs. Third, what I'll call the ordinary workers, the great mass of people who are not absolutely poor, nor are they at all rich, who work hard, experience precariousness at times, and so on. And fourth, the workers who come from other countries, immigrants, including undocumented workers, and so on.

We can say that, in France, there exist different movements with respect to these four groups: for example, many student demonstrations about many issues, riots by youth in the *banlieues,* with cars burned and so on, a sort of violent revolt without any continuity. There are the big demonstrations of ordinary workers—in December 1995 in France, for example, with millions of people, lasting many weeks. And there are also organizations and big demonstrations by immigrants and workers. So all four of these groups are capable of revolt. But the point is that that sort of revolt is practically always the revolt of *one* of these four components. And so I'd say that something like this is your idea of a new grouping. I name "revolt" or, simply, "movement," when there are demonstrations, riots, and so on of *one* of these groups. But *politics* begins when we have something that's not reducible to revolt or movement because there are two, three, or four components or groups involved in the movement. So politics is really the construction of a *new* grouping that's not reducible to the four groups. And politics always involves creating a passage, a pas-sage between one group and another group.

So a "surprising grouping" is a mixture of two, three, or four groups that are representative of the components of our society. One by one we have only revolt or movements, but when we have something beyond one by one we have a political possibility. A very important part of the action of the State is to create the pure *impossibility* of something of that sort, to create the impossibility of an alliance between two or more components of the social organization. On this point I have proof. I have the proof that many laws, many decisions of the State, many activities of the police, and so on are entirely organized not only by the possibility of preventing a movement, and so on, but more important, by creating the impossibility of *politics*, if we name "politics" the creation of a passage between two different groups. So the situation today is that, in opposition to that sort of activity of the State, politics involving two components sometimes exists—in France at least; I can't say anything about here—for example, an alliance, limited but real, between some students and some workers who come from other countries. The movement of undocumented workers in France, which is a significant movement, with enormous difficulties, is really a movement that's a mixture, an alliance between some intellectuals, some students, and some workers from Africa, and it's something that has existed now for more than ten years; it's not something that has come and gone. Sometimes there's also a relationship between a fraction of the students and ordinary workers; that's been the case for the past three years.

So the relationship between two groups, which is the beginning of a new grouping, hence the beginning of politics, exists in a limited way, but exists. The union of all four groups would be the revolution, naturally, which is why the State creates the absolute impossibility of such a union. I don't know any circumstances in which the union of all four components really exists. Maybe it's only in extraordinary circumstances that something like that is possible—war, for example. This is a lesson of the past century, because the Russian Revolution, the Chinese Revolution, the various popular liberation movements, and so on, were all in the form of war. So the question is also: What is revolutionary politics when it's not war but *peace*? And we don't know, really. We don't have any example of a complete union of the different popular components of the situation without that sort of terrible circumstances, exceptional circumstances, like war.

So the political problem today is really, first—I agree with you—one of a new grouping, and the problem is probably how to go from two to three, something like that. Two exists in some limited fashion, but there's the question of the passage from two to three, and three perhaps creates the possibility of four, the possibility of global change. So my answer, my complete answer is that we can define precisely what the beginning of politics is, which is always to create a small passage from one group to another group, and thus a small, real novelty in the organization of politics. But we also know what the current stage of all this is: the passage from two to three, in my opinion. Four is an event. Four is the number of an event. And three is the number of new forms of organization. One is nothing, movement and revolt. Two is the beginning of politics. Three is the beginning of new forms of organization. And four is change. So we can hope.

NOTES

1. This interview, which has been edited for publication, took place at the Western Infirmary Lecture Theatre, University of Glasgow, on February 13, 2009, and was conducted as part of "Paul, Political Fidelity, and the Philosophy of Alain Badiou: A Discussion of *The Incident at Antioch*," a conference at the University of Glasgow, February 13–14, 2009. The interview was immediately preceded by the first public reading of scenes of the play in English.

2. Alain Badiou, *Saint Paul: The Foundation of Universalism*, trans. Ray Brassier (Stanford, CA: Stanford University Press, 2003), 1.

3. *Saint Paul*, 1.

4. Alain Badiou, "Rhapsody for the Theatre: A Short Philosophical Treatise," trans. Bruno Bosteels, *Theatre Survey* 49 (2008):187–238.

BIBLIOGRAPHY

Badiou, Alain. *Almagestes*. Paris: Seuil, 1964.

———. "L'Antiphilosophie (3): Lacan." Seminar 1994–1995. Notes by Aimé Thiault and Daniel Fischer, transcription by François Duvert. http://www.entretemps. asso.fr/Badiou/94-95.htm (accessed December 12, 2011).

———. *Being and Event*. Translated by Oliver Feltham. London: Continuum, 2006.

———. *Can Politics Be Thought?* Translated by Bruno Bosteels. Durham, NC: Duke University Press.

———. *The Century*. Translated by Alberto Toscano. London: Polity Press, 2007.

———. *The Communist Hypothesis*. Translated by David Macey and Steven Corcoran. London: Verso, 2010.

———. *Conditions*. Translated by Steven Corcoran. London: Continuum, 2008.

———. "Le Courage du présent." *Le Monde*, February 13, 2010. Translated by Alberto Toscano as "The Courage of the Present." http://www.lacan.com/ symptom11/?p=163 (accessed December 14, 2011).

———. "The Democratic Emblem," in *Democracy in What State?* Translated by William McCuaig. New York: Columbia University Press, 2011.

———. *L'Écharpe rouge*. Paris: François Maspéro, 1979.

———. *Ethics: An Essay on the Understanding of Evil*. Translated by Peter Hallward. London: Verso, 2001.

———. "The Factory as Event Site." Translated by Alberto Toscano. http://www. prelomkolektiv.org/pdf/prelom08.pdf (accessed December 14, 2011). Originally published as "L'Usine comme site événementiel," in *Le Perroquet*, no. 62–63 (April 22–May 10, 1986).

———. *Infinite Thought: Truth and the Return to Philosophy*. Edited and translated by Oliver Feltham and Justin Clemens. London: Continuum, 2003.

——. "Is Communism the Answer to the Crisis?" Interview with Steven Sackur, BBC *Hardtalk*, 3/24/09. Transcript by Richard James Jermain. http://www.lacan.com/thesymptom/?page_id=1512 (accessed December 14, 2011).

——. *Logics of Worlds.* Translated by Alberto Toscano. London: Continuum, 2009.

——. *Metapolitics.* Translated by Jason Barker. London: Verso, 2005.

——. "On the Truth Process." Lecture, European Graduate School, August 2002. http://www.egs.edu/faculty/alain-badiou/articles/on-the-truth-process/ (accessed December 14, 2011).

——. "Politics and Philosophy." Interview with Peter Hallward, in *Ethics: An Essay on the Understanding of Evil.* Translated by Peter Hallward. London: Verso, 2001.

——. "Politique et vérité." Interview with Daniel Bensaïd. *Contretemps* 15 (2006), 47–56.

——. "Pour aujourd'hui: Platon!" Seminar, École Normale Supérieure, Paris. 2009–2010. Notes by Daniel Fischer. http://www.entretemps.asso.fr/Badiou/09–10.htm; transcription by Philippe Gossart. http://www.entretemps.asso.fr/Badiou/09–10.2.htm (both accessed December 14, 2011).

——. *La République de Platon.* Paris: Fayard, 2012.

——. "Rhapsody for the Theatre: A Short Philosophical Treatise." Translated by Bruno Bosteels. *Theater Survey* 49, no.2 (2008):187–238.

——. *Saint Paul: The Foundation of Universalism.* Translated by Ray Brassier. Stanford, CA: Stanford University Press, 2003.

——. *La Tétralogie d'Ahmed (Ahmed le subtil, Ahmed philosophe, Ahmed se fâche, Les Citrouilles).* Paris: Actes Sud, 2010.

——. "Théâtre et philosophie." *Les Cahiers de Noria*, no. 13 (1998), 14.

——. *Théorie de la contradiction.* Paris: François Maspero, 1975.

——. *Theoretical Writings.* Edited and translated by Ray Brassier and Alberto Toscano. London: Continuum, 2004.

——. *Theory of the Subject.* Translated by Bruno Bosteels. London: Continuum, 2009.

——. "'We Need a Popular Discipline': Contemporary Politics and the Crisis of the Negative." Interview with Filippo Del Lucchese and Jason Smith. *Critical Inquiry* 34, no. 4 (2008), 645–59.

——, and Fabien Tarby. *La Philosophie et l'événement.* Paris: Éditions Germina, 2010.

Benjamin, Walter. *Selected Writings*, vol. 4. Cambridge: Harvard University Press, 2003.

Claudel, Paul. *La Ville.* Edited by Jacques Petit. Paris: Mercure de France, 1967. Translated as *The City* by John Strong Newberry. New Haven: Yale University Press, 1920.

Cohen, Paul. "The Discovery of Forcing." *Rocky Mountain Journal of Mathematics* 32, no. 4 (2002).

Engels, Friedrich. *Germany: Revolution and Counter-Revolution*. New York: International Publishers, 1969.

——. *Dialectics of Nature*. New York: International Publishers, 1940.

Feferman, Solomon. "The Gödel Editorial Project: A Synopsis." http://math. stanford.edu/~feferman/papers/Goedel-Project-Synopsis.pdf (accessed Dec. 12, 2011).

Goethe, Johann von. *Faust I & II*. Translated by Stuart Atkins. Princeton, NJ: Princeton University Press, 1994.

Hallward, Peter. *Badiou: A Subject to Truth*. Minneapolis: University of Minnesota Press, 2003.

Heraclitus and Charles H. Kahn. *The Art and Thought of Heraclitus: An Edition of the Fragments with Translation and Commentary*. Cambridge: Cambridge University Press, 1979.

Jech, Thomas. "What Is . . . Forcing?" *Notices of the AMS* 55, no. 6, 692–693.

Johnston, Adrian. "Courage Before the Event: Alain Badiou and the Force of Affects." *Filozofski vestnik* 29, no. 2 (2008), 101–33.

Konstantinov, F. V., et al. *The Fundamentals of Marxist–Leninist Philosophy*, 2nd revised edition. Translated by Robert Daglish. Moscow: Progress Publishers, 1974.

Lacan, Jacques. *Écrits: The First Complete English Edition*. Translated by Bruce Fink. New York: W.W. Norton & Co., 2006.

Lenin, V. I. "The Lessons of the Moscow Uprising," in *Collected Works*, vol. 11. Moscow: Progress Publishers, 1965.

Mao, Zedong. "Introducing a Co-operative," in *Collected Works*, vol. VIII. http://www.marxists.org/reference/archive/mao/selected-works/volume-8/mswv8_09.htm (accessed December 14, 2011).

Marx, Karl, and Friedrich Engels. *The German Ideology*. Translated by C. J. Arthur. New York: International Publishers, 1970.

McNulty, Tracy. "Feminine Love and the Pauline Universal," in *Philosophy and Its Conditions*. Edited by Gabriel Riera. New York: SUNY Press, 2005.

Reinhard, Kenneth. "Forcing the Messiah: Paul, Rosenzweig, and Badiou." *Rosenzweig Jahrbuch* 4 (2010).

Sartre, Jean-Paul. "*Dirty Hands*," in *No Exit and Three Other Plays*. Translated by Lionel Abel. New York: Vintage Books, 1989.

Tiles, Mary. *The Philosophy of Set Theory: An Historical Introduction to Cantor's Paradise*. Mineola, NY: Dover Publications, 1989.

Žižek, Slavoj. *Welcome to the Desert of the Real: Five Essays on September 11 and Related Dates*. London: Verso, 2002.

INDEX

Aeschylus, xxv

Ahmed Gets Angry (*Ahmed se fâche*; Badiou), viii, xxi

Ahmed the Philosopher (*Ahmed philosophe*; Badiou), viii, ix, xxi, 134n4

Ahmed the Subtle (*Ahmed le subtil*; Badiou), vii, viii, ix, xxi. See also *The Pumpkins*

Almagestes (Badiou), xxi

Amphitryon (Plautus), ix

Antigone, xliii

Antioch, xv, xxviii, 132n18; incident at, xi, xxix, xlvi, 123n1

Aperghis, George, vii

Arianism, xxxi

Aristophanes, ix

Arnim, Bettina von, 130n62

atheism, xi, xxxix, 128n52, 134n1, 143

Athena, 128n46, 130n65

Auden, W. H., xxxix

Avare (*The City*), xxxvii–xxxviii, xli–xlii, 124n14

banlieues (poor suburbs), xiv, xv, xl, xlii, 123n3, 148

Barnes, Djuna, 130n62

Being and Event (Badiou), xxxiv, li, 123n13, 138

Benjamin, Walter, xxvii, xxxvi, 122n9

Bérénice (play; Racine), 124n7

Besme, Isidore de, xxxvii, xli

Besme, Lambert de (*The City*), xxxvii–xxxviii, xli, xliii, xlvi

Bible, xiv, 124n9; Corinthians, xxx, 121n2(Intro.), 133n24; "incident at Antioch" in, xxix, xlvi, 123n1

Blanton, Ward, ix, 142–50

Boyer, Élisabeth, viii

Break of Noon (*Partage de midi*; Claudel), xxxi, 121n3

Brecht, Bertolt, xxxvi

Britannicus (play; Racine), 126n24

Calme bloc ici-bas (Badiou), xxi

Camille (*Incident*), xiv, 126n27

Cantor, Georg, xxxiii

Caravaggio, Michelangelo da, xliii, 127n41

Catherine the Second (Catherine the Great), 130n62

Catholicism, ix, 147; of Claudel, xxxvi, xxxix, 140, 141–42; and Paul, xxii, 143

The Century (Badiou), xxxvi, xxxix, 135n9

Cephas (*Incident*), x, xiii, xl, xliii, xlix, 122n12, 134n5; *vs.* Avare, xli–xlii, 124n14; and language, xvii, xli, 124n9; name of, xv; and Paul, xi; and Paula, xlv, xlvi–xlviii

Châtelet, Madame du, 130n62

Christianity, l, li, 142, 145, 147; in *Incident*, xv, xxviii–xxx; *vs.* Jewish Law, xi, xxix–xxx, xlvi, xlvii, 122n7

the Church: Badiou on, 143–44, 147; and the Party, 142–43. *See also* Catholicism

The City (*La Ville*; Claudel), ix–x, xi, 134n1; characters in, 124n14; and *Incident*, xiii, xvi, xvii, xxii, xl, xli, xliii, xlv, xlvi, li, 140; plot of, xxxvii–xxxix; religion in, ix, xxxix, 142

Claudel, Camille, xliv, 129n62

Claudel, Paul, ix–x, xi, xxxi; Badiou on, 140–42, 143–44; and *Incident*, xiii, xvi, xvii, xxxvi–xl; language of, xxxvi, xxxix, 142; and *Red Scarf*, xxii, 140

Cœuvre (*The City*), xxxvii, xxxviii, xxxix, xli, 134n1

Cohen, Paul, xxii, xxvii, xxxiii–xxxvi, xxxix, xl, li

communism, ix, 133n25, 145; in *Incident*, x, xi, xl, 127n36

The Communist Hypothesis (Badiou), 123n1

Communist parties, 130n62, 134n5, 135n11, 135n12

Constantine, Emperor, xxx

continuum hypothesis, xxxiii

Corneille, Pierre, 140

Council of Nicea (325 CE), xxx–xxxi, xlviii

Curie, Marie, 129n62

Damascus: in *Incident*, xv, xxviii, xxxi, xxxii, xl, xliii, xliv, xlv, xlix; Paul's conversion on road to, xi, xv, xxviii, 124n5, 128n48

David (*Incident*), x–xi, xv, xlvi, xlviii–l, 125n20

democracy, x, xi, 124n8

Derrida, Jacques, 145

Dickinson, Emily, xliv

Diderot, Denis, 140

Dmitrieff, Elisabeth, 129n62

Docetism, xxxi

En partage (film), viii

Engels, Friedrich, xiv, 128n53, 131n7, 134n4

Event, xxiii, xxxiii, xl, xlix, 125n20, 136n22; Badiou on, 146–47; site of, 135n16; theater as, xxv, xxvii

Ferdinand (*The Story of Ferdinand*; Leaf), 131n3

film, viii, xxvi

forcing, xxii, xxvii, xxxiii–xxxvi, xxxvii; in *Incident*, xl, xlix, l, li; of the Messiah, xxxv, 122n8

formalization, xiii, xliv, 127n39, 128n53, 128nn49–50, 130n64, 147

Freud, Sigmund, 134n4

The Frogs (Aristophanes), ix

Germain, Sophie, 129n62

The German Ideology (Marx and Engels), xvii, xliv, 128n53

Germany: Revolution and Counter Revolution (Marx and Engels), 131n7

Giraudoux, Jean, ix

Gödel, Kurt, xxxiii

Goethe, Johann Wofgang von, xiv, 131n66, 134n4
Gracq, Julien, 126n25

Hallward, Peter, 124n6, 135n9, 135n18
Hegel, G.W.F., 121n3, 125n18, 134n4, 135n13, 145; dialectics of, xxx, xxxi
Heidegger, Martin, 127n38, 134n4
Heraclitus, xiv, 133n30
Hervey, Sandor, xiv
horlieu (place outside of place), xxxi, xxxix, xliii–xliv, xlviii
Hypatia, xliv, 129n62

"In Memory of W. B. Yeats" (Auden), xxxix
The Incident at Antioch (*L'Incident d'Antioche*; Badiou): comedy in, xiv–xv; performances of, ix, xxvii, li, 121n1(Intro.), 137; plot of, xl–l; rediscovery of, viii–ix; revisions to, vii–viii, 137; structure of, xxviii–xxxii, 137–38
individualism, xxiv, 128n53, 129n56, 143

Jerusalem Conference (50 CE), xxix
Jiang Qing, 130n62
Joan of Arc, xliv
Judaism: and Christianity, xxix–xxx, 147; and forcing of the Messiah, xxxv, 122n8; Law of, xi, xxix–xxx, xlvi, xlvii, 122n7

Kafka, Franz, xxxvi
Kant, Immanuel, 132n14
Kleist, Heinrich von, ix
Kollontaï, Alexandra, 130n62

La Fayette, Madame de, 130n62
La Fontaine, Jean de, xiv, 134n8
La République de Platon (Badiou), 125n18
Labé, Louise, 130n62

Lacan, Jacques, xliii, xliv, 122n10, 123n13, 127n40, 131n4, 132nn19–20
Lâla (*The City*), ix, x, xxxvii–xl, xli, xliii, xlvi, li, 125n18
Lambert. *See* Besme, Lambert de
language, 128n50; of Cephas, xli, 124n9; of Claudel, xxxvi, xxxix, 142; and effect of strangeness, xiv–xv; of *Incident*, xi–xii, xiii–xvii, xxii; Marxist, vii, xiv
Law, ix, xli; Jewish, xi, xxix–xxx, xlvi, xlvii, 122n7; and revolution, xi, xlv, 124n15; splitting, xliii, xlvii
Lenin, V. I., 131n7, 134n5, 136n23
Litvak, Joseph, viii
Logics of Worlds (Badiou), 138
Lubetkin, Zivia, 130n62
Luxembourg, Rosa, xliv, 130n62

Mallarmé, Stéphane, 126n31, 133n28, 133n29
Mansfield, Catherine, 130n63
Mao Zedong, xxx, 134n5, 136n19
Marx, Karl, xiv, xxx, 128n53, 131n7, 145
Marxism, xxii, xlii, 137, 139
mathematics, xxxiii–xxxvi. *See also* Cohen, Paul
Maury brothers (Jean and Pierre; *Incident*), x, xiv, xvii, xl, xliii, xlvi
May 1968 demonstrations, xxii, xxviii, xxxvii, xl, li, 133n25, 138
The Meaning of Sarkozy (*De quoi Sarkozy est-il le nom?*; Badiou), 127n36
Michel, Louise, 126n27, 129n62
Mitterrand, François, vii, 123n1, 132n13
Mokhtar (*Incident*), xlii, xlviii, l, 126n29, 127n35, 136n20; language of, xiv, xvii; name of, xv; and Paula, x, xlv, xlvi
Molière, ix, xxvi, 140, 141

Murasaki, Lady (Murasaki Shikibu), 130n62
music: in *Incident*, xvi–xvii; in *The Red Scarf*, vii, xvi

Nancy, Jean-Luc, 145
New Philosophers, xxii
Nicea, xv, xxviii; Council of, xxx–xxxi, xlviii
Nicene Creed, 134n1, 135n10
Nietzsche, Friedrich, 121n3, 134n4
nihilism, ix, x, xxxviii; Badiou on, 143, 144
Nœther, Emmy, 129n62

The Opposing Shore (*Le Rivage des Syrtes*; Gracq), 126n25

Paris Commune (1871), ix, xxxvii, xl, li, 127n35, 129n62. *See also* May 1968 demonstrations
Parmenides, xiv
the Party: Badiou on, 134n5, 139–40, 142–43; in *Incident*, x, xi, xliii, xlix, 134n5; in *The Red Scarf*, xxii. *See also* Communist parties
Paul, Saint, xxii, xxvii, xl, li, 122n7, 125n18; Badiou on, 143–44, 145–47; Caravaggio's painting of, xliii, 127n41; conversion of, xi, xv, xxviii, 124n5, 128n48; in *Incident*, xxviii, xxix–xxx; on Jewish Law, xi, xxix–xxx, xlvi, xlvii, 122n7, 133n24; and Paula, xliii, xlvii, 144; and Peter, xi, xxix, xlvi, 122n7. *See also* *Saint Paul: The Foundation of Universalism*
Paula (*Incident*), xxx, xxxvi, xli–l, 123n1, 125n20, 134n6; atheism of, 134n1; Badiou on, 138, 142, 143, 144–45; disappearance of, x, xlviii; on equality, 125n18, 125n21; and Lâla, x, xxxix, xli; and language,

xvii; name of, xv; red scarf of, xlii, 125n17, 126n26, 126n27; return of, x–xi, xlviii–l; revelation of, xliii–xlv, 127n41; and revolutionaries, xi, xvii, xliv, xlv
Peter (Cephas), xi, xxix, xlvi, 122n7, 123n2
Pintre, Madame (*Incident*), xiv, xlii, xliv, xlvi, xlviii
places, allegorical (*lieux*), xv, xxviii–xxix, xxx, 123n4. *See also* *horlieu*
Place of Choices, xxviii, xxix, xxx, xxxii, xliii, xlvi
Place of Foundations, xxviii, xxix, xxxi, xxxii, xlviii, l
Place of Politics, Official, xxviii, xxix, xxx, xxxii, xl, 127n34
Place of the War Reserves, xxviii, xxix, xxx, xxxii, xlii, xlv, xlvi, 123n4
Place of Truths, xxviii, xxix, xxx, xxxii, xliii, xlvi
Plato, xxiv
politics: Badiou on, viii, xxi–xxii, 138, 139, 144–45, 147, 148–50; of Claudel, xxxix, 141; emancipatory, 124n6, 134n5; of equality, xlix–l, 123n1, 125n18, 133n23; factory-based, 132n8; and forcing, xxxiv–xxxv; French, 137, 138, 148–49; identity, 125n18; in *Incident*, x–xii, xlviii; and mathematics, xxxiii–xxxvi; and revolution, xxx, 148–50; and the state, l, 148–49; and theater, xxi–xxii, xxv–xxvii; without power, xlii, 138, 144–45
Portulans (Badiou), xxi
positivism, ix
Pottecher, Maurice, xxxvi
The Pumpkins (*Les Citrouilles*; Badiou), viii, ix, xxi

Racine, Jean-Baptiste, xiv, 124n7, 126n24, 140

The Red Scarf (*L'Écharpe rouge*;
    Badiou), viii, xxi, xxii; and
    Incident, 126n27, 139; as
    romanopéra, vii, xvi; and *The Satin
    Slipper*, ix, 140
Reinhard, Ken, viii, ix, xix, 123,
    127n40, 128n51
religion, xi, xiv, 141; in *The City*, ix,
    xxxix, 142; and Paula, 142, 143.
    See also Catholicism; Christianity;
    Judaism
revolution, 125n17, 127n35; Badiou
    on, 133n25, 139, 142, 148–50;
    and the Church, 140; failures of,
    123n1; *vs.* Law, xi, xlv, 124n15;
    and politics, xxx, 148–50; and
    the State, xi, xxxi, xlv, xlvi, xlviii,
    xlix, 134n5. *See also* May 1968
    demonstrations; Paris Commune
"Rhapsody for the Theatre" (Badiou),
    xxiv, xxv–xxvi, 147
Richard III (Shakespeare), 131n4
romanopéra (novelopera), vii, xvi
Rousseau, Jean-Jacques, 140

*Saint Paul: The Foundation of
    Universalism* (Badiou), xiii, xxiii,
    xxix, xxxv, li, 128n48, 137, 144
Sappho, xliv, 129n62
Sartre, Jean-Paul, 135n12, 140
The Satin Slipper (*Le Soulier de satin*;
    Claudel), ix, xxii, 139, 140
Schiaretti, Christian, viii
Seghers, Anna, 130n62
set theory, xxxiii–xxxiv
Shakespeare, William, xiv
socialism, ix, 123n1, 132n13
Socrates, xliii, 125n18
Spitzer, Susan, viii, xii, xxi, xlv,
    122n12, 137–42
Stalin, Josef, 132n11
the State: Badiou on, 143, 144,
    145; and politics, l, 148–49; and

revolution, xi, xxxi, xlv, xlvi, xlviii,
    xlix, 134n5; and theater, xxv–xxvi
subjectivity, xxiii, xxiv; Badiou on,
    139, 141, 142, 145; becoming-
    Subject, xiii, 142

Taylor, Mark C., 145
temporality, xxxi, 122n7, 133n27; and
    theater, xxiv, xxvi–xxvii
Teresa of Avila, Saint, 130n62
theater: Badiou on, xxiii–xxiv, xxv–
    xxvi, xxvii, 140–41; as experiment,
    xxiv, xxvii; and philosophy, xxiii–
    xxviii; and politics, xxi–xxii, xxv–
    xxvii; tragic, xxv
"Théâtre et philosophie" (Badiou),
    xxiii–xxiv, xxvi, xxvii
Theodora of Byzantium, 130n62
Théorie de la contradiction (Badiou),
    xxviii
Theory of the Subject (Badiou), xxiii,
    xxx, xxxi, xxxiv, xliv, li, 122n7,
    137, 138
Treml, Martin, ix
The Tricks of Scapin (*Les Fourberies
    de Scapin*; Molière), ix, 141
truth: *vs.* knowledge, xxiii, xxiv–xxv;
    theatrical, xxiii–xxiv, xxvii
truth-event, xlix, 146
truth procedures/process, xxv, xxvi,
    125n18, 126n21, 132n21, 147

universalism, xxiii, xxxv, 123n1,
    143, 146. See also *St. Paul: The
    Foundation of Universalism*

Villembray, Claude (*Incident*), x,
    xl–xlv, l, 132n12; and language,
    xvii; and Maurys, xliii, xlvi;
    murder of, x, xlviii; and Paula,
    xliii, xlvi
Vitez, Antoine, vii, viii, xxvii, 137
Voltaire, 140

the wager, xxiv, xxxv, 125n20, 133n28

Wagner, Richard, 122n11

Weigel, Sigrid, ix

women, xliv, 123n13; Badiou on, 125n18, 144–45; equality of, 125n18, 125n21

Woolf, Virginia, 130n63

workers, xlii–xliii, 126n30; Badiou on, 135n18, 148, 149; and the Church, 140; immigrant, xxxiv, xl, 148, 149

Zassulitch, Vera, 130n62

Zenobia, 130n62